The Tanner Lectures on Human Values

THE TANNER LECTURES ON HUMAN VALUES

18
1997

Hill, Scalia, Said, Bloom, Schuller,
Maguire, O'Neill

Grethe B. Peterson, *Editor*

UNIVERSITY OF UTAH PRESS
Salt Lake City

Copyright © 1997 University of Utah Press
Copyright © 1996 Edward L. Said

All rights reserved
ISBN 0-87480-543-0
ISSN 0275-7656

∞ This symbol indicates books printed on paper
that meets the minimum requirements of
American National Standard for Information Services —
Permanence of Paper for Printed Library Materials,
ANSI A39.38–1984.

THE TANNER LECTURES ON HUMAN VALUES
was composed in Intertype Garamond with Garamond Foundry display type
by Donald M. Henriksen, Scholarly Typography, Salt Lake City.

THE TANNER LECTURES ON HUMAN VALUES

The purpose of the Tanner Lectures is to advance and reflect upon scholarly and scientific learning that relates to the entire range of human values.

To receive an appointment as a Tanner lecturer is a recognition of uncommon capabilities and outstanding scholarly or leadership achievement in the field of human values. The lecturers may be drawn from philosophy, religion, the humanities and sciences, the creative arts and learned professions, or from leadership in public or private affairs. The lectureships are international and intercultural and transcend ethnic, national, religious, or ideological distinctions.

The Tanner Lectures were formally founded on July 1, 1978, at Clare Hall, Cambridge University. They were established by the American scholar, industrialist, and philanthropist, Obert Clark Tanner. In creating the lectureships, Professor Tanner said, "I hope these lectures will contribute to the intellectual and moral life of mankind. I see them simply as a search for a better understanding of human behavior and human values. This understanding may be pursued for its own intrinsic worth, but it may also eventually have practical consequences for the quality of personal and social life."

Permanent Tanner lectureships, with lectures given annually, are established at nine institutions: Clare Hall, Cambridge University; Harvard University; Brasenose College, Oxford University; Princeton University; Stanford University; the University of California; the University of Michigan; the University of Utah; and Yale University. Other international lectureships occasionally take place. The institutions are selected by the Trustees.

The sponsoring institutions have full autonomy in the appointment of their lecturers. A major part of the lecture program is the publication and distribution of the Lectures in an annual volume.

The Tanner Lectures on Human Values is a nonprofit corporation administered at the University of Utah under the direction of a self-perpetuating, international Board of Trustees. The Trustees meet annually to enact policies that will ensure the quality of the lectureships.

The entire lecture program, including the costs of administration, is fully and generously funded in perpetuity by an endowment to the University of Utah by Professor Tanner and Mrs. Grace Adams Tanner.

Obert C. Tanner was born in Farmington, Utah, in 1904. He was educated at the University of Utah, Harvard University, and Stanford University. He served on the faculty at Stanford University and was a professor of philosophy at the University of Utah for twenty-eight years. Mr. Tanner was also the founder and chairman of the O. C. Tanner Company, the world's largest manufacturer of recognition award products.

Harvard University's former president Derek Bok once spoke of Obert Tanner as a "Renaissance Man," citing his remarkable achievements in three of life's major pursuits: business, education, and public service.

Obert C. Tanner died in Palm Springs, California, on October 14, 1993, at the age of eighty-nine.

GRETHE B. PETERSON
University of Utah

THE TRUSTEES

RICHARD ATKINSON
President of the University of California System

GILLIAN BEER
President of Clare Hall, Cambridge

LEE C. BOLLINGER
President of the University of Michigan

GERHARD CASPER
President of Stanford University

DAVID PIERPONT GARDNER
President Emeritus of the University of Utah
President Emeritus of the University of California System

THE RT. REV. CAROLYN TANNER IRISH
Salt Lake City, Utah

RICHARD C. LEVIN
President of Yale University

O. DON OSTLER
Chief Executive Officer, O. C. Tanner Company

CHASE N. PETERSON
President Emeritus of the University of Utah

NEIL L. RUDENSTINE
President of Harvard University

HAROLD T. SHAPIRO
President of Princeton University

ARTHUR K. SMITH, CHAIRMAN
President of the University of Utah

LORD DAVID WINDLESHAM
Principal of Brasenose College, Oxford

CONTENTS

The Tanner Lectures on Human Values v

The Trustees vii

Preface to Volume 18 ix

Thomas E. Hill, Jr. Respect for Humanity 1

Antonin Scalia Common-Law Courts in a Civil-Law System: The Role of United States Federal Courts in Interpreting the Constitution and Laws 77

Edward W. Said On Lost Causes 123

Harold Bloom   I. Shakespeare and the Value of Personality 155

              II. Shakespeare and the Value of Love .. 179

Gunther Schuller   I. Jazz: A Historical Perspective 203

              II. Duke Ellington 224

              III. Charles Mingus 237

Mairead Corrigan Maguire Peacemaking from the Grassroots in a World of Ethnic Conflict 253

Onora O'Neill Kant on Reason and Religion 267

The Tanner Lecturers 309

PREFACE TO VOLUME 18

Volume 18 of the Tanner Lectures on Human Values includes lectures delivered during the academic year 1995–96.

The Tanner Lectures are published in an annual volume.

In addition to the Lectures on Human Values, Professor Tanner and the Trustees of the Tanner Lectures have funded special international lectureships at selected colleges and universities which are administered independently of the permanent lectures.

Respect for Humanity

THOMAS E. HILL, JR.

THE TANNER LECTURES ON HUMAN VALUES

Delivered at

Stanford University
April 26 and 28, 1994

THOMAS E. HILL, JR., is professor of philosophy at the University of North Carolina at Chapel Hill. He graduated *magna cum laude* from Harvard University, was awarded a Rhodes Scholarship to Oxford University, and received his Ph.D. from Harvard University in 1966. He has taught at Johns Hopkins University and Pomona College, was a visiting associate professor at Stanford University, and from 1968 to 1984 was at the University of California, Los Angeles, where he served as acting chair of the department from 1983 to 1984. He is a member of the American philosophical Association and the North American Kant Society. He is the author of numerous articles on Kant, and his books include *Dignity and Practical Reason* (1992) and *Autonomy and Self-Respect* (1991).

I. BASIC RESPECT AND CULTURAL DIVERSITY

1. *Prologue*

History echoes with passionate pleas for *justice* and *charity*, but in our times, increasingly, what we hear are demands for *respect*. In a world where interests are diverse and often conflicting, justice is needed to assure each person a reasonable prospect of security, liberty, and other basic conditions of a tolerable life. Charity can fill gaps, rendering aid that cannot be demanded as a right and ameliorating the harmful consequences when justice fails. Respect, as a moral ideal, answers to a deep and pervasive human need beyond the more concrete needs that characteristically lead to demands for justice and charity.[1] Even though they have long benefited from charity and have now won concessions to their just demands, people stigmatized as inferior may still feel, quite rightly, that they "get no respect." The respect that they want is something more than material benefits, more even than such benefits offered in a charitable spirit or from recognition that they are owed. What they want, I believe, is something to which we should

---

What I present here is a slightly revised version of Tanner Lectures given at Stanford in April 1994. I am grateful to those who were responsible for making that opportunity possible, especially Obert Clark Tanner and Grace Adams Tanner, the trustees of the Tanner Lectures, its director, Grethe Peterson, and officials at Stanford University, notably President Gerhard Casper, Susan Okin, and Michael Bratman. Barbara Herman and Jeffrie Murphy, as expected, provided encouragement and constructive suggestions as well as acute and insightful criticisms, which were highlights of the occasion. I also want to thank the audience at the lectures and participants in the accompanying seminars for their challenging, but respectful, comments. I regret the long delay in making these lectures available for publication and apologize to all concerned, especially given that I never managed to do the more extensive revisions for the sake of which I postponed timely publication.

[1] Justice, charity, and respect are different concepts, none of which reduces to the other, but this is not to deny that they can overlap in various ways. All of these may recommend the same course of action on a given occasion, for example, and one important way to demonstrate respect is to grant another person (willingly and for the right reasons) what he or she is owed in justice.

presume every human being has a claim, namely, full recognition as a person, with the same basic moral worth as any other, co-membership in the community whose members share the authority to determine how things ought to be and the power to influence how they will be.[2]

The long and ugly history of struggles against racial bigotry, gender oppression, and cultural imperialism seems to reveal an unfortunate pattern. Deep injustices, once partially hidden by the conspicuous but inadequate charity of the privileged, become more glaring, and so the less privileged increasingly demand their *rights* rather than hope for generosity. But, unfortunately, as major battles for justice are won, mutual respect is slow to follow. For example, slavery was replaced by official segregation, and this in turn has given way to greater legal equality for African Americans; but the struggle has left a nasty residue of racial contempt. Legal disregard for women has been partially overcome, and other unjust social barriers to women may be yielding to protest; but here, again, victories for justice are often followed by a backlash of mutual contempt rather than an increase of respect. Unabashed colonial exploitation commonly passes over into a phase of hypocritical paternalism, which, under pressure, then retreats to a more distant indifference to the troubles of former colonies left behind. In each sphere, as chances for reconciliation are lost in empty rhetorical exchanges, naive hope and premature trust can easily turn to bitter resentment, cynicism, and ultimately mutual contempt.

Although less angry and violent than the reaction to open enmity, this final *contempt* poses problems that may be even harder to resolve. One can at least confront and respectfully negotiate

---

[2] Note that I use here the cautious terms "we should presume" and "a claim," leaving open for now whether the initial presumption can be overridden and under what conditions one's "claim" must be fully and immediately honored. Obviously not everyone should now be trusted, without qualification, with the same full rights and responsibilities as persons who are mature, competent, and conscientious adults. Qualifications are needed regarding infants, the mentally incompetent, mass murderers, sociopaths, etc. These special cases will be discussed to some extent in my second lecture.

with a single-minded, unpretending enemy; but contempt is a deep dismissal, a denial of the prospect of reconciliation, a signal that conversation is over. Furious argument and accusation, and even sharp-tongued deflation of hypocrisy and self-deception, leave some space to resume communication; but cold, silent contempt does not. The one demands to be heard, while the other walks away in disgust. Moral argument, however impassioned, is addressed to a person, acknowledged as "one of us": perhaps delinquent, misbehaving, outrageously deviant from our common standards, but still "one who can be reached," or so we presume. Increasingly, and sadly, it seems to me, we are in a place and time when, having at last achieved some success in combating the most overt forms of bigotry, oppression, and imperialism, we are in danger of sliding into a stage of mutual contempt and dismissal, affecting all sides of racial, gender, and cultural divides.

But if there is a trend toward separation, dismissal, and contempt, there are also healthy reactions as increasingly minorities make the demand for "respect" their common theme, women refuse to put up with sexual harassment, and university students prod reluctant traditionalists toward greater respect for cultural diversity. This loud and many-sided call for respect loses much of its potential force, however, and even begins to sound thin and trite, when made indiscriminately, without ground or context. "Respect me!" everyone shouts; but if the demand comes from intolerant racist and sexist bigots, one cannot help but doubt its force. Similarly, when the demand comes from a gang member with a knife at your throat, an ideological terrorist, or a student who refuses to read any literature written by Eurocentric white males, then one begins to wonder. Why should I respect everyone? What does respect entail? Is it compatible with deep disagreement and disapproval? Does respect need to be earned? Can it be forfeited? Is respect due to persons *as members of groups* or only *as individuals*? Does proper respect mean refusing to make comparative judgments of merit? On the contrary, are not some writings trash, some cultural practices immoral, and some people utterly contemptible?

I am not a sociologist or historian, and so it is not my place to identify and analyze social trends; but my impression that we face the broad trends that I have sketched is partly what prompts my current reflections on the ethics of respect for persons. They pose immediate practical problems to which, I believe, some old philosophical ideas are still quite pertinent.

2. *The Project, Theoretical and Practical*

My plan in these lectures is to return to a certain stage in Western intellectual history in order to draw out some ideas that are pertinent to current problems. To do so is to risk both distorting history and offering anachronistic solutions to new problems; but occasionally we can find in old texts bits of wisdom that are worth reshaping for current debates, especially if the problems we face are in fact perennial issues of human conflict in a new guise.

Specifically, the plan is to describe and extend the core of Immanuel Kant's idea of human dignity, with its fundamental requirement of respect for persons. Although Kant himself is often criticized for lapses into dogmatic rigorism, his principle of respect for persons is the product of his deep dissatisfaction with dogmatic, uncritical, and pseudo-scientific moral theories that would impose their parochial norms on a world of richly diverse people, who are capable of critical reflection and making their own choices.[3] Respect for persons, Kant realized, presupposes a prac-

---

[3] Although, as I shall argue, Kant's fundamental moral theory is potentially liberating and duly respectful of all persons, in his specific comments on women, unfortunately, he remained a man of his time, taking for granted stereotypes that denied the equal competence and potential intellectual, social, and political independence of women. See, for example, Immanuel Kant, *The Metaphysics of Morals*, trans. Mary Gregor (Cambridge: Cambridge University Press, 1991), 125–26, and various remarks in his *Observations on the Feeling of the Beautiful and the Sublime*, trans. John T. Goldwait (Berkeley: University of California Press, 1960), and *Anthropology from a Pragmatic Point of View*, trans. Mary Gregor (The Hague: Martinus Nijhoff, 1974). Kant was also more keenly aware of conflicts between individuals and nations than of deep cultural conflicts and misunderstandings, but again his theory, I believe, is pertinent to the latter as well.

tical conception of persons that must be normatively grounded, systematically developed, and responsive to a realistic (but not cynical) view of the human predicament. It must not merely reflect the substantive norms of particular communities or traditions, for it is needed as a framework for guiding moral reform within cultures and mediating conflicts among them.

As expected in any time-bound philosophy, Kant's ideas come with excess baggage that clear-thinking people cannot easily carry across centuries and continents. So among my tasks will be to propose developments, or modifications, of the initial Kantian ideas to make them more tenable to those who can draw on two hundred more years of experience and philosophical reflection. It is not immodest to suppose that we can propose improvements on venerable ideas from the past; what would be presumptuous is only to suppose that future reflection can never improve on our own proposals. In the present case, the proposals needed are of two kinds: first, that we strip from the core of Kant's ethics certain unnecessary doctrines, no matter how dear to the old man's heart these may have been; and, second, that we render some of Kant's abstractions more concrete, in particular, by augmenting his abstract conception of *free and principle-governed rational agents* with a conception of *culturally embedded social persons* who not so much "create" values as "find" what is valuable to them in their historical contexts. This augmentation of Kant's theory is especially important because it seriously addresses the most persistent source of dissatisfaction with Kantian ethics voiced in recent times.

After sketching, filtering, and augmenting the Kantian idea of basic respect for humanity, I propose to draw out some of its implications regarding the attitudes we should take toward cultural diversity. Here, as we apply the augmented Kantian idea to an urgent contemporary problem, its moral significance should become clearer. In effect, it offers a reasonable ground on which mutually respecting persons can stand, despite deep cultural differences, an intermediate ground between a dogmatic moralism that would impose all of our values upon everyone and an uncritical relativism that would accept anything, no matter how cruel, in the name of diversity.

In concluding this lecture, I shall venture a few comments on how basic Kantian respect might be relevant to a more immediate issue: How far should the traditional university curriculum be modified in response to the challenge of multiculturalism? In my second lecture I sketch more fully the Kantian grounds for respect for persons and address the particular question, Why shouldn't we say that criminals and bigots, and others we perceive as immoral, have *forfeited* all respect as human beings?

The practical problems raised here are major, complex problems in the real world, and so, one may wonder, what has *philosophy* to do with them? Obviously, mere thinking will not make the problems disappear. Nor does one presume, when offering philosophical reflections, that everyone will be convinced. The major questions that moral philosophy addresses are, in the end, normative ones that each of us must answer for ourselves. They ask, Where should a reasonable person stand? on various issues, and Why? One obvious reason that moral philosophy cannot eliminate concrete problems, such as bigotry and intolerance, is that it can never make itself heard beyond a limited audience; but even when serious people listen, it has no magical power to coerce assent. At best, by doing moral philosophy one can offer *others* only the product of one's efforts to think through normative problems honestly and clearly, together with a commitment to live by the results. For *oneself*, engaging in moral philosophy can help to structure a life of integrity, by identifying what one can conscientiously live for, the normative ground where one finds one must finally stand after scrutinizing one's initial beliefs for hypocrisy, self-deception, parochialism, and prejudice. By philosophizing with others, one can hope for greater agreement, within limits; but, beyond that, when agreement proves impossible, one can only hope for *respectful* disagreement.

3. *Human Dignity and the Background in Earlier Moral Theories*

In his *Groundwork of the Metaphysics of Morals*, Immanuel Kant famously argued that it is a fundamental moral principle, a Categorical Imperative, that we should treat humanity, in every person, as an end in itself, never as a means only. The idea had many implications, for example, regarding justice and the limits of expediency in politics; but one especially important implication concerned the basic attitude that human beings should take toward each other. In the second part of his later work, *The Metaphysics of Morals*, Kant spelled out this implication in discussions of "duties to oneself" and "duties to others."[4] Self-respect, he argued, requires that we avoid servility and other forms of self-degradation. The key idea was that, as a human being, everyone has an equal worth, independent of social standing and individual merits. To grovel and humiliate oneself before others, in shame or even guilt, is to deny one's equal status as a human being. If guilty, one should reform, making one's conduct more appropriate to the dignity of one's status; but that status itself is unconditional, not something one earns or can forfeit.

Equally, Kant maintained, it is a duty to respect others as human beings. Contrary to aristocratic doctrine, he argued for a basic respect for persons as human beings that is not grounded in (and so should not vary with) heredity and social rank. Contrary to meritarian individualism, he claimed that this respect is also not based on (and so should not be extended or withheld according to) individual talents, accomplishments, earned social position, or even — surprisingly — moral goodness. The requirement of respect, instead, is rooted in the dignity of humanity, an unconditional and nonquantitative value attributed to everyone with the potential capacities to be a moral agent.[5] This value, Kant main-

[4] See *The Metaphysics of Morals*, 214–36 and 254–64.

[5] Immanuel Kant, *Groundwork of the Metaphysic of Morals*, trans. H. J. Paton (New York: Harper and Row, 1964), 102. References and more interpretative com-

tained, is "above all price" and "without equivalent." It sets firm limits to what one human being may do to another, even in a good cause. And, significantly, it is fundamentally a requirement of attitude and policy, not a specific act-principle.

Kant's idea of human dignity was bound up with his particular conception of persons and embedded in a many-sided, systematic ethical theory that, you may be glad to hear, I shall not describe in detail. What I propose to do instead is to survey some background in the history of ethics that may help to explain the appeal of Kant's basic idea.

Oversimplifying, we might characterize some major steps in previous moral philosophy as follows. From Plato and through many centuries, moral philosophers asked their audiences to pose *for themselves* the questions What is a good life? and What sort of life would a wise and reasonable person choose, given the human condition, the assets and limits of human capacities? The answers were partly given in terms of the kinds of ends the philosophers thought worth pursuing, but the ancient philosophers also acknowledged, in various ways, that the fact we live among other people imposes limits on what we can wisely and reasonably conceive to be the good life for ourselves. Justice, the bonds of friendship, and the needs of the *polis* were seen not merely as pragmatic, prudential constraints but also as limits inherent in the structure of a good life. The philosophers differed, of course, about what the good life is, and so certain higher-order philosophical questions became prominent: *Why* is one way of living better than another? What *reason* is there to prefer the life of an Athenian over the life of a Spartan, or vice versa? How can one know or justify one's opinion that a life of so-called virtuous moderation is better than a life of pleasure? In other words, how are values grounded? What, if anything, makes them more than mere preferences?

---

ments on this basic idea of human dignity can be found in my *Dignity and Practical Reason in Kant's Moral Theory* (Ithaca: Cornell University Press, 1992), esp. chapters 2 and 10. See also Alan Donagan, *The Theory of Morality* (Chicago: University of Chicago Press, 1977), and my "Donagan's Kant," *Ethics* 104 (1993): 22–52.

Responding to early Sophists who regarded values as conventional and relative, Plato offered one of the main answers that has influenced the Western tradition: true values are grounded in an unchanging reality beyond this world we see and feel. Like numbers, and other abstractions, they exist independently of all human thought and history. They can be known through reason, but only through the trained and dialectically disciplined reason of experts, who, as it happens, are none other than philosophers. Although dialectical argument must precede the discovery of what is good, in the end, the good must be "seen" or intuited by the most highly educated. Common folk are only dimly aware of true values and so must be instructed by the experts. Ordinary feelings and thoughts about what is valuable are essentially worthless. The Platonic idea, however obscure, has persisted in modern and less elitist guises. Later versions concede that most human beings, with a bit of effort, can "see," intuit, or have revealed to them the realm of independent values, which somehow exist "out there" as models, but are not made or changed by human needs, thought, or social development.

Later Greeks, including Aristotle, realized the implausibility of the Platonic vision, even if they were not as repelled as we are by the elitism that accompanied it. For them, starting with Aristotle, the biologist, the good life could be determined by the study of human nature. They saw nature as having a purpose or *telos* for our species, and this is supposed to be discernible in common human tendencies. The purpose of human life, and the virtues that enabled the wise and fortunate to achieve it, turned out to be remarkably reflective of the ideals and needs of the particular cultures in which these philosophies developed and competed: a balanced and moderate life of activity, guided by reflection, according to Aristotle; a life free from pain, according to Epicurus; and a life of disciplined self-mastery, according to the Stoics. The theories rested upon what now seem dubious assumptions about human nature: a *teleological* structure and *common* capacities, aims, and requirements for happiness.

Medieval thinkers introduced a theological perspective and eventually grafted this onto the ancient teleology. Ultimate values are grounded in the mind or will of God, they argued; voluntarists saying that God created values by his arbitrary will, and traditionalists saying (with Thomas Aquinas) that eternal values were not created by God but merely promulgated to us, finite beings, as divine commands.

All three views sought to ground values in something deeper, more lasting, and more impressive than fluctuating human desires and preferences. But modern thinkers, notably at first Thomas Hobbes, challenged their basic presuppositions. Abstractions do not exist as things to be perceived, he argued; and, famously, David Hume later added that even if they did, mere "perception" of them (by "reason") would not move anyone to action. Human motivation, for good or ill, is rooted in desire and feeling, and so, Hume and his friends said, any plausible conception of objective value must be grounded in universal, or almost universal, human sentiments. According to the British empiricists, the good life is not grounded in anything outside of the lives of ordinary human beings, but rather in certain mundane commonalities in what we like and dislike. Platonic forms, ancient teleology, and even theology were increasingly rejected as ultimate grounds for value judgments; and, especially after Hume, it seemed more and more plausible to see values as little more than matters of taste and useful conventions. Privileged access to values by the elite became a less popular idea, for, though philosophers were supposed to have a more "scientific" understanding of values, the feelings that make up "the moral sense" (as well as other matters of taste) were thought to exist in everyone — everyone, at least, who grew up with the benefits of Western civilization.

The British empiricists helped to bring the idea of values down to earth, but their positive views raised problems. Would the empirical study of human nature really confirm the uniformity of human feelings on which their account of morality rested? Could the fact that human beings happen to be disposed to similar feelings of approval and disapproval adequately account for the common belief in the authority, binding force, and universality of basic moral principles? Wouldn't conventional theories of justice, like Hume's, leave dominant societies without any good reason for respecting weaker societies?[6]

Natural law theory and social contract theory, in many varieties, also developed in the same modern period. Though almost always tied to theological premises, the former offered the hope that *reasonable* people, of all cultures, could survive and thrive together if they would just govern their interactions by a minimum common framework that respects the rights and value of all human beings.[7] But the idea that natural laws are simply "discerned by reason" was too reminiscent of Plato. It invited philosophers to declare dogmatically which precepts were "laws of nature," thereby enabling them to dress up their favorite maxims in a cloak of authority. Increasingly one could wonder, how can one know what laws of conduct nature or God prescribes? How was the thought of such external laws supposed to *motivate* free and critical thinking persons, who have desires and plans of their own? When, as was common, natural law theory reverted to divine sanctions to provide motivation for obedience to its laws, it took on again many of the old problems of traditional theological ethics. For example, its appeal to divine sanctions left unexplained the common moral idea that one should do what is right without regard for reward or punishment.

---

[6] Hume said, for example, that justice could not bind us with respect to animals, even highly intelligent animals, if they lacked the power to *make* us respect them, and tragically Europeans continued to treat less powerful cultures as if they were animals.

[7] In theory natural rights and equal (basic) moral standing were typically extended to all human beings, "men," or "mankind," but in recent years many have raised reasonable doubts about the extent to which various natural law and social contract theorists actually intended to include women and "savages" when they wrote grandly of the rights of "man."

Social contract theories came in many varieties, and they offered some promise of grounding moral and political values more squarely in the problems and possibilities of the human condition. But various difficulties undermined the promise. Some theories, such as John Locke's, presupposed a historical fiction; others, such as Hobbes's, underestimated the human resources for peace and so proposed draconian means to end war. Jean-Jacques Rousseau deeply influenced Kant with his vision of what it would be for a community of free persons to live in mutual respect, listening to each other, working together, despite their differences, and governing themselves, in their public life, by the general will of all citizens. Though human-centered, egalitarian, and inspiring, Rousseau's political ideal nonetheless invited abuse of power by the self-appointed interpreters of the general will; it required invasive measures and a secular religion to promote patriotic spirit; and it gave little reason for decent treatment of "aliens," outside the ideal community.

This, briefly (and oversimply), was the context of moral philosophy as Kant might have seen it in 1785. Previous moral theories had failed. They preached specific values without adequate grounding, or else they undermined the authoritative mediating role of morality by reducing it to something contingent, relative, and in effect variable with culture. Crucially, Kant thought, they did not seek the source of all human values in humanity itself, that is, in the distinctively human capacities for thoughtful evaluation. Kant proposed a new perspective, which acknowledged contingent values that vary from person to person, and from society to society, and yet also endorsed a common formal framework for moral thinking. He tried to draw *both* of these, the variability of particular values and the common framework, from the idea that human beings themselves are the ultimate source of all our (human) values, moral, aesthetic, and personal. Endorsement under conditions of reasonable reflection, not mere sentiment, is what grounds values; and, significantly, the idea of *reasonable* reflection presupposes a willingness to listen to the voice, and to heed the interests, of others. Reasonable reflection also requires a kind of deliberative freedom, which, in practice, implies that one must try to see one's situation realistically, counteracting one's natural tendencies to self-deceit, self-serving bias, and local prejudice. A central point was that, although the values of individuals and societies may vary widely, their expression must be constrained by whatever basic framework for human interactions would be accepted by reasonable, autonomous, and mutually respectful persons.

Kant's theory is complex, and, whatever its virtues, they are entangled in metaphysical and moral views that are at least controversial, at worst obscure and unduly rigoristic. I propose simply to set aside these features for now, in order to concentrate on the central idea of human dignity and respect for persons.

(1) For example, let us disregard Kant's conviction that reason prescribes quite specific absolute duties, such as that one ought never to tell a lie, and also set aside his empirically unfounded and obviously culture-bound ideas about the particular nature of women, sex, and animals.[8]

(2) Also, when Kant tried to *interpret* everyday moral concepts in a larger philosophical context, he introduced certain metaphysical Ideas that he thought presupposed in the moral perspective. These Ideas, including "the intelligible world" and a "free will" independent of space and time, have understandably led to skepticism about Kant's whole philosophical system. I believe, however, that these metaphysical extensions of Kant's normative concepts are to a considerable extent separable from the central points in his moral philosophy, at least separable from the main points that I shall stress in these lectures.

(3) Again, although Kant himself was optimistic that all reasonable and autonomous persons would agree to *the same* moral

---

[8] See, for example, *The Metaphysics of Morals*, 225–27, 220–22, and 238, and also "On a Supposed Right to Lie because of Philanthropic Concerns," in the 3rd edition of *Grounding of the Metaphysics of Morals*, trans. James W. Ellington (Indianapolis: Hackett Publishing Co., 1993).

principles, that optimism is very difficult to share in our contemporary world. But, as I explain later, sharing that optimism is not necessary for our purposes; for we can treat Kant's proposals as a standard of *conscientiousness*, rather than absolute moral truth, and for this purpose assurance of universal agreement is not needed.[9]

(4) Similarly, though Kant may have assumed it, we need not insist that every sane adult member of *Homo sapiens* has a conscience and that all human children have the capacity and predisposition for it. Instead, one can say more modestly that, for practical purposes, our morality of respect presumes, until proved otherwise, that virtually all human beings, except perhaps the severely brain damaged, have enough potential for developing the capacities for reciprocity and self-restraint to qualify for human dignity. Again, unless proved otherwise, we presume that aware, functioning adults, who have a language and engage in social interactions, are not beyond the reach of reasonable moral discussion.

All of these modifications, I would argue, are compatible with the core idea of human dignity: that is, human beings are to be regarded as worthy of respect as human beings, regardless of how their values differ and whether or not we disapprove of what they do.

To avoid misunderstanding, I should anticipate now a point to be discussed more fully in the next lecture. That is, it is crucial to notice that in our ordinary ways of thinking we often use an idea of *respect* quite different from Kant's idea of respect for persons *as human beings*. This is the idea of respecting individuals *for special merit or achievements* that they may have to varying degrees. Respect for merit must be earned and can be forfeited. Kant's more controversial idea, by contrast, is that, simply by

---

[9] I discuss this modification, or extension, of Kant's moral theory, and the need for it, along with some other needed developments, in "A Kantian Perspective on Moral Rules," *Philosophical Perspectives* 6 (1996): 285–304.

virtue of their humanity, all people qualify for a status of dignity, which should be recognized respectfully by everyone.[10]

4. Persons Conceived as the Source of Values

The idea of respecting persons remains rather empty until the underlying (normative) idea of persons is specified. *How* we respect persons as sources of value, as well as *why*, depends on how we suppose they come to value what they do.[11] This is not to say we need, or could use, a full-blown metaphysical theory or complete human psychology here. To base an ethics on either would introduce complexity and controversy of the very sort that simple respect principles are meant to bypass. What should suffice, for present purposes, is a review of some general points about how human beings come to form values — points that, on reflection, may be obvious but help to specify what it might mean to respect human beings as sources of value. I shall distinguish six points. The first few are Kant's; but the rest are necessary supplements.[12]

---

[10] The basic distinction here and refinements have been frequently discussed. See, for example, Stephen L. Darwall, "Two Concepts of Respect," *Ethics* 88 (1977): 36–49, and my *Autonomy and Self-Respect* (Cambridge: Cambridge University Press, 1991), chapters 1, 2, and 11.

[11] My main concern in this lecture is, not with the grounds, but with the *content*, or practical implications, of the Kantian idea that human beings should be respected as valuers, i.e., as rational persons whose valuing various sorts of things, under appropriate conditions, is the source of all values (at least as we can know them). The *grounds* of this basic Kantian notion that what is valuable is somehow constituted by the reflective endorsement, under certain conditions, of rational agents (conceived in a certain way) are, of course, open to controversy. Although in my second lecture I reconstruct some aspects of Kant's defense of this idea, there is much more that needs eventually to be said. In particular, I want to make clear that I do not endorse a simple argument pattern that says *without further argument and explanation*: persons should be respected as such; they are sources of value (i.e., their valuing things, in appropriate conditions, makes those things valuable); human persons, we discover empirically, value such-and-such things in these-and-those ways; therefore, persons should be respected, as valuers, by helping them continue to value things in these-and-those ways (as in fact they tend to do) and by providing them as far as possible with such-and-such (the things they in fact value). There is something to this line of thought, but, as it stands, there are too many gaps. My subsequent list of "ways human beings value" (in section 4), then, is meant only to point the way toward certain principles (in section 5) about how we should respect human beings, but it is not meant, by itself, to establish or justify these principles.

[12] Here I sketch these points about values only briefly. Each needs further explanation, and the relations among them should be clarified. All but the first two

(1) Most obviously, individuals value the realization of various personal goals and projects and, derivatively, many other things as means to this. Traditionally, human beings, as opposed to inanimate things, plants, and animals, are conceived as having characteristic capacities of understanding, memory, foresight, use of language, rational reflection, and awareness of others.[13] They have, at least potentially, an ability to constrain themselves by principles and norms seen as providing reasons for acting. They have some capacity to reflect on their immediate desires, impulses, and preferences and from this to form more settled goals, plans, and policies, while aware of elementary facts of life, such as that desires conflict and one "cannot have it all." They adopt ends, recognize means, and are disposed to take the necessary means to their ends, when available. These points correspond in Kant's theory to the ability to "set onself ends," to use hypothetical imperatives, and to make plans free from immediate control by animal instinct and impulse.[14] Having these general capacities implies little or nothing about the specific values that human beings have. It does not imply, for example, that they are selfish; nor does it imply that they are altruistic.

(2) The capacities of "humanity" that qualify persons as "ends in themselves" include some minimum capacity for reci-

---

points, in effect, propose incorporating into Kantian moral theory ideas that are usually thought to be reserved for theories hostile to Kantianism. These ideas are admittedly important and yet either omitted or not stressed in Kant's writings and in Kantian ethics as usually interpreted. To develop these ideas and to show their compatibility, even fruitful companionship, with what I consider the most important, basic features of Kant's moral theory is a large project, to which I hope to contribute in future work.

[13] I say "characteristic" here to avoid controversies about how to classify infants, severely brain damaged (human) accident victims, etc., issues to be considered, at least briefly, in my second lecture.

[14] Kant, *Groundwork of the Metaphysic of Morals*, 80–88. Later Kant calls these capacities "the predisposition to humanity," as opposed to the (moral) "predisposition to personality." See *Religion within the Limits of Reason Alone*, trans. T. M. Greene and H. H. Hudson (New York: Harper and Row, 1960), 21–23.

procity and recognition of the moral standing of others.[15] This is not to say that everyone is morally good or even has a developed conscience. The point is just that basic respect is attributed on the presumption (even if just faith) that the persons respected have at least the capacity to be touched and moved by considerations of reciprocity and recognition of (all) other persons as having moral standing.[16]

On the Kantian view, we conceive of persons as (at least potential) *valuers*, whom we respect as the *source of all (human) values*. But persons are valuers in different ways or senses. Under point (1) above, we consider them as *valuing* goals, policies, and derivatively means, where *valuing* involves some degree of reflective endorsement, which is more than merely *desiring*. Under point (2) above, we consider persons as at least potentially recognizing the (equal) status of all persons and then as valuing being in reciprocal relations with others on mutually agreeable terms.[17]

---

[15] This feature of what, in his *Groundwork*, Kant calls "humanity" corresponds to what, in *Religion*, he calls the "disposition to personality" (222–23). Kant regarded *humanity* (and later *personality*) as more than a latent capacity, like the ability to learn French or set theory. This included a predisposition toward developing and exercising the capacity, a predisposition that sometimes fails to develop fully, but, absent conflicting tendencies (e.g., sensuous desires), it would. Kant regarded these dispositions to be innate, not learned, aspects of human nature, but contemporary Kantian theory, I think, might concede that it is sufficient that the capacity *to acquire* (or "learn") the predisposition is a natural or an almost invariable feature of human beings. Such a concession would not be without consequences, but I shall not pursue the issue further here.

[16] I am inclined to add "equal moral standing," but Kantians should want the threshold for respect kept low enough to include, for practical purposes, virtually every functioning adult human being. Perhaps capacity to recognize equality is not so essential here as the capacity to recognize everyone as having *at least a quite substantial moral standing* ("substantial" here implying much more than a minimum recognition of someone's "moral standing," say, as "lowest caste human"). For now I leave open just what is involved in "recognizing moral standing" and "reciprocity." Eventually, of course, these need to be spelled out, but for now the main point is just that human beings are presumed to be, in some appropriate sense, able and disposed to acknowledge and respect rights and interests of others and to join others in accepting (and following)) various mutually advantageous principles and conforming to them.

[17] This corresponds, roughly, to "a capacity for a sense of justice" and to the capacity for being "reasonable," in John Rawls's *Political Liberalism* (New York: Columbia University Press, 1993), 81ff.

But there are still other ways in which persons may be considered sources of value.

(3) People have not merely ends and means according to their likes and dislikes, they also tend to have some values that are essential or virtually indispensable to them. I have in mind two quite different sorts of things. First, there are some general aims, characteristic of human beings, apparently so common, so deeply rooted, and so vital to decent human life everywhere that they are understandably taken, for practical purposes, as *essential* to human nature. Happiness, broadly construed, is perhaps the most common term for these aims, when appropriately combined, but more specific elements often cited include self-preservation, freedom from pain, the development and exercise of our physical and mental powers, companionship, social standing, self-respect, and so on. Less controversial are associated needs that (virtually) everyone seems to recognize as vital to human life, whatever its particular forms: for example, food, water, shelter, community support, and freedom and opportunities of various kinds. Second, there are the various particular projects, associations, and cherished ideals with which individuals come to identify themselves. Among these are the "ground projects" that Bernard Williams talks about, commitments so deep that the person who has them might not care to live without them and such that we might say that the person would not be "the same person" if he or she lost them.[18] Kant himself acknowledged indispensable values of the first kind but not, at least explicitly, those of the second kind.[19] Nevertheless, that people often have such individual ground projects and ideals is an important fact about them as persons, a fact that needs to be recog-

---

[18] Bernard Williams, "Persons, Character, and Morality," in Bernard Williams, *Moral Luck* (Cambridge: Cambridge University Press, 1981), 1–19.

[19] See Kant's *The Metaphysics of Morals*, 189–92, and his *Critique of Judgment*, trans. Werner S. Pluhar (Indianapolis: Hackett Publishing Co., 1987), 317–21. The significance for Kantian ethics becomes clear in Jeffrie G. Murphy, *Kant: The Philosophy of Right* (London and New York: Macmillan, 1970), 94–108, and Barbara Herman, *The Practice of Moral Judgment* (Cambridge, Mass.: Harvard University Press, 1993), chapter 3, 45–72.

nized in any full account of what it is to respect persons as persons.[20]

(4) Human beings do not form values as abstract, ahistorical rational beings completely free from cultural context, but neither are they fully programmed robots lacking in the critical ability to contribute to the shape of their lives. As many have recently emphasized, people come to value what they do in a particular setting, influenced by dominant cultural patterns as well as crosscurrents of contrary social influences.[21] We are embedded in intertwining networks of cultures and subcultures; and however independent and thoughtful we may become, these no doubt constantly influence and impose outer limits on what we come to like and to dislike, to cherish and to hate. However, for practical purposes, the Kantian warns that we should not overestimate the irresistibility of these cultural bonds by assuming that reflective persons can never see good reason to set aside a part of their heritage. As existentialists saw (but exaggerated), we are not like *personae* in a play of life for which the script has already been completely written. We stand neither totally outside, nor totally within, the roles in which we find ourselves. Up to a point, at least when the cross-currents of the context permit, people can take responsibility, and hold others responsible, for trying to resist and remold features of a culture deeply at odds with respect for humanity.

(5) Human beings are disposed to seek what is valuable to them, and sometimes they find it — often where they were not looking.[22] Too often Kantians, like existentialists, talk as if "free"

---

[20] I thank Cynthia Stark and Robin Dillion for helping me to appreciate this point.

[21] Alasdair MacIntyre is perhaps the philosopher who has, in recent times, most vividly and influentially emphasized the importance of this point. See, for example, his *After Virtue*, 2nd edition (Notre Dame, Ind.: University of Notre Dame Press, 1984).

[22] Here, as in (1) and (3), and to some extent in (4), I am thinking of "values" as the various things people cherish other than morality itself (e.g., the minimum framework of respect I have alluded to). For example, art, customs, rituals, religious traditions, family relations, work, games, foods, literature, myths, patterns of humor, etc., of various kinds, the sort of things, aside from morality, that characteristically differentiate one culture from another.

individuals "choose" their nonmoral values, picking them from thin air, as it were, for no reason. They suggest, misleadingly, that (acausally) free agents simply "dub" certain goals as valuable to them, by sheer radical choice, thereby *making* them rationally important to themselves and morally significant to others.[23] In fact, I think, for the most part we simply *find* certain things in our experience to be valuable to ourselves and others like us, and other things we find indifferent, ugly, deplorable, despicable, or disgusting. Like what is "funny," "interesting," and "entertaining," what is seen as intersubjectively "valuable" in this way is judged to be, as we say, "worthy" of attention among some relevant group, but this carries no implication that "value" is a real intrinsic property of things in the world or even the dispositional property of causing pleasure to everyone who experiences the thing. To say that we *find* things valuable even when we were not especially looking for value (e.g., suddenly coming upon a gorgeous sunset) is not to make a metaphysical point but only a phenomenological one.[24]

[23] Some of my earlier papers (e.g., "Pains and Projects," in *Autonomy and Self-Respect*, chapter 12, and "Kant's Theory of Practical Reason," in *Dignity and Practical Reason in Kant's Moral Theory*, chapter 7) may veer close to these implausible claims. Christine Korsgaard too at times seems to suggest something of the same sort, but I suspect she intends something more subtle.

[24] I mean here to make clear that, despite my talk of "finding" values, the point does not imply commitment to G. E. Moore's theory of intrinsic value or to any "naturalistic" reduction of "value" to "fact." I also want to leave open the plausible *psychological* explanation of judgments of value as rooted in natural responses of persons of a certain kind, developed in a certain way, to facts they encounter or at least perceptions they have. Thus, the causal account of value judgments may refer to a relation between persons, as responders, and facts or perceptions about the valued objects. But this is not to say that to *experience something as good* is to *think of it as* causing favorable responses in me and persons like me. I assume here too, as earlier, that to value something, to find it valuable, and to judge it of (intersubjective) value are more than merely desiring, liking, or experiencing some inclination toward the thing. In the first case one finds, or judges, or sees something as *worthy* of desiring and endorsing for choice, at least in appropriate contexts. More needs to be said on these distinctions, of course. Finally, I conjecture that these commonsense points about how we find various things valuable, and disvaluable, are denied by philosophical extremists regarding value—both voluntarists and realists—because they overreact to the inadequacies of the opposite extreme view. Once we concede that values are neither "created" as such by free, unmotivated "dubbing" nor discovered as intrinsic features of the world we experience, then there should be little resistance to the commonplace observation that we typically "find" some things valuable and others not.

It is *as if* we *just see* that some things are good to us and, we assume, to others like us, and other things bad; these "discoveries" come and go, whether we are looking or not, often not all at once, but gradually.

I should emphasize that none of this implies that the same things will be, or even can be, found valuable in every culture; to the contrary, I assume that we cannot even understand, much less appreciate, some experiences without the cultural background of those to whom it is valuable.

(6) Finally, human beings value much, if not most, of what they do *as social beings*. Kant, too much influenced by Hobbes, tended to think of the moral life as a constant struggle between reasonable moral constraints and *self-serving* individual desires. But it is part of our problem, as well as its solution, that as social beings we care deeply for joint projects, interlocking social networks, and common histories. It is a misleading but all too familiar Enlightenment picture that independent individuals are always beset by discrete self-referring desires and then from these choose for themselves a series of personal "ends" that are definable without mention of others, except perhaps as competitors. But this picture of what and how people value what they do is seriously distorted in several ways.

Consider, for example, the fact that many of our projects are *joint projects*. That is, like members of an orchestra we aim to produce something, over time, that cannot be done alone. More significantly, the goal itself is conceived as doing something well *with others*, where each does his or her part not in isolation but with the aim and wish to do it with the others.[25]

Moreover, *historical particulars* are typically important in what we value. We do not, for example, want just that some good

---

[25] The general point is recognized by many people, but I am indebted especially to the following: Robert M. Adams, "Common Projects and Moral Virtue," *Midwest Studies in Philosophy* 13 (1988): 297–307, Nancy Sherman, "The Virtues of Common Pursuits," *Philosophy and Phenomenological Research* 53, no. 2 (1993): 277–99, and various works of Michael Bratman.

music be played by someone, but that we, the orchestra members (Ursula, Kareem, Hsu, Dmitri, Joe, et al.), play Beethoven's Seventh Symphony well together now. Feuding families want not just to confirm the abstract proposition "Unprovoked aggressors will be made to suffer"; they want to make sure that they themselves avenge the aggression of their particular enemies immediately.

Some of our deepest values may also be *reciprocal and layered*.[26] For example, I may value the fact that you respect and trust me, and you value the fact that I respect and trust you; moreover, I value the fact that you value the fact that I respect and trust you, and you value the fact that I value the fact that I respect and trust you, and so on. The values here are obviously deeply entwined and not individually satisfiable.

Again, philosophers often oversimplify life by treating all values as present-time desires for goals, which are seen as discrete states of affairs or events, but many of our values, I think, are *cross-time wholes*, involving our joint histories with other people.[27] Producing a piece of music, with a temporal beginning, middle stages, and a conclusion, is an example. As Aristotle suggests, we can assess a human life as exemplifying the final good for human beings, and as a "happy" life, only by considering the whole life as it has been (or is anticipated to be) completed.[28] Moreover, what counts, as we reflect, is not just whether the discrete moments were (or will be) pleasant (or intrinsically desirable) but also the pattern and the conclusion, how the parts of the life fit together, how each stage complements or completes the earlier stages, for good or ill. A meaningful life is not measured, on the model of account-

---

[26] This idea is vividly presented by Thomas Nagel in his essay "Sexual Perversion," *Journal of Philosophy* 66 (1969): 5–17.

[27] This is a major theme of MacIntyre's *After Virtue*. I note its potential relevance to a practical problem in "The Message of Affirmative Action," in *Autonomy and Self-Respect*, chapter 13, especially 201–11.

[28] Aristotle, *Nicomachean Ethics*, in *The Basic Works of Aristotle*, ed. Richard McKeon (New York: Random House), Book I, chapters 10–11 [para. 1100a–1102a], 946–49.

ing, in terms of pluses and minuses for independently good or bad moments; but rather, as Alasdair MacIntyre has stressed, its value is often assessed more in the *narrative terms* of stories (e.g., histories, biographies, novels, legends, and folktales). Here the connections between the parts of a life matter, like the connections among the chapters of a book. The terms of assessment, not reducible to any fixed rules, include initiation, unfolding, tensions, disruptions, growth, character, climax, resolution, and fitting (or unfitting) endings.

We can observe, too, that the whole of a life, a personal history with loved ones, and significant episodes within these often have for us an *organic value*, that is, a value in the whole that cannot be equated to any sum of values of "parts."[29] Like the beauty of a painting or the personal "meaning" of complex social experience, such things cannot be evaluated by dividing them, assessing the parts, and somehow "adding up" the results. The great moral philosophers, including Kant, must have had some practical awareness of these rather obvious facts; but, as contemporary critics are fond of repeating, their value theories are often expressed in special, semitechnical terminologies that oversimplify the familiar experiences of evaluation that they were meant to clarify.

A final caution. These various complex ways in which social beings have values should not be confused with the simple idea that people (at times) care for the welfare of others. That, I think, is obviously true, but such simple benevolent desires are far from the whole story of our being social. We also hate, resent, and

---

[29] G. E. Moore emphasized the idea that intrinsic values have an organic unity, the sum of the value of the whole not always being equal to the sum of the intrinsic value of its parts. However, Moore worked with a metaphysical idea of intrinsic goodness as an intuited, simple, nonnatural property, which is opposed to the Kantian conception, and Moore was also more willing than one should be, I believe, to talk as if intrinsic values could be compared in terms of the *quantity* of value in each, thereby taking too literally the metaphors of "sums" of value. See G. E. Moore, *Principia Ethica* (Cambridge: Cambridge University Press, 1903, reprinted 1959), 27–36.

despise others; we find our lives deeply attached and entwined with others we do not even like; many joint projects of one group are aimed at the destruction of another group; and many prefer narratives and histories that end with one's group gleefully gloating at the suffering of some group of outsiders. Human sociability, and the sense of connectedness with others, is part of the context of human life, for good or ill; it is not, by itself, the solution to its conflicts.

5. *What Would It Be to Respect Persons as Valuers?*

To review, on the Kantian perspective, the ultimate source of human values is not Platonic forms, natural teleology, divine will, or universal human sentiment. Ultimately all that is valuable for us stems somehow from the reflective endorsements of human beings. *Particular* ends, means, ground projects, discovered delights, joint endeavors, social networks, and histories are valued differently by different individuals and cultures. But the common framework Kant proposes as worthy of reflective endorsement by all is a basic requirement, across cultures and individual differences, to respect every human being as a source of value.

How can we make this more specific? The key is that persons are to be respected as the sources of (human) value and that we value things in the six ways reviewed in the last section. More specifically, then, how should we respect every person?

(1) Insofar as we value and respect persons as capable of reflecting on their desires, setting their own ends, and rationally pursuing means to them, we have some (presumptive) reason to allow them the space and opportunity to do so and even to aid them in the pursuit to some extent, provided their means and ends are compatible with due respect for all others. Since there are millions of people on earth, each with many diverse ends and entitled to some life of his or her own, the general duty *to aid* their pursuits, as Kant said, can only be an "imperfect" one: a relevant consideration but indefinite as to whom, when, where, and exactly how to

help. The presumption against interference with others' innocent projects, however, stands as a constant constraint on our pursuit of our own interest as well as a permanent bar against excessive paternalism—the attempt to make people happy only by *our* vision of the good rather than theirs.

(2) Insofar as we value and respect persons as moral agents, with the capacity to reciprocate and acknowledge the moral standing of others, we must not "write them off" as creatures who can only understand and respond to power, bribery, and manipulation. Morality itself is constituted, on the Kantian view, by what fully reflective, autonomous, and reasonable persons would agree to as a fair and mutually agreeable framework for human interactions. Hence no one has privileged access to what morality prescribes, and no one's voice on moral matters should be arbitrarily discounted. What mutual respect requires more specifically must itself be worked out, in many-sided conversations, in which the biases of each of us are amply exposed to the contrary perspectives of others. The (modified) Kantian conception of morality does not entail that to be respectful one must indiscriminately celebrate, accept, or even tolerate all the different practices endorsed by some cultural group. Given cultural diversity, the lesson to draw, rather, is that we cannot have proper respect and work out what this requires in particular contexts unless we try to think from an inclusive human perspective, with moral humility, willingness to listen, to rethink, at times to suspend judgment, and often to compromise.

(3) Insofar as we value and respect persons as having the two kinds of indispensable values, (a) the necessary means of life and (b) self-identifying ground projects, we have presumptive reasons both for noninterference and for aid, provided the projects and the means themselves are compatible with due respect for others. Importantly, we have here grounds for setting limits to our tolerance and approval of what others do; for when the powerful are denying the weak the basic necessities of life, to stand up for the weak is often more respectful to all than standing idly by.

Respect for persons as deeply identified with certain (permissible) ground projects requires respect for them as the particular individuals they are, not merely as fellow members of common humanity. That is, what is called for is not merely respect for the general capacities and rights they share with others but also appropriate attention and response to what they, as individuals, count as most significant about "who they are." [30] Respecting humanity, then, requires more than a proper attitude toward people in the abstract; it requires respect for people as particular individuals, whose "identity" (as we say) is bound up with particular projects, personal attachments, and traditions.[31]

(4) Insofar as we respect persons as embedded in a cultural and historical context, though capable to some extent of reflectively criticizing and rejecting it, we must avoid two extremes. On the one hand, we must not discount the significance of culture in determining what treatment is properly respectful; but, on the other hand, we must not simply assume that to treat them *as their dominant culture dictates* is always respectful to *them*, the individuals. Understanding the individuals' own conception of their relation to their culture is important, but not always decisive. For example, to condemn someone for what we regard as immoral conduct, in total disregard of what that conduct meant and whether it was prescribed or condoned in the agents' own culture, would fail to respect them as human beings, like us, who are partially shaped, unconsciously limited, and deeply influenced by cultural environment. But to refuse to make any judgment at all about those in "other cultures" is disrespectful to them, for it treats them

---

[30] *Appropriate* respect here does not mean indiscriminate aid or toleration of all personal projects; it must take into account the fact that some personal projects, even "ground projects" crucial to an individual's "identity," may be deeply immoral and contemptuous of others.

[31] The notion of "identity" here is normative and slippery, though important. It is not the same as the more minimal "personal identity" generally discussed in the metaphysical debates of philosophers concerning split brains, brain transplants, memory discontinuity, etc.

as the fixed product of societal influences with no moral power to understand and be moved by moral criticism of it.

(5) Insofar as we respect persons as generally "seekers" and sometimes "finders" of value, we should be ready to make some effort to appreciate the different values others have found. At the same time we should not assume that they are perfectly set and satisfied with what they have found, and so uninterested in communicating and sharing new experiences. Ideally, value systems of individuals and groups would evolve, as people have the power and freedom to explore, and to widen the range of their experience, as well as to retreat and protect themselves from constant massive exposure to unwelcome forms of life. Diversity would not be valued just for the sake of diversity, but for the way it allows some to live out the best values they have found and enables others to seek out something better.

(6) Finally, insofar as we take seriously the idea that persons have social values (joint projects, reciprocal and layered values, etc.), we can no longer imagine that we can respect persons just by dealing with them, one by one, as if isolated sources of individual interests. We respect someone only by acknowledging and taking fully into account the importance to that person, and others, of the networks of relationships in which that person finds life meaningful. Group ties, traditions, family connections, and deeply layered hopes may mean more to persons than anything they value just for themselves. Respect for individuals, properly understood, should not compete with community values, for the only way to respect the social values of individuals is to honor, so far as one legitimately can, the groups within which the individual finds his or her life valuable. The limits to how far we can honor group ties, of course, lie in the general requirement to respect all persons. Insofar as group loyalty feeds on hatred and contempt of others and expresses itself through war and humiliation, then those who would respect all humanity must disengage their basic *respect for*

the individual members from the *respect for their group* that otherwise would be its corollary.

6. Basic Respect and Multiculturalism in the University

So far my remarks have been quite abstract, wide-ranging, perhaps too concerned with theory for the general reader. Thus, in conclusion, let me try to compensate in a small way by talking more specifically about how the idea of basic respect for persons might apply to the controversial question, How should universities respond to the facts of cultural diversity?

The issue is complicated because of the diverse nature of universities themselves. They are many-sided institutions that have evolved for various purposes, serve different constituencies, and are answerable to many contributing and engaged parties. What these elements should be, and how they should be ranked, will no doubt always be a matter of controversy. To simplify, then, I shall comment only on the educational or teaching commitment of universities, particularly in undergraduate general studies courses.

The question, then, is this: What is a reasonable and respectful attitude to take, when confronting decisions about university general education, given heightened sensitivity to (what I shall call) the facts of cultural diversity? First, let us review some of these facts. I take it that the following four points are fairly uncontroversial.[32]

(1) People in different cultures, both across time and now, deeply differ in their ways of life, their social norms, their conceptions of law and interpersonal relationships, their highest aspirations, and also in their mundane everyday tastes and preferences. There may be also overlapping similarities, perhaps even some universal convergence points; but because of difficulties of cross-

---

[32] The "facts" that I select to emphasize here are, admittedly, far from all the relevant facts that need, ultimately, to be taken into account. I deliberately stress what I take to be facts about deep differences, difficulties in cross-cultural communication, and oppression of the weak by the strong because these are, I believe, major sources of the most urgent obstacles to mutual respect in multicultural contexts.

cultural understanding, we do not know how deep and pervasive these similarities, or the differences, are.

(2) Although cultures evolve and intermingle, and individuals sometimes rebel and advocate radical changes, most people tend to seek and find what is valuable and meaningful to them within their own cultural settings. Individuals are embedded in cultures and often identify themselves and their ground projects in terms intelligible only in the cultural contexts.

(3) Although, when conditions are right, social criticism and independence of mind are possible and important, we all inevitably tend to misinterpret others and to be biased by our own heritage whenever we try to think through issues that cross cultural borders. This includes, of course, philosophers who lecture on respect and cultural diversity.

(4) All the various cultures, and subcultures, are not equal in power, and throughout history powerful groups have tended to persecute, exploit, and try to dominate weaker groups, sometimes with open group enmity but often in the name of universal ideals. The means have been many, including not only war, slavery, and genocide but also subtler symbols of moralistic disapproval or contemptuous dismissal. These are reflected in folklore, histories, literature, and philosophy, as well as in everyday jokes and conversations. The almost universal tendency to bias and the frequent moral imperialism of dominant groups understandably lead to skepticism about the objectivity of cross-cultural judgments, especially the judgments of the relatively privileged.

Some apparently think that these "facts" warrant an attitude of extreme relativism about values, which draws no limits. Since there are such deep differences in beliefs, they say, there is no good reason not to accept "respectfully" whatever values prevail within a culture. Or, if they confess disgust for foot-binding, clitorectomies, wife burning, child prostitution, or other practices condoned in different cultures, they must be careful, they think, to explain that this is a mere "personal preference." Since whatever passes within a culture is to be respected for that place and time, extreme relativists have no moral ground, besides changing local fashion, for trying to reform even their own society. "Whatever is, is right"; or, to put the point in more postmodern terms, the ideas of "right" and "wrong," and "better" and "worse," need to be deconstructed and then discarded with other myths of the past.

As elementary philosophy texts have explained time and time again, admitting the facts of cultural diversity in no way supports this whole-scale resistance to making cross-cultural value judgments with its indiscriminate acceptance of whatever has the endorsement of some culture. Moreover, the rejection of all cross-cultural standards opens the door to the very sort of power-driven cultural imperialism that culturally sensitive, gentle relativists want to resist. Controlling and subordinating those who are weaker may be an essential value in some dominant cultures, as, for example, in the American subculture of *macho* men with respect to "their" women. When this happens, indiscriminate toleration amounts to politely condoning abuse, exploitation, and humiliation. Even the *hypocrisy* of oppressors who dominate others in the name of high moral ideals cannot be condemned by the extreme relativist, except perhaps with the mild rebuke, "My friends and I dislike what you are doing."

We should not be smug, though, just because we can see the self-defeating character of the extreme relativist position. The facts of cultural diversity do not support *that*, but we should not be so arrogant as to think that they have no implications for us at all. In particular, for those who, like me, endorse at least basic respect for persons, there are strong implications. Among these, I believe, are the following.

First, we cannot fully respect people of diverse cultural backgrounds, within our own country or elsewhere, without making serious effort to understand and *appreciate*, so far as we can, features of their cultures that they cherish and see as crucial to their particular identity. Given the inevitable predisposition to cultural bias, we can progress toward such understanding and appreciation only by engaging with the voices of the people within those cultures, through their literature, their histories, and their folklore, and ideally with the help of teachers who themselves represent the cultural heritage.

Of course, limited time, opportunity, and other circumstances severely limit the extent and depth to which any one person can study and engage with other cultures. As teachers and students, perhaps, we have more contact with other ethnic groups than the average person does; but the more diverse our local environment, the more obvious it becomes that we can begin to understand only a small fraction of the many traditions represented by the people we meet. To study a wide range of cultures superficially, like sampling many dishes at a smorgasbord, may be personally rewarding, but is unlikely to contribute significantly to overcoming the problems of cross-cultural misunderstanding and disrespect.

A more realistic ideal would be deeper engagement with one or a few different cultures. Becoming fully "bicultural" in one's experience, analogous to being truly bilingual in speech, is probably beyond the reach of most of us, nor is it clear that this is generally desirable. What is important, however, is to challenge one's customary ways of thinking, feeling, and perceiving so that one becomes more open to the possibility of values that we could never imagine when bound within a single cultural experience. This increased sensitivity to alternatives may lead to new sources of personal enrichment, in music, art, literature, and personal friendship; but, more important, it is needed for *meaningful* tolerance and respect. Without the openness stimulated by appreciation of some other cultures, we might proclaim commitment to these ideals but fail to see *when and how they give us reasons* for acting (and for restraint) in contexts of cultural conflict. Respect is blind if uninformed about relevant values and the reasons they provide; and it inevitably remains uninformed if nothing shakes us from our habits of seeing everything exclusively from our primary culture's perspective.[33]

Second, in trying to understand and appreciate different literary values, traditions, rituals, music, languages, patterns of personal relation, and so forth, respect calls for us *to confront our biases*, to try to recognize and counteract our initial inclination always to judge by comparison with what is most familiar. With regard to diverse *moral* practices, all the more, basic respect calls for modesty and caution to curb our arrogant bias in judging others whom we hardly understand. This requires not merely self-discipline but also, so far as possible, respectful confrontation and communication with representatives of cultures whose practices we are initially inclined to condemn; for, on the modified Kantian view proposed here, moral insight is not the special endowment of any group but is something that can only emerge gradually as diverse but mutually respectful human beings engage seriously in communication about how best to live together despite their differences. Thus, openness in confronting other cultures is needed, not only to respect individuals who are different from us, but also, more generally, to curb our moral arrogance and to further moral understanding. This is not to say that morality is simply a hodgepodge of standards picked indiscriminately from a variety of cultures and thrown into a multicultural pot. The point is rather that no single group, within the bounds of one heritage, can by itself achieve that diminution of bias, awareness of options, and appreciation of human limits and possibilities necessary to warrant confidence that it possesses the best, or most human and just, moral system.

Third, it is not respectful to people of other cultures, or to ourselves, to condone and tolerate all cultural practices, no matter

---

[33] Barbara Herman has been particularly helpful in stressing that what is needed (and possible) is not so much full knowledge of every culture but rather *openness* and sensitivity to possible facets of the cultures we confront that may affect what reasons we have to act one way or another.

how harmful and restrictive they may be. On the modified Kantian conception that I am proposing, human beings are seen as culturally embedded but nonetheless as (to some degree) capable of critical judgment, independent thinking, recognition of the moral status of other persons, and constraining themselves by principles based on the ideal of mutual respect among all persons. To respect this moral capacity, as the key to a morality of respect, we must, however modestly and cautiously, condemn practices that, even after closest study, seem obviously and deeply dismissive of certain classes of human beings. To condemn cultural practices, elsewhere or at home, one must take a stand, and in taking a stand one takes a *risk* that bias has corrupted one's judgment. But respect for all, unlike more parochial principles, can be conscientiously defended to all, and those who endorse it show no respect to themselves or others when, through excess caution, they refuse to condemn what they see as deeply contemptuous practices. An important implication for issues regarding curriculum is that the respect that calls for widening cultural understanding does not require, or allow, us to suspend our most basic standards of judgment — for example, to read the diaries of Anne Frank and Joseph Goebbels, or the autobiography of Frederick Douglass and the speeches of John C. Calhoun, with the same morally detached interest that might be appropriate in the study of set theory, abstract art, and geology.

Fourth, to say that moral judgment should not be suspended when reading, discussing, or selecting curricular materials does not imply that moralistic criteria should dictate what is to be read. To purge the reading lists of everything considered immoral, replacing these with works more uplifting or "politically correct," would be to undermine any hope of the sort of cross-cultural understanding to which universal respect aspires. Listening appreciatively to history's victims is no doubt long overdue, but we should also hear the false rhetoric of oppressors and the banal excuses of the overly tolerant, if we hope to gain more than a skewed and superficial grasp of the complex dynamics of cultures. Curriculum development requires judicious selection, but understanding and respect require listening to many voices we dislike and deplore — not listening passively merely, but with minds and hearts fully engaged.

Fifth, how far should a curriculum go in replacing the old, Western, white male authors, such as Shakespeare, Hobbes, Gibbon, and Darwin, with writers representing other perspectives (e.g., contemporary, non-Western, non-European, and feminist)? I do not pretend to have a definite answer; and, even if I did, the appropriate forum to which it should be presented, with due respect, would not be the audience at a public lecture but a diverse deliberative committee with the authority and commitment to work out the details together. One implication of what I have been saying today, however, seems clear and relevant. As human beings, we tend not only to hold on to what we now value but also to seek out more of what we may find valuable, and we find it in many places we could not initially anticipate. But finding something valuable is not the same as having an initial untutored desire for it or even liking it upon first exposure. Many, if not most, of the long revered works in the now much disparaged "canon" for college students were there because people who devoted time to them experienced in them something that enriched their lives. These works have, then, a strong, though not exclusive, claim on our attention. The claim stems not so much from our respect for the authors themselves, much less from their origin in a European, white male tradition, but from respect for those who might be the readers. One does not have to argue that these works are "better" than each competing nonstandard selection, by some standard neutral among all cultures, but only that they have been persistently found to be among the best or most valuable to the reflective readers within the tradition they represent. Nor, for reasons just given, need they be "morally pure." What does matter is that they have been challenging, stimulating, illuminating, and life-enriching to a sufficient number of intelligent and diligent readers to warrant a prediction that they will continue to be found so by others.

My remarks here are not meant to favor "the canon" more than innovation and diversity in the curriculum, for the case for each seems strong. Here, as elsewhere, dogmatism is out of place. There are no precise lines to be drawn in choosing among a wealth of riches. So what proper respect calls for, surely, is open discussion and listening, broadly inclusive procedures for decision making, and eventually compromise. If a curriculum did not give substantial place for *establishing excellence* within the dominant Western tradition, it would not respect those who are deeply influenced by that tradition and so have special reason to try to understand it and find what has been thought most valuable in it. If, however, a traditional curriculum did not diversify in a serious and substantial way, it would continue to reinforce cultural bias or at least fail to help students to develop their resources to fight it. Moreover, this extreme conservatism would fail to respect students as persons who, despite being embedded in a culture, can enrich their lives by learning to appreciate values of another kind — or at least to respect those who do.

II. Must Respect Be Earned?

In my last lecture I sketched (and modified) an old idea drawn from Immanuel Kant, the idea that the ultimate source of human values is humanity itself, rather than Platonic forms, natural teleology, God's commands, universal human sentiments, or particular social conventions. Humanity is attributed only to those presumed to have certain basic normative capacities and dispositions. These include the ability to reflect on one's desires and circumstances, to set ends for oneself, to form coherent plans, and to be willing to reciprocate with others in endorsing principles that respect each person as a potential sourse of legitimate values. In Kant's philosophy these ideas were accompanied by a moral rigorism and a radical "two perspective" metaphysics that few philosophers today can accept; but I treat these as associated ideas that are inessential to Kant's central moral insights. In his vigorous defense of individual responsibility, Kant seems to have exaggerated the power of autonomous individuals to set themselves ends and to adopt principles independently of others, but his view can be coherently supplemented, I suggested, with a more realistic account of how, rather than dubbing individual goals to be valuable by acts of free choice, we tend to *find* our values, as social beings, within our familiar cultural contexts. Applying this suggestion, I argued that *if* we respect persons as sources of value, understood in this more realistic way, *then* we are committed to certain attitudes about cultural diversity. In particular, this respect has implications for *how* different cultures should be represented in a university curriculum. For example, proper respect calls for caution and modesty in moral judgment but not for unlimited tolerance or passive acceptance. It requires effort to appreciate other cultures but not moralistic dismissal of our Western heritage. Mutual respect, in a pluralistic world, urges us to acknowledge that we are all embedded in cultural contexts that unavoidably *limit* our understanding, skew our judgment, but do *not preclude* our responsibility to confront and diminish our prejudices in wider cross-cultural communication.

Supplementing Kant's own account of how we form our values, I called attention to six points about how a commitment to basic respect for human beings as sources of value might work out in practice. Each of these prescriptions should be considered, for now, as *prima facie* or *defeasible*, for in particular cases what is recommended by one consideration may be in tension with what is recommended by another. For example, the presumption that one should not tolerate or condone culture practices that are deeply contemptuous of women can be in tension with the *prima facie* consideration that we should respectfully acknowledge that individuals tend to identify themselves by their traditional roles within a culture. How in practice these tensions should be resolved will require further reflection, perhaps case by case. Inventing further rules for these problems may not be helpful. In any case, my argument left the details of these matters open, in order to stress more general points. That is, *if* we accept basic Kantian respect, *then* (1) there are limits to what cultural practices we can condone, but (2) we have at least *prima facie* reason not to interfere coercively or manipulatively with the cultural values that others find, and reflectively endorse, as central to "who they are," and (3) we must try, so far as possible, to encourage changes in disrespectful cultural practices, at home or elsewhere, but only by means that respectfully address, as moral agents, those with whom we disagree.

Although these conclusions may seem obvious to many, they are not uncontroversial. Even if our values stem ultimately from the reflective endorsements of human beings, we may wonder, *why* should we respect and value every person as a source of values? It does not follow from the fact that everyone *has values*, or finds things valuable, that these things *are valuable*, or ought to be regarded by all as valuable. It is natural to wonder, *why* should we respect those who refuse to respect others, who blatantly disregard even the minimum demands of a morality of respect for persons? To be blunt, are not some people, as a former colleague would say, "moral garbage," mere "scum" that pollutes rather than enriches life for the rest of humanity? How can we respect such people in any meaningful sense? Why suppose that we are committed to respecting those who have done nothing to *earn* it? Even if we grant that everyone initially is owed some respect as a human being, is there any reason to deny that some extremely bad characters, by their immoral deeds, *forfeit* all respect, justifying our viewing them with utter contempt?

These are the issues to which I turn in this second lecture. Whereas before we focused on *how* to respect humanity (in multicultural contexts), we now ask *why* and *within what limits*? These are large questions that I cannot pretend to answer adequately here. What I can offer is only a sketch of some ways a Kantian might interpret and respond to them. The sketch is meant partly to reflect Kant's own basic strategy of argument, fine points aside, and partly to suggest lines of response, broadly consistent with Kant's ethics, that might be developed more fully in time.

1. *Respect for Humanity vs. Respect for Merit: Reformulation of the Issues*

One might suppose, mistakenly, that doubts about the propriety of respecting *all* human beings could be dismissed by making a simple distinction. To those who think that we should respect only those who have *earned* respect, for example, we can imagine an analytic-minded philosopher responding as follows. We need a distinction, he or she says, between two kinds of respect: *respecting persons for their merits* and *respecting persons for their social positions*.[1] Consider the first. When we mean to acknowledge the present of individuals' distinctive merit or excellence, we can say such things as "One must respect Perlman as a violinist," "She won the respect of the team for her efforts," "I respect him as a politician, but not as a saxophonist," "I respect her as an artist, but not as a person." Respect here amounts to confidence in a person's ability or esteem for her excellence in a context of comparative or scalar evaluation.

Again, we often respect persons for *performing well in a social position*, but then we are not respecting them merely because they occupy the position but rather because they are good at the tasks associated with the position. When we have in mind respect for merit, for example, to say "I respect her as a lawyer" means "I respect her because she is a *good* lawyer," not "I respect her because she *is* a lawyer." For similar reasons, respecting someone as a safecracker does not mean respecting the person simply *because* he or

---

[1] See Stephen Darwall, "Two Concepts of Respect," *Ethics* 88 (1977): 36–40. His terms are "appraisal respect" and "recognition respect." A similar distinction is an important part of my discussions in *Autonomy and Self-Respect* (Cambridge: Cambridge University Press, 1991), especially chapters 1 and 11.

she *is* a safecracker but rather respecting the person for his or her safecracking skills.

Now consider the second kind of respect: respect for a person's social position. Suppose someone says, "She has not been a particularly good mother, but she is my mother, after all, and I must respect her as such." Here the point is not to make a comparative evaluation, but rather to acknowledge that merely holding a certain position, or standing in a certain relation to another, is sometimes enough to warrant a (presumptive) claim of respect. This should not be surprising because social roles, positions, and relationships are often defined in normative terms, by the rights, responsibilities, and privileges that are constitutive of them. To take another example, suppose I say, "I cannot abide his views, and I do not trust him, but he is, after all, the president, and we must respect him as such." Here I would imply that office-holders are to be respected on account of the position they hold, not because they are doing well at fulfilling that position.

How is this distinction relevant to our concerns? Consider our previous question, whether we must respect those who refuse to respect others. Now armed with the distinction between two kinds of respect, our hypothetical defender of the Kantian position might try to dismiss this worry as a mere verbal confusion. Of course, he or she might say, immoral, vicious people do not deserve *respect* in the first sense, for they are not especially good or meritorious as persons; but, nonetheless, we must *respect* them *as human beings*, in the second sense, for *humanity* (or being human) is itself a moral status or position that calls for respectful recognition. In support, he or she might cite the point, noted by Locke and others, that "person" often functions as a "forensic notion," defined, as it were, as "one who possesses such and such rights and duties." Similarly, he or she might argue, the terms "humanity" and "human being" are often used as labels for those presumed to have a certain moral status worthy of respect. If so, it seems we can coherently respect even viciously immoral people *as human beings*, even though, as individuals, they fall far short of how human beings should conduct themselves.

This reply calls attention to an important distinction, but it fails to meet the underlying concern of those who wonder why they should respect all human beings. To be sure, if we share the same moral attitudes, we may come to conceive of "being human" as a moral status with given rights and duties, just as aristocrats once conceived of "being a duke" as a quasi-moral status with rights and duties. In this context of agreement, to say "She is a human being, so treat her accordingly," would be a way of expressing a familiar moral judgment. This would be like saying, in an earlier time, "He is a duke, so treat him accordingly." But playing with these conceptual implications will not get us very far toward a deep justification. Even if it is, for some speakers, a tautology that human beings should be treated with respect, we may still wonder why we should elevate even the most vicious members of our biological species to the normative status of "human being." Similarly, even if, for some, "Dukes are entitled to special honor" is true by definition, we may still doubt whether certain corrupt characters who were called "dukes" are entitled to that richly normative label. Building entitlements into the definition of the terms "human being" and "duke" makes it all too easy to defend the propositions "Human beings should be respected" and "Dukes are owed special honor," for it simply turns them into tautologies. Once we do this, however, the moral controversy merely shifts to another question, namely, what entitles anyone to the labels "human being" and "duke"? We may still wonder why respect *this or that particular* lying freeloader or sociopathic murderer.

The moral of these linguistic reflections is simple: although the demand to *respect people as human beings* treats "being human" (or "having humanity") as a moral status, it leaves open to question what rights and responsibilities should belong to that position. "Respect her as a human being" does not mean "Esteem her as a comparatively superior human being" but rather "Accord her all the respect (presumptively) due to anyone who has the status of being human." But specifically *what* respect is (presumptively) due to all human beings, and whether it can be forfeited, so far remains an open issue. Given this, our initial question about why we should respect all human beings can be reexpressed, in a more refined way, as follows: *(1) Why grant to all members of our species, or even to all with certain basic normative capacities, a moral status (of "humanity") that includes the presumption that anyone who has the status should be respected by all?*

If we can answer these concerns about the *presumption* that respect is owed to every human being, then a further question still arises: *(2) Granted that all human beings have a defeasible right to respect as human beings, is there any reason to suppose that they cannot forfeit this right?* This question is pressing because analogies suggest that all role rights can be forfeited by gross misconduct. For example, even though "doctor" and "president" refer to roles that are usually accorded a presumption of due respect, some doctors and presidents are so corrupt that, by general agreement, they forfeit their initial claims to respect on account of their positions.

Suppose that we can see *some good reasons* for *trying* to respect even the worst persons as human beings *if this is possible and compatible with our other responsibilities.* Our agreement with Kant that no one can altogether forfeit respect as a human being would still be *conditional* on satisfying ourselves regarding a remaining question: *(3) How, in practice, can we defend ourselves, punish criminals, and express our outrage at bigotry and corruption if we must treat all the unjust, corrupt bigots with respect?* This question seems pressing especially if we come to doubt the answer so often given in theory, but rarely in practice, namely, "Condemn and despise the sin, but not the sinner." With experience, we may well wonder: Is this psychologically possible? Even so, would it really be respectful? Can we respect either ourselves or the perpetrators of heinous crimes if we refuse to hold them *responsible* for their choices?[2]

In what follows, I address all of these concerns briefly. To preview: First, I sketch a Kantian line of reasoning for the presumption that respect is owed to all human beings. There are two main steps, outlined in the next two sections: (1) a description of a Kantian moral framework and efforts to show that this articulates and develops moral concepts to which we are already committed and (2) a claim that some formal requirements of respect are implicit in the Kantian framework and more substantive requirements can be defended by reasoning from it. Second, I consider how a Kantian perspective might lead us, for moral and practical reasons, to try to adopt the attitude that no one can completely forfeit all respect as a human being, provided this is possible and compatible with our other responsibilities. Third, to satisfy the last proviso, I suggest reasons for thinking that basic respect for all humanity, as understood here, is possible and fully compatible with our responsibilities to protect ourselves, to support just punishment, and to censure the perpetrators of evil (not merely their "deeds").

Together, these points have important practical implications regarding how we can legitimately respond to immorality and crime. We should respect even vicious and unremorseful people *as human beings*, but we can do so without tolerating their behavior, trusting them to reform, or forgiving them. Far from being empty, however, the requirement of respect limits the kinds of moral censure and punishment that we can fairly use. The Kantian ideal of respect should also temper our responses on campus to

[2] The general policy of separating the "sin" from the "sinner," condemning the former while never attributing blameworthiness to the perpetrators, seems disrespectful to oneself as it denies one the expression of legitimate resentment and indignation, and it seems disrespectful of the offender because it places him or her in a category outside normal interactive moral relationships.

those whom we believe to be racists and sexists, replacing contemptuous dismissal with firm but respectful confrontation.

2. *Interpreting the Issue: Why Should We Respect All Human Beings?*

At first glance, this seems a simple question, for we are used to many ways of answering questions of the form "Why should we . . . ?" On reflection, however, it is not so obvious how we should understand the question. What sort of answer might one be looking for? Often we answer "Why should we . . . ?" questions by pointing out desirable consequences, but the basic Kantian claim is not amenable to this sort of defense. Even if we could show empirical evidence that adopting a policy of universal respect proves to be generally advantageous to everyone, this would not justify holding it, as Kantians do, as a deep, necessary feature of the basic moral framework for deliberating about all specific issues. Granting everyone due respect is a basic moral requirement not derivative from the desirability of promoting other good consequences. Although it is a welcome fact that according people due respect tends to promote other goods, Kantians take the principle of respect for humanity as standing independently of this fact and serving as a limit to what we may legitimately do in our efforts to promote the general welfare.

Again, given Kantian denials of intuitionism, naturalism, and sentimentalism as theories of value, it is not open to "justify" respect for humanity by pretending to find "in" humanity some intuitable, natural, or sentiment-evoking property of "worthiness of respect."

Kant himself wrote eloquently of the reverence and awe that seem forced from us as we contemplate "the moral law within," and this may suggest that Kant's only ground for making universal respect so central in his ethics is his belief that everyone will, necessarily but inexplicably, "find" that this moral predisposition commands their respect wherever it is found, even in those who in fact flagrantly fail to follow it. One famous passage in Kant's *Groundwork*, in fact, might seem to offer just this sort of argument. That is, one might take Kant to be arguing as follows: All of us first recognize "humanity" in ourselves; we cannot help but regard this humanity in us as "Awesome!" ("an end in itself," loosely interpreted); seeing that the "awesome" thing is also in every other moral agent, we should acknowledge that the same attitude is appropriate to humanity in everyone;[3] hence we should respect everyone's humanity.

Now even if Kant at times suggests this sort of argument, it does not provide the kind of deep grounding that one might hope to find for his central principle of respect for humanity. Many will no doubt refuse to concede that they find either "humanity" or "the moral law within" as awesome as Kant does, and by Kant's own principles he should not be appealing either to intuition or to contingent sentiments (as, it seems, the argument above does) to support his account of the basic features of the moral point of view. One might try to argue that the initial recognition of humanity as "awesome" is neither an intuition nor an emotional response, but rather a *necessary* aspect of a *rational* agent's inevitable consciousness of being subject to moral constraints (i.e., part of "the fact of reason" that Kant discusses in his second Critique).[4] But, for this proposal to amount to more than an appeal to "intuition" or common sentiment, it needs to be more fully explained *why* seeing one's own "humanity" as an "end in itself" is necessarily something we do *because we are rational*.[5]

[3] See Kant, *Groundwork of the Metaphysic of Morals*, trans. H. J. Paton (New York: Harper and Row, 1956), 96. The argument would be fallacious in moving to the requirement to respect humanity in others if what one recognized in oneself was just that one's own humanity was of great value to oneself (as, perhaps, one sees one's own pleasures). The argument presupposes that one sees humanity, in one's own case, as *in itself respect-worthy*, not just something valuable to one because it is one's own.

[4] *Critique of Practical Reason*, trans. Lewis W. Beck, 3rd edition (New York: Macmillan Publishing Co., 1993), 30–32.

[5] Even if it gives a plausible reading of Kant's argument, the fuller explanation needed would make the argument in question far more complex than the simple,

What, then, is the Kantian ground for the idea that we should respect all human beings as such? With apparent simplicity we can say, as commentators often do, that the ground is "humanity" itself, or "rational nature," or "autonomy." This, however, only indicates *what* qualifies moral agents as objects of basic respect as human beings; it does not spell out *why*. The reference (to "humanity," etc.) points to what Kant *believed* a creature needs in order to be owed such respect; but it does not, by itself, provide an argument that addresses the concerns of those who have yet to accept the Kantian moral framework. Is there more we can do?

We can "justify" some features of a system of thought by showing their connections with other beliefs we share, for example, by showing how they are entailed or presupposed by deep and pervasive commitments that we would find difficult, if not impossible, to discard. Proofs and "justifying" arguments come to an end at some point, but we can often satisfy the actual "Why should we . . . ?" concerns that prompt the search for justifications. Sometimes we do this by revealing that the "We should . . ." in question turns out to be, in effect, the expression of an attitude to which we are already committed by other beliefs and attitudes that we see no adequate reason to abandon. The conceptual connections may be far from self-evident, revealing themselves only by deep analysis of the normative concepts we employ. The mode of argument, then, would not be quick appeal to intuition, linguistic or otherwise, but a process of gradually unfolding and articulating more clearly the implications of modes of thought that we actually rely upon and could not give up, at least not without radical reorientation of our lives.

This is the sort of "justification," I believe, that Kant offers in response to the concerns underlying the question "Why should we

---

facile ("intuitive") line of thought that the interpretations I am examining in this section take it to be. That fuller account would need, I think, to make use of at least some of the background ideas that I develop in the next two sections. Thus, although I believe there is something to the proposed interpretation, I shall not try to develop it here.

respect all human beings?" Briefly, we *should* because such respect is an essential aspect of the moral framework for deliberation to which we are in fact committed by our concept of ourselves as moral agents, subject to duties, once this is properly understood. In the next sections, I describe some general features of the Kantian moral framework (as I reconstruct it) and sketch strategies Kant suggests for showing that in fact we presuppose it. Then, in the following section, I consider how this basic moral framework leads to the presumption that all human beings should be respected in certain (formal and substantive) ways. As always for Kant, "we should" refers to what "we would" do *if*, though able and sometimes tempted to do otherwise, we acted in a fully rational way. "Why should we . . . ?" questions, then, in effect translate into questions about what is rational, or reasonable, for us to do.[6]

3. *The Kantian Moral Framework and Kant's Strategies for Showing It Presupposed in Common Moral Concepts*

Kantian ethics acknowledges a need for a common moral framework for thinking about specific moral issues. That is, its ambition is to attempt to resolve more particular controversies by appeal to widely shared standards for moral deliberation and argument, standards providing criteria regarding what is morally relevant and procedures for working toward reasonable resolutions of conflict. Many familiar perspectives on morality (for example, those inherent in various religious sects) quite frankly call for an antecedent conversion to a quite specific value system. Thus, they do not well serve, and were not meant to serve, the desired mediating role of a general framework for discussion, mutually acceptable to a wide range of people with diverse moral convictions. Utilitarianism, in its several forms, has been attractive partly be-

[6] As will be evident, I often use "reasonable" to express in commonsense terms what Kant seems often to mean by "rational." The latter term in recent times is usually used to describe conclusions based entirely on instrumental reasoning and individual preferences rather than prescriptions based on thinking from the common point of view of all moral agents (i.e., what I call "reasonable").

cause it seems to serve that mediating role, in effect asking people who are quarreling over particular day-to-day moral issues to frame their disputes in terms of a common overarching commitment to whatever seems, on best evidence, to promote the greatest satisfaction of human preferences, impartially considered. Utilitarian theories, however, raise many (now familiar) problems, most notably that, even though committed to "counting" each person's preferences, they leave open the possibility that, in the end, the good of some may be totally sacrificed to satisfy the preferences of others.

What I propose, then, is to sketch an alternative moral framework, drawn from Kant, which is meant, like utilitarianism, to be a mode of thinking that can help to mediate moral disputes. But, unlike utilitarianism, this Kantian alternative refuses to reduce moral deliberation to unconstrained quantitative thinking that treats all individual aspirations as just so many preferences in a common pool, which are to be denied or approved according to a global maximizing strategy. The framework I shall sketch is Kantian in a broad sense because it draws from several of Kant's formulas of the Categorical Imperative, but I have not time here either to trace its heritage or to fill in all the necessary details.

The basic idea is that, for purposes of thinking about what particular moral principles we should endorse, how they are to be interpreted, and what exceptions should hold, we can appropriately think of moral principles as principles that all *reasonable* human beings would accept, as justifiable to themselves and others, under certain ideal conditions. The idea of the "reasonable" here, as in John Rawls's work, is broader than the idea of "the rational," as contemporary decision theorists understand this; for reasonableness includes a willingness to reciprocate with others on mutually agreeable terms.[7]

---

[7] Commonsense and Kantian ideas of the reasonable, as I understand them in contrast with other models of the rational, are discussed more fully in my paper "Reasonable Self-Interest," in *Social Philosophy and Policy* (forthcoming, 1997).

The conditions for ideal reasonable legislation include sober and realistic awareness of the contexts in which the principles are to be applied, sensitivity to the diverse values that people have, willingness to set aside personal differences that are morally irrelevant to the task, and effort to review principles on their merits, without undue reliance on one's own familiar traditions, antecedent cultural or religious loyalties, and personal attachments.[8] A key stipulation is that each person, in reviewing possible moral requirements, must acknowledge that, ideally, every person subject to the requirements shares equally the authority to make and interpret them. Everyone is, as it were, an equal co-legislator in what Kant calls "a kingdom of ends," in which the legislators together must "make" the "laws," settling on moral standards that, they agree, should take precedence over their individual policies. That is, they are seen as, ideally, the joint authors of principles that trump the policies that *otherwise* they might adopt to satisfy their personal desires.

This ideal "moral legislation" is not arbitrary but is supposed to be guided by legislators' mutual commitment to essential features of a moral perspective that, like constitutional constraints, are not themselves "legislated." The latter, basic ideas implicit in the various forms of the Categorical Imperative, are meant to be constitutive aspects of the ideal of living in community with other free, equal, and reasonable moral agents who constrain their personal pursuits by mutually agreed standards. We are to think of substantive moral principles, beyond the constitutive standards, as binding a person only if they are justifiable to that person insofar as that person too considers the issue from the ideal perspective of a co-legislator. Thus, human beings are viewed as if they were

---

Unfortunately, the same term serves for both the rational and the reasonable in Kant's texts.

[8] My idea of Kantian moral "legislation" as a framework for deliberating about more specific issues and various problems it raises are discussed more fully in "A Kantian Perspective on Moral Rules," *Philosophical Perspectives* 6 (1992): 285–304.

jointly authors of binding principles and individually subject to them, once the principles are finally decided.

In this ideal model, all moral agents are assumed to have *autonomy*, which means, in part, that no one is morally bound by demands imposed from any other source, unless such demands are backed by more basic principles that all rational agents with autonomy would accept. Autonomy implies, further, that in moral legislation one does not accept principles simply because they are traditional, currently accepted, sanctioned by religious authorities, or especially favorable to the interests of one particular group rather than another. The *humanity* of each person is treated by the others as an "end in itself," at least in the "thin" sense that the "reasonable will" of each person, along with every other, is what counts as the final authority. Hence all accept the constraints that they jointly will as legislators, giving them priority over the various (contingent) ends and means that otherwise they might like to adopt. That is, if they believe that the appropriate joint deliberation of all who have humanity, or reasonable wills, would converge on certain general principles, then they acknowledge those principles as the final, unconditional authority regarding what ends they should seek and what means they may, and may not, use.

The general idea here has affinities, not only with Kant, but with Rousseau's political ideal, John Rawls's theory of justice, Thomas Scanlon's idea of moral justification, and no doubt other views as well. Many details need to be filled in, and problems must be faced, before any heuristic model of this kind can be fairly assessed or confidently used. But, long before that, it is natural to wonder: What could lead one to think of ideal moral reflection in this way? Kant tried to show that the Kantian legislative perspective is implicit in the attitudes of ordinary conscientious people. His reasoning took two lines, which converged on the main point.

One line of thought starts this way. What fundamental priorities express the attitude of conscientious persons, independently of the specific views they may have about what is right and what is wrong? Well, at least this: they have the attitude that if they judge, upon full and reasonable deliberation, that they are morally required to do something, then they must do that, even if other goods have to be sacrificed. In other words, they treat what Kant calls their "good will" as good "above all else," "without qualification."[9] This is not to say that they hold that morality generally requires the radical sacrifice of other goods, such as health, wealth, knowledge, and happiness; it means only that, if the only way they can gain one of these other goods is by doing what they are convinced is wrong, then they are committed to foregoing that other good. This is an old and, to many, trivial point: one should not sell one's soul (or moral integrity) for anything, no matter how attractive it may appear. So far, of course, this tells us nothing substantive about what sorts of acts are immoral; but it reveals a conscientious attitude as one that accepts that there are reasonable constraints on the pursuit of personal goods, including happiness. Upon further analysis, this attitude is revealed as a matter of *respect* for moral principle, something distinct from wanting to achieve a desired goal.[10] The attitude turns out, on reflection, to be respect for "objective principles": that is, principles to which anyone, *if fully reasonable*, would conform his or her personal policies ("maxims").[11]

Another line of thought runs in the same direction, but a bit further.[12] Different people have different ideas about what particular duties they have, but what is it *in common* that they are thinking when they think they are morally required to do or to refrain from various acts? For one thing, they think they *ought* to do it; and this thought may be interpreted as the idea that what they ought to do is what, upon full and reasonable deliberation,

---

[9] *Groundwork*, 61–62.

[10] Ibid., 68–69.

[11] Ibid., 69–70, especially 69n.

[12] The following paragraphs, to the end of this section, are meant to be a very loose reconstruction of lines of thought in *Groundwork*, chapter 2, esp. 80–104.

they would do if completely rational and reasonable, though they are quite aware that they might not do it.

There are many things, however, that they believe they ought to do that they do not regard as *moral* requirements, and so more must be said. The something more is apparently this: when conscientious persons accept something as a moral requirement, they see it as nonoptional, that is, as what they ought to do, whether or not they feel like doing it, and not just because it serves their personal interests. Unlike what is "necessary" to fulfill an optional plan, they feel, one cannot simply change one's plans and thereby escape the "ought" judgment. What accounts for their sense that they "must" or "ought" to do what they believe is morally required, then, is not their belief that doing it will get them something they want, such as wealth, friendship, or happiness. Since thinking one *ought* to do something, in general, implies thinking that it is reasonable to do, they must presuppose that there is some other kind of reason why they ought to fulfill particular moral requirements. They must, then, be presupposing, among their deep commitments, some general principle, or point of view, that would explain why they regard it as reasonable to judge that they ought, on particular occasions, to do the morally required things, whether they want to or not.[13] In other words, they are committed to there being some standards of reasonable conduct, which they count as

---

[13] The point is independent of whether there is general agreement on the particular duty. Some may think that it is a duty to lie on a certain occasion, and others think that it is a duty not to lie; but what they have in common is the supposition that reason requires them to do the various things that they believe to be morally required, whether this serves their particular wants and plans or not. And this, presumably, needs explanation and support from a more general account of what it is to be reasonable. As I noted earlier, I am systematically substituting "reasonable" for "rational" in the discussion of moral deliberation because I think this is less misleading to modern audiences. Also note that the argument presupposes an internalist view of reasons and "ought"; that is, if I judge that I have reasons to do something, or ought to do it, I am thereby to some degree disposed to do it and I acknowledge that there is something I favor or am committed to that is positively connected with it. "Committed" here, though, does not mean wholeheartedly or all-considered finally resolved to do it, but leaves open that I could merely acknowledge its "authority," believe it is what I would do if doing my best, etc.

authoritative for them, that indicate that certain things ought, and others ought not, to be done, and not just because this serves the specific aims and interests that the agent happens to have.

To put the thought in Kant's terms, the idea of duty presupposes that there is a Categorical Imperative, that is, a general principle reasonable for all, that can guide moral judgment and support particular moral beliefs. This cannot be merely the Hypothetical Imperative, "It is rational to take the necessary means to your ends," for this supports no requirement independent of one's aims and wants.[14]

At this point we must look around for candidates. Most alleged moral principles are too specific and substantive to be plausibly advanced as principles reasonable for everyone to adopt, no matter how diverse their aims, values, and traditional ties. For example, "Follow the will of the god X," "Follow the example of those judged wisest and best in your community," "Live by the code of your ancestors," "Obey the law," "Follow the promptings of your natural sympathy"; all these, and many more, are too limited in application, or too controversial in their priorities, or both, to gain wide acceptance as the comprehensive, universally reasonable standard that people who believe in moral requirements presuppose as the source of these requirements. Many people may be persuaded to accept them, but why should one expect all reasonable people, regardless of their particular differences, to find such specific, substantive principles authoritative for them? If they fear the consequences of violating tradition, law, or religious precepts, this would make conformity to those principles quite sensible, but it could not justify thinking of them as *moral requirements*, that is, as how one ought to act, regardless of one's personal wants, hopes, and fears.[15]

---

[14] My understanding of this nonmoral general principle of reason is more fully spelled out in my collection of essays on Kant's ethics, *Dignity and Practical Reason in Kant's Moral Theory* (Ithaca: Cornell University Press, 1992), chapters 1 and 7.

[15] See *Groundwork*, 108–12, and contrast 88. Here I try merely to articulate the spirit of Kant's opposition to substantive accounts of the fundamental moral principle, deliberately omitting Kant's more direct lines of argument for his "universal law" formula of the Categorical Imperative and its relation to later formulas.

The inadequacy of the other candidates to explain the idea of duty makes the Kantian proposal look more promising. The core idea is that the Categorical Imperative, that most comprehensive principle behind the belief in particular duties, is "conform to universal law," which, liberally reconstructed, means to restrict one's personal acts and policies to those compatible with whatever general principles everyone would accept if "legislating" from the moral perspective that I sketched earlier. Morally binding "laws" are not to be found in a vision of Plato's world of Forms, in God's mind, or in secular conceptions of nature. Rather, we must try to work out together what a moral point of view requires in various situations by trying to think realistically, to transcend particular biases and special interests, and to find a common core of ideals and standards that we can justify to each other, despite our differences. What makes this formal prescription a candidate for being a "principle of reason" is that what it enjoins is simply an interpretation, for the human condition, of the abstract rule "Govern yourself, constrain your desires and plans, according to what is reasonable." The interpretation, which begins to add some teeth to the precept, holds that what is reasonable is (ideally) to be worked out jointly in ongoing, mutually respectful deliberations in which everyone must try to justify proposed policies and principles to everyone else who is willing to reciprocate.[16]

4. *Formal Respect for All Implicit in the Kantian Moral Framework and Substantive Respect Defensible from It.*

The Kantian moral perspective implicitly contains within it an important, though relatively formal, requirement of respect. In accepting moral constraints as what, ideally, all human beings would agree upon in reasonable joint deliberations, we are, in a sense, respecting each person as a potential co-legislator of the

[16] Here I interpret and extend ideas Kant presents in *Groundwork*, 88–104, along lines discussed more fully in *Dignity and Practical Reason in Kant's Moral Theory*, and some later essays, including "Donagan's Kant," *Ethics* 104 (1993): 22–52.

basic principles we must all live by. The aim is to see that our conduct can be justified to others who are able and willing to take up the moral point of view. This does not mean that we may do only what others like, but only that we must avoid conduct that we believe would be prohibited by principles that all reasonable people (taking the moral perspective) would agree on.[17]

If some people are not now willing and able to deliberate morally, though they have the potential capacity to do so, their interests and voice can to some extent be represented by proxy: that is, by others trying to give weight to what those not now able to deliberate would agree to if they could and would take up the requisite point of view.[18] In this way we may think of children as

---

[17] Perhaps it is worth calling readers' attention here to an important qualification I introduce later when trying to accommodate the ideal Kantian model to the reality that reasonable people will not always agree: that is, one can view the model as a standard of individual *conscientious decision*, rather than *moral truth*. Moral truth, one might say, would be the ideal point on which all reasonable persons' moral deliberations would converge. But since we do not often know that, we can say that a conscientious choice is one based on what, after due deliberation, consultation, and taking seriously the opinions of others, the moral agent sincerely judges to be the best candidate for reasonable acceptance by all, even though he or she is aware that reasonable people may disagree.

[18] In this way, I am supposing, infants (at least all but the severely brain damaged) might have their interests represented and protected. Those who can now deliberate morally must do so in such a way that they could reasonably hope to justify their principles, eventually, to all with "humanity," the basic capacities and dispositions that enable a person to be a moral agent in human conditions. These capacities can be ready and developed, as Kant seemed to be supposing in most of his ethical writings; or they could be latent, as in young children. Much discussion would be required to decide, as interpretation of Kant or as independently defensible theory, where to draw these lines; but for now I assume that those with the latent capacities of humanity (e.g., young children) are among those to whom moral deliberators must try to imagine themselves justifying their policies. This involves trying to estimate, difficult as this might be, what the children would say was justifiable treatment when they are mature, aware of their basic human needs, but have not lost sight of their childhood interests. Alternatively, perhaps the hypothetical justification should be addressed to proxies who both understand and are fully devoted to the children's interests. These issues, I realize, are too complex and difficult to resolve here, and the same can be said of fetuses, the comatose, the permanently retarded, etc. They are issues that should not be swept aside; for unless they can be satisfactorily addressed within a Kantian framework, that framework remains subject to significant doubt.

represented in the moral deliberation process, even though not now ready actually to take part.[19]

A different sort of proxy argument from the Kantian framework might call for decent treatment, kindness, and even a kind of "respect" for nonhuman animals and members of our species born without any potential for moral deliberation; but such an argument, obviously, could not support a presumption of *respect for them as* (even potentially) *fellow "legislators" of moral principles.*

Although I shall not try to construct the argument for decent treatment of animals and brain-damaged human beings here, one point at least is worth noting now. Critics often assume that basic Kantian ethics can offer no better case for decent treatment of animals than the contingent, empirical argument Kant himself offered for an "indirect" duty not to be cruel to animals: that is, cruelty to animals is likely to foster habits of cruelty that are likely to be turned against human beings.[20] A common cause of this mistaken assumption, I suspect, is a confusion between the essential point in basic Kantian theory that "humanity" is *the source of moral duties* and the independent and, I believe, inessential point (un-

[19] The same might be said for any adults whom we *knew* to be so blindly devoted to *authorities* for answers to moral questions that they actually cannot yet engage in reasonable deliberation about moral issues on any other ground. Jeffrie Murphy feared that my presentation implied that many Roman Catholics must be denied basic respect because of their loyalty to their church and Scriptures; but I cannot see how this follows from my reconstructed Kantian view. First, it would be arrogantly presumptuous to suppose we *know* that the believers in question have no grasp of the moral considerations themselves, only blind acceptance of "orders" understood only as that. Typically, to the contrary, Catholics that I know have a good sense of morality *together with* a faith that, properly understood, authoritative church prescriptions are based on good moral reasons. Second, even if a given believer is not currently able to engage in moral dialogue and deliberation with anything more than appeals to authority, the Kantian perspective, as I understand it, does not deny that person respect as a human being; for we have no good reason to suppose such a person permanently and unalterably unresponsive to moral considerations presented as reasons for action rather than as commands.

The practical point of insisting on active capacities of independent reflection, autonomy, etc., in the *ideal* of moral deliberation is not to deny respect to imperfect deliberators, but just to indicate that in our *hypothetical* reasoning from that ideal construct we need not imagine that good moral arguments are constrained by a need to convince people when they are relying exclusively on authority.

[20] See *The Metaphysics of Morals*, 238.

fortunately also accepted by Kant) that "humanity" fully specifies and restricts the range of creatures toward whom we have direct moral duties. The latter implies, for example, not only that we have no duties "to" animals, but also that decent treatment of animals is morally required only insofar as indecent treatment of them would damage vital human interests. But this repugnant doctrine does not follow from the fundamental Kantian point that moral duties get their authority and direction from the ideal deliberations of reasonable human beings. If, as most of us believe, there are good reasons to deplore and prevent the needless suffering of animals, one should not assume, without further argument, that our reasonable Kantian moral "legislators" are precluded from taking these considerations into account and setting their moral standards accordingly. Some ways of expressing such reasons, admittedly, are incompatible with Kantian value theory, but we are not restricted to these.[21] The crucial point to remember in debates on this issue is that the fact that only human beings have moral duties (and the capacity to determine specifically what their duties are) does not entail that they can reasonably ignore the miseries of the beings who lack the capacity for morality but who nevertheless suffer in many of the ways that we do.

The idea of all human beings as potential co-legislators is admittedly a metaphor that abstracts in many ways from the imperfect conditions of real moral deliberation and discussion. Nevertheless, it is an ideal that makes vivid and brings together important aspects of what moral deliberation may be thought, at its best, to be. If we take the ideal seriously, we can see that it implicitly presupposes certain standards of respect that are, comparatively speaking, formal or procedural. For example, legislators

[21] Here I have in mind, for example, the old utilitarian idea that pains, whether human or animal, are "bad in themselves," where intrinsic badness is interpreted as a real metaphysical property that exists and is discernible as such independently of considerations about what it is reasonable to choose to pursue or to avoid. The contrast with a Kantian value theory, as I see it, is characterized in my *Autonomy and Self-Respect*, chapter 12.

sincerely trying to find reasonable agreements must *listen* to one another, take seriously the arguments of those who reject one's initial position. They must be *sincere* in their proposals and *nonmanipulative* in their arguments, for their aim is not to gain power through debate but to *convince* others that their position is justifiable. Efforts to *broaden one's knowledge*, to *see issues from others' point of view*, and to *invite criticism* of one's reasoning are all needed in honest attempts to locate and remove the sources of disagreement. Granting that no one has privileged access to moral truth requires us to *acknowledge the fallibility* of our moral judgments when we realize that others sincerely disagree. Even when we acknowledge persons only as *potential co-legislators*, as we do with young children, this suggests we should promote the development of their capacities to become mature moral deliberators. There is reason, then, to make education undogmatic, to encourage critical thinking, empathy, and communicative skills. Manipulative, seductive, deceitful, and overpowering rhetoric should be out of bounds both in moral education and in public discussion of moral issues. All these requirements are implicit in the idea that all are potential authors of the moral law, and, importantly for our purposes, they are all forms of respect. Thus, to accept the Kantian moral framework itself is already to acknowledge at least a presumption that all human beings should be accorded these forms of respect in moral discussion and education, in the ways appropriate to their level of development.[22]

Importantly, a ground for presuming more substantive requirements of respect for all human beings may be found when we actually try to take up the Kantian moral perspective,[23] rather than

[22] Note that the first reason for the presumption of respect for all, which I try to draw from the moral perspective itself, corresponds to what I was thinking of in "Donagan's Kant" as the "thin" notion of humanity as an end in itself. It is a minimum kind of respect built into the relatively formal idea that morality requires treating what "humanity," or rational willing, in each person legislates as supremely authoritative over one's other concerns.

[23] By "substantive requirements of respect" I have in mind the more specific prescriptions, beyond those I have just labeled "formal," that I discussed in my first

merely thinking about the formal constraints implicit in it.[24] Each rational person, Kant says, necessarily regards his or her own humanity as an end in itself, on the same ground as do others; and so, Kant argues, we must regard humanity in every person as an end in itself. There are various ways to read this argument; some render it fallacious, others (including one I discussed earlier) merely make it implausible.[25] A more promising idea suggested by the passage is this. Suppose we ask what do people, despite their diverse backgrounds and values, typically regard as especially important, of highest priority, about themselves and how they are to be treated by others? Deep reflection, we can conjecture, will typically downgrade many of the momentary, superficial concerns we have and focus our attention on matters such as having a life, freedom, security, opportunities, self-respect, and the substantive forms of respect from others. We tend to regard concern for these things, which Kant associates with our "humanity," as more than mere personal preferences, in fact as (objectively) higher-order values on which we have a legitimate claim. Placing a high priority on being respected for one's humanity, or rational nature, may even be thought to be implicit in the common (rather thick) concept of a rational person, one who lives a life governed by reason.[26]

---

lecture. Ideally, in a fuller argument, these would be reviewed and explained in detail, but for now I am concerned mainly to sketch the *pattern* of the argument from the Kantian legislative perspective to justify requiring more substantive forms of respect.

[24] This corresponds to my conjecture, in "Donagan's Kant," that one might argue from the moral perspective defined with a "thin" idea of humanity as an end to a "thicker" or richer normative conception of humanity as an end. The key would be arguing that any reasonable person who acknowledges all persons as "ends in themselves" in the thin sense would, because of some plausible but contingent premises about what people deeply care about, try to protect as nearly absolute (and as not subject to trade) certain other values that earlier (in *Dignity and Practical Reason*, chapter 2) I described as implicit in Kant's idea of "humanity as an end in itself." For example, the value of (honorable) life, not being deprived of one's rational capacities, claims to a fair share of external liberty, symbolic expressions of respect from others, etc.

[25] See section 2, paragraphs 3 and 4, of this lecture.

[26] This suggestion is in line with the interpretation I mentioned but did not pursue in section 2, paragraph 4. I intend to return to this on another occasion.

In any case, the key assumption for present purposes is just that, in the absence of strong contrary evidence, we can reasonably presume that, when thinking clearly and deeply, people tend to place a high priority on being respected as human beings, in important substantive ways, independently of whatever respect they might earn for special merit.[27]

Supposing this is generally true of human beings, then we all have reason to *propose* moral constraints to protect these essential or high-priority values, including substantial forms of respect, and on the same grounds we have reason to *hope that others will endorse* these constraints as well. In the moral legislative model, the condition of insisting on protection for oneself is willingness to concede that one must grant a similar protection for others. So, assuming, as I suggested, that having the respect in question is among the higher-priority shared values, then we can suppose that everyone deliberating from the Kantian legislative perspective would endorse at least the presumption that every human being is to be respected so far as possible in the substantive ways that we so highly value. Since not all human beings have special skills or unusual merit, compared to others, the respect we presume required cannot be *respect for a person's merit* but rather *respect for a person's position*, which in this case must be just the position of "being human."

Having now sketched the patterns of argument for presuming that respect for all human beings is morally required, we must face a *recurring objection*. Kant's arguments assume that all "human

---

[27] Note I did not say "absolute priority." The point is compatible with people thinking that they would sacrifice, subordinate, or only conditionally value the respect under some imaginary circumstances (e.g., if the price of insisting on universal respect was tolerance of evil). But if they realize that, as I suggest later, we could have and give an unconditional respect to every human being, as such, without losing our right to self-protection, moral criticism, and punishment, then they may see no need to qualify the value they place on such respect. We can conceive a world where everyone unconditionally respected every person as a human being (though not for merit), where this respect is never forfeited, without supposing that in that more respectful world we would have to tolerate, avoid censuring, or even try to like people who behave outrageously.

beings," or persons with "humanity," have, at least potentially, the capacity and predisposition to deliberate from a moral perspective and to act accordingly, and Kant apparently had faith that virtually all the (adult) people we are likely to meet, perhaps outside institutions for the insane, in fact have the essential attributes of "humanity." Today, however, we may question this assumption. Are there reasonable doubts sufficient to undermine even the modest claim that we should, *for practical purposes, presume* that all the cognitively competent, functioning people we encounter in daily life qualify for our respect as human beings?

Kant, like most others in his era, seemed to accept without much question the predisposition to morality as a basic feature of human nature.[28] He granted that human beings have, in addition, an innate tendency to evil, but even that, as Kant interpreted it, was just a tendency, under temptation, to refuse to follow a moral law that in our hearts we acknowledge as authoritative for us.[29] No human being, he supposed, loves evil for evil's sake; and no one mature enough to understand morality could be indifferent to it. Even the worst murderers when facing the gallows, he thought, could not help but feel remorse and sense the justice of their punishment. There are two aspects to the human will: one, our practical reason (*Wille*), acknowledges the reasonableness of moral considerations and makes us respect their authority; the other, our power of choice (*Willkur*), enables us to choose in practice to follow that authority or else to violate it. A moral choice, Kant thought, preserves integrity and self-esteem, but an immoral choice inevitably results in internal conflict of will and discontent with oneself; conscience, an internal judge, is inescapable.[30]

Are there, despite Kant's faith, functioning adult members of our biological species who do not have, even potentially, the ca-

---

[28] Immanuel Kant, *Religion within the Limits of Reason Alone*, trans. T. M. Greene and H. H. Hudson (New York: Harper and Brothers, 1960), 21–23.

[29] *Religion*, 23–40.

[30] *The Metaphysics of Morals*, 233–35.

pacity for morality? There are several different categories to consider. First, literature is full of grand tales about *defiant immoralists*, who, like Milton's fallen angel, take as their motto, "Evil, be thou my good!" There are also stories about completely *innocent amoralists*, who somehow manage to grow up and interact with others, like gentle but intelligent animals, but remain conscience-free and impervious to moral concepts. Turning from fiction to more troublesome real cases, *sociopaths*, we are told, can have an intellectual grasp of moral concepts but remain inwardly unmoved by them. They can manipulate others by moral arguments, but, having never internalized any moral standards, they have no conscience to violate.

Obviously, the severely brain damaged can lack moral capacities, but our question is a more difficult one: Can human beings with a full range of cognitive and linguistic capacities nonetheless be *utterly unable* to acknowledge and be moved by moral considerations? If so, our previous Kantian arguments would apparently give us no reason for respecting them as human beings, for those arguments presupposed that they were potentially among those whose acknowledgment of the basic moral framework made them respect-worthy co-legislators of moral principles. Even if morality is like a fair, mutually beneficial game for all who can accept and play by its rules, we could not be sure that everyone has the *ability* to do so. Given this, for all we know, some who otherwise appear mature and responsible adults deserve neither the benefits nor the burdens of being respected as human beings with moral capacities. It is often thought, for example, that empirical evidence shows that this is how "sociopaths" should be viewed.

The issue, whether in fact those labeled "sociopaths" really lack all capacity and disposition to morality, can be settled only by empirical investigation, not philosophical speculation. It should be noted, however, that the issue is not as easy to revolve as it might seem at first. Sociopaths no doubt display ample evidence that they *do not* constrain themselves by familiar moral principles, but much more is needed to demonstrate that they *cannot*. They have developed their amoral habits and policies in response to particular circumstances, and we lack adequate evidence whether they would remain equally unresponsive in all circumstances. Perhaps they have seen all too well how cynically some self-professed moralists use moral discourse to their own advantage. Perhaps they have never experienced anything they trusted as genuine, rather than self-serving, judgmental, and manipulative, moral discourse and interaction with others. Like everyone else, they display evidence of their predispositions by their responses in a certain corner of our very imperfect world, which is not a world ideally designed always to bring out a latent moral predisposition if there is one. Therapists working within a mental health model are not trained or expected to engage their clients in genuine moral dialogue, as equals, providing the recalcitrant with the good and sincere moral arguments needed to elicit a moral response if that is possible. So a sociopath's resistance to therapy is not necessarily the same as irremediable insensitivity to moral concerns.

Given our ignorance or uncertainty about the empirical issue, there is a practical moral consideration that should suffice to make us quite reluctant to identify classes of aware and functioning people as nonetheless utterly lacking in the potential for morality. History is stained with a bloody record of what happens when people too lightly dismiss as "inhuman" other people they dislike and fail to understand. Greeks thought the barbarians incapable of reason and virtue; Europeans and early Americans viewed black Africans and their descendents that way; and there is a long record of men thinking that women are human enough to follow, but not to lead, to be gentle and compassionate, but not to be just and courageous. We are obviously tempted to take the failure of others to conform to *our own* moral ideas as sufficient evident that they *cannot* think morally and do not deserve the respect of moral dialogue. Since this temptation has been for centuries an unfair source of misery to people misjudged to be "less than human," it seems wise to counteract the temptation with a strong contrary presumption that, until *proved* otherwise, virtually all the cognitively able and functioning people we meet have at least the *potential* capacity and disposition to engage with others in mutually respectful, reciprocal moral relations.

Since we must act under uncertainty about whether sociopaths, and other apparent amoralists, are *incapable* of morality, we risk error however we treat them. The practical question, then, is: which error would be worse? From a moral point of view, I suggest, it is generally worse to risk denying respect where it is due than to risk granting respect where it is not due. In the first case, we risk wrongfully casting a potentially responsible human being out of the moral community, whereas in the second case we only risk wasting our moral scruples where they are not needed. So, again, for practical purposes, we should presume that respect is due to all.

5. *Conditional Grounds for Refusing to Allow That Basic Respect Can Be Forfeited*

Assuming for now that there is a strong presumption that every human being should be respected as such, can they, by persistent and unrepentant immorality, *forfeit* all the respect that was presumptively due to them as human beings? In other words, can a person's conduct be so contemptuous of others that it defeats and cancels our (presumed) obligation to respect him or her as a human being? Many seem to think so; Kant did not, but, in any case, it is a practically important, but complex, issue.

To avoid misunderstanding, note that *forfeiting* occurs when *moral agents*, who are responsible for their actions, violate important rules so flagrantly that their *culpable* misconduct removes from others the moral obligation to treat those persons (in certain respects) as otherwise their standing would have required. Thus, for example, an ordinary felon forfeits a right to vote, and club members delinquent in their dues may forfeit their club privileges.

If a creature that we formerly took to be a responsible moral agent did things so wild, destructive, and unresponsive to reason that we concluded that we owed "it" utterly no moral consideration, this would not necessarily be a matter of judging that a person *forfeited* all his or her rights. Forfeit presupposes responsible moral agency, and our changed attitude might simply reflect our opinion that earlier we misjudged the *causal responsible* agent to be morally responsible as well. Rather than grounds for forfeit, the person's deplorable conduct may be viewed as evidence that we have misclassified the agent, supposing "it" more like an animal or an unsocialized, wild child than a responsible human adult.

Two quick caveats are needed here. First, there are strong practical and moral reasons, as I noted earlier, for being very reluctant to reclassify any functioning adult as "merely an animal," and my hypothetical example above is not meant to deny this. The point of introducing it is simply to stress that saying that a moral agent *forfeits* all rights and standing as a human being is quite different from saying that someone does not qualify as a moral agent, responsible for his or her conduct. Second, because of the extraordinary difficulty of fully understanding the psychology of Hitler, Attila the Hun, Jeffrey Dahmer, and the like, these extreme cases are not good test cases for a *general policy* about what rights criminals and other moral offenders forfeit. So, for now, let us concentrate on more easily intelligible cases, admitting that more may need to be said about cases in which the evil — or madness — is apparently so extreme as to defy understanding.

From the Kantian perspective, there are several possible ways of arguing that no one should be seen as having totally forfeited all respect as a human being. Our considerable ignorance of the deep motives and character of offenders is significant. Also, since lawful conduct is no guarantee of moral attitudes, we are to a considerable extent ignorant of the *comparative* moral worth of overt offenders and law-abiding citizens. Again, since we cannot help risking that we will misjudge people, we need to consider whether it is better to err one way rather than the other. Is it not better to err by giving offenders more respect then they are due than to err by denying offenders respect that is due? Can any of us with genuine moral humility, rooted in honest scrutiny of our own characters and motives, confidently deny all force to the thought "There, but for circumstance (God's grace, luck, or whatever), go I?" Are we willing to live in a world where everyone judges us, up to the point of utter contempt, by the loose standards of evidence needed for anyone to reach a verdict on another's ultimate moral deserts? Further, would not treating criminals and other offenders with utter contempt, as Kant suggests, cast a shadow of dishonor on all human beings? After all, by hypothesis, if culpable, those we condemn are "responsible" moral agents, and so they retain at least some minimum responsiveness to moral concerns. Moreover, their failings, broadly speaking, are similar to ours in kind even if not in degree.

The Kantian framework, as presented here, suggests another line of argument. This relies more heavily on empirical assumptions than Kant would have liked, but nonetheless it seems relevant. If we address the issue of forfeit from within the Kantian framework, it boils down to whether appropriately situated "legislators" of (derivative) moral standards would cancel the presumed obligation to respect all human beings for the special case of heinous crimes and moral offenses. Since this is a question about real, quite imperfect human circumstances, it requires a shift from ideal to nonideal theory and hence some appropriate adjustments in how we conceive the Kantian moral deliberators addressing the issue.

Let me pause briefly to explain. In ideal theory we ask, What principles would moral legislators make under the assumptions that the legislators will agree and that each will accept and follow their joint decisions? But the principles that would be reasonable if we could assume universal conscientious compliance may be quite unreasonable, even disastrous, if applied to the real world, where noncompliance is frequent and compliance must often be forced by threat of punishment. This does not mean that ideal theory is useless. It is often helpful to think *first*, What would be the ideal principles, that is, the principles most reasonable to adopt *if* all would conscientiously follow them? This is helpful, however, only so long as we are willing to think again, more realistically, about the differences between that ideal world and ours. Then the issue becomes, How must those ideal rules be modified to accommodate the facts of the actual world — for example, the facts that even the most conscientious people commonly disagree about moral principles and that the less conscientious often violate even their own principles? If we accept the legislative model, the strategy for addressing such issues is to consider what modifications ideal legislators would make in their principles if they knew they were legislating for people who are quite imperfect in specified ways.

Consider, for example, the problem raised by *moral disagreement*. In the most abstractly conceived Kantian moral legislature, "the kingdom of ends," individual differences among members are discounted and so no disagreements are anticipated. But how are we to apply the ideal to our circumstances, where, even with the best efforts to eliminate bias, disagreements persist? The best move toward a solution, I suggest, would be to adjust the Kantian framework as follows. As more ideal moral legislators presumably would recommend *for moral deliberation in our imperfect world* where moral disagreements are pervasive, our best possible human deliberators should (1) acknowledge their liability to disagreement while continuing to seek as broadly based and well grounded agreement as possible. To this end, they would also (2) prescribe a variety of strategies to reduce deep disagreements, such as encouraging cross-cultural understanding, broadening the scope of moral dialogues, looking for common values beneath superficial differences, accepting mediating procedures when substantive disagreement proves unresolvable, and so on. Then, aware that these strategies are not always successful, they would (3) recommend both *moral humility* and *conscientiousness*, as the best attitudes in a world where moral certainty and universal agreement are impossible. By this I mean that when moral disagreements persist, despite our best efforts to reduce them, then the best we can do is to admit our fallibility,[31] and then, each of us, act on the principles that we honestly judge to be *the most plausible candidates* for being justifiable to all. With this amendment, reflections from ideal theory can help to guide *conscientious* personal choice even though they offer no assurance of moral *"truth."* [32]

Now to return to the issue of forfeit, we need to consider how such moral deliberators would modify ideal principles if deciding standards for a world (like ours) that is imperfect in another important respect besides its liability to moral disagreement—namely, even when there is agreement on what is morally required, *noncompliance is frequent and coercion is necessary*. In particular, would they withdraw the presumption that everyone should be respected as a human being?

Recall that our hypothetical moral deliberators are now concerned to settle on rules for an imperfect world, like ours, in which even conscientious people have lapses and no one is completely immune from corruption. Although character and conduct are not entirely matters of luck, they know that, in our imperfect world, luck provides very unequal opportunities, temptations, and social pressures. Even if, as relatively comfortable and educated folk, they are fairly confident that they, and their loved ones, will never commit the most serious crimes, they know that other less fortunate or more impulsive people will do so despite the fact that they

---

[31] Strictly, one should admit not only fallibility (i.e., that one may be in error about what is the best candidate for justifiability to all), but also that there may be no fact of the matter about which of several candidates is better.

[32] By moral "truth" within the framework considered here we must mean what all human beings, as ideal co-legislators, from the moral point of view would agree on. Conscientiousness requires merely trying one's best to think issues through from that point of view, in consultation with others, and acting on the outcome.

are not beyond redemption or utterly lacking in concern for others. They know too that the children and partners loved by many respectable people will turn to crime, for reasons we cannot fully understand. Their confidence that they themselves, and their own children and loved ones, will never turn out like this may not be as justified as they think. In any case this special feature of their own case is more relevant to their private wishes than to what they should approve as general moral policy.

Another important fact that they must keep in mind is that all systems for imposing punishment and moral sanctions are subject to error, both unintended mistakes and deliberate abuses. Adding this to the previous considerations, the result is that the moral deliberators should be aware that a policy allowing that serious offenders forfeit all respect would, over time, authorize utterly contemptuous treatment for some innocent people, many of mixed character, some who now fully intend to be law-abiding, and many loved by them.

Before a policy is settled, moral deliberation should also include vivid representation of what utterly contemptuous treatment can amount to. First, there are many practices actually employed in prisons today: for example, deemphasizing individuality by giving prisoners generic haircuts, uniforms, cells, and identification tags; moving them by physical force whether needed or not; using basic comfort and opportunities for physical exercise, mental stimulation, and companionship as special "treats" to manipulate behavior; ignoring prison rapes and beatings; and unrestrained verbal abuse from guards. Next, we must recall the many contemptuous forms of punishment employed in various places throughout history: physical beatings and burnings, sleep deprivation, prolonged solitary confinement, "silent treatment," exiling, ostracizing, public humiliation by branding, tarring and feathering, coerced false confessions, "brainwashing," drawing and quartering, public display of heads on pikes, refusal of burial, expunging names from records, and blacklisting heirs. More informal expressions of contempt should also not be forgotten: cursing, spitting, mocking, gratuitous denial of innocent wishes, and other efforts to express disdain (treating someone "like dirt," "like a worm," or "like garbage"). Especially when based on the thought that the guilty person has *forfeited* all moral standing, these punishments and symbolic humiliations are ones that we are naturally very reluctant to risk incurring or imposing on anyone about whom we care. This is not only because we hate pain but because we could hardly bear the utter contempt these practices express, which is far more, and worse, than mere retribution, vengeance, indignation, and angry rebuke. It represents the will of others, collectively, to deny any remaining worth to our existence, and it would be a rare person who could maintain his or her self-respect, or even self-love, when forced to confront that message.

Recall, too, that those who accept the Kantian framework are not self-centered or "mutually disinterested," like Rawls's "original position" members. They are committed to regarding humanity in each person as an end in itself, and at least formal requirements of respect for persons as co-legislators of moral standards are implicit in the basic framework for deliberation. Also, with some minimal empirical assumptions, we can argue *from* the Kantian framework *to* reasonable presumptions of further (substantive) respect, as we did above. Similar argument would support *prima facie* requirements of mutual aid and promoting the happiness of others, since no appropriately impartial legislator would deny that meeting vital needs and promoting happiness are good to do at least *when there is no relevant reason not to.*

Given all this, it seems incredible to suppose that all Kantian deliberators would agree that criminals and other moral offenders can altogether forfeit respect and that, therefore, we may treat them with utter contempt. There is good reason to suppose that to be subjected to such contempt is too awful to risk, not only from an individual's point of view but from that of any representative person reflecting on general policies in advance of involvement in particular cases. They would not want to risk being treated with utter contempt; nor would they want to risk this for anyone else because, by hypothesis, they care (to some degree) about everyone.

This conclusion needs to be qualified, however. All have *good reasons* not to accept a policy that risks utterly contemptuous treatment for them or anyone they care for; but, for argument's sake, we must concede that there could be *overriding reasons*, warranting the risk. Our conclusion that respect cannot be forfeited seems clear, then, provided one further condition can be met. This remaining condition is that the attitude of not permitting respect to be forfeited is possible for us and is compatible with our other responsibilities, in particular, to protect ourselves, to maintain just punishment, and to speak out forcefully against moral atrocities. Do we need to treat serious offenders with utter contempt in order to protect ourselves, to give them their just deserts, or to express our reasonable outrage? In the next, and final, section, I suggest that, to the contrary, we can continue to respect offenders as human beings without sacrificing any of these concerns.

6. *The Possibility of Respectful Self-protection, Punishment, and Moral Censure*

My claim in this final section is the following. The proviso we left open in the argument above is satisfied because we can treat everyone with basic human respect and still meet our other responsibilities. Thus, our presumption that all moral agents should be respected as human beings should stand even for perpetrators of serious crimes and moral offenses. Even they should not be seen as forfeiting all respect.

First, is self-protection compatible with respect? Many of us would agree with Kant that, properly constrained, self-protection is a right and a responsibility. We may resist unlawful threats with force, and we should not let anyone "walk all over us." Measured, proportional responses to unwarranted threats, however, are not contemptuous of the attacker. Even lethal force in self-defense is permitted by traditional moral standards, widely agreed to be justifiable to virtually all reasonable persons. Nor do we need to return mockery and degrading insults to those who hurl them at us, for there are more effective ways to combat verbal abuse. A policy of trusting the demonstrably untrustworthy is not a requirement of respect, but merely foolishness. Tolerating others' abuse and contempt is not a way of respecting them, or oneself; it only smooths the way for continuing maltreatment. Respectful self-protection leaves the door open for negotiation and reconciliation, when possible, but it does not require dropping one's guard prematurely.

Even when self-protection warrants lethal force against an aggressor, readiness to kill *when absolutely necessary* need not express the *contemptuous attitude* that the aggressor has forfeited all considerations as a human being. The respectful self-defender would *prefer*, if possible, that aggressors retreat peacefully, that they not suffer permanent pain and humiliation, and that ultimately they would rejoin the law-abiding community and thrive in their legitimate concerns. Utter contempt shows in the use of unnecessary force, disregard for peaceful options, and, generally, regarding unjust aggressors as nothing but obstacles to be eliminated.

Second, is basic respect compatible with reasonable effective and just punishment? What is needed are public systems that protect legitimate interests, discourage further violations of reasonable laws, and yet also respect everyone, including criminals, as human beings. Granted, our own coercive social systems fall short, but that does not mean that effective systems of protection, deterrence, and punishment must necessarily deny basic respect to offenders. Surely neither the draconian methods of punishment nor the attitudes of utter contempt reviewed in the last section are necessary; and history does not record that they have been remarkably effective.

In any decent social order with a proper respect for its members, there will need to be fair, public rules designed to ensure the members a secure life with opportunities to pursue what they find valuable, provided the pursuits are compatible with others' right to similar pursuits. Universal respect does not require *tolerance* of willful violations of the rights of others. In principle, and approximately in practice, a society can respect all the members by maintaining laws and other social norms, guaranteeing, to all who will cooperate, security and opportunities that would be impossible without rule-governed mutual constraints. By limiting surveillance and the constant presence of armed guards, the members trust each other, conditionally, to comply with the laws from a conscientious regard for what they can see as a fair basis for cooperation. Even this (cautious) trust is a form of respect. Once the trust has been breached, we can show basic respect by providing fair trial, access to legal defense, consideration of mitigating circumstances, avenues of appeal, respectful demeanor and speech in legal processes, abolition of degrading forms of punishment, resources to encourage reform, appropriate criteria for parole, and prison conditions that do not add gratuitous degradation to just punishment. To ensure *respectful just punishment* we need reforms in both our practices and our attitudes, but neither experience nor philosophical argument has shown that this is an unattainable goal.

Third, similar considerations apply when we turn to moral censure, outside the legal system. Just as some systems of punishment are disrespectful and others are not, moral blame and disapproval can be respectful or not. There are many ways these can be disrespectful. For example, an unwarranted, disrespectful superiority is displayed when we self-righteously blame others for overt offenses no worse than our private ones. Again, we show disrespect when we make oral accusations based on flimsy evidence, class stereotyping, and no genuine effort to understand. Also, manipulative blame, meant merely to condition subjects to associate unwanted behaviors with bad feelings, ignores the reason and judgment of those who are blamed, in effect denying their moral agency. It is how we train pigeons and rats that we regard as incapable of responsible choice. Finally, hurling epithets at someone in contempt, merely to vent one's hostility, to cause pain, or to please a sympathetic crowd, fails to address the offender as a person because there is no willingness to hear a response.

We are not forced to choose between disrespectful blame and cold, contemptuous dismissal because *respectful moral accusation, argument, and censure* are possible. Moral blame, properly conceived, is a judgment addressed to someone presumed capable of hearing it as such and responding appropriately. Blame is not merely a pain inflicted to deter future misconduct by inducing an expectation that similar pains will recur when misconduct recurs. The most painful and disturbing moral censure, in fact, presupposes that the person blamed is "one of us," guilty of betrayal of shared commitments and capable of feeling the bite of the censure just because he or she has internalized moral ideas of mutual respect under which he or she stands accused. To express moral disapproval is all the more appropriate when the accuser is not a moralistic busybody, quick to judge, but is the very person the offender has most disrespected by his or her conduct. Judicious moral blame is a judgment that itself respects the accused as a moral agent, capable of hearing and heeding the relevant moral point. Although notoriously those of us in glass houses should be reluctant to use it, moral blame can be loud, vehement, and pointed while at the same time respectfully addressing the conscience of the accused.

I hasten to add that my remarks here are not meant to encourage a moralistic, judgmental attitude, for this too is a serious vice that mutually respectful people have many reasons to avoid and discourage.[33] My point is just that since *respectful blame* is an option in response to extreme immorality, one cannot argue that

---

[33] In fact in my previous writings I have so emphasized the merits of not being judgmental, rather than the possibility of respectful moral judgment and censure, that I fear this may have encouraged the suspicion that Kantian respect is incompatible with vigorous moral blame. My last remarks are meant, in part, to correct that impression.

all respect is forfeited by serious moral offenders because to think otherwise would be to condone their offenses. Since just and respectful punishment and moral censure are available to express appropriate moral attitudes and protect legitimate interests, there is no good reason to set aside our initial presumption that all human beings have dignity, a respect-worthy status that need not be earned and cannot be forfeited.

This conclusion is pertinent to our initial concerns, in the first lecture, with moral debates on university campuses. For example, both sides in disputes about sexism and racism are usually convinced that their stand is conscientious and correct. No one admits to being either a bigot or an unfair accuser of bigotry; and so the problem has more to do with "erring conscience" and moral insensitivity than with willful immorality. Here, more than ever, there is a need and an opportunity for mutually respectful moral discussion because, unlike in criminal cases, typically both sides are already publicly committed to being conscientious in their judgments. Moreover, the confrontations take place within universities, which are institutions, more than any other, opposed to dogmatism, empty rhetoric, and manipulation of opinion and committed, instead, to listening to evidence, accepting criticism, and understanding alternative points of view. That is the theory, anyway; and mutually respectful moral debate should be part of the practice.

Common-Law Courts in a Civil-Law System: The Role of United States Federal Courts in Interpreting the Constitution and Laws

ANTONIN SCALIA

THE TANNER LECTURES ON HUMAN VALUES

Delivered at

Princeton University
March 8 and 9, 1995

ANTONIN SCALIA is Associate Justice of the United States Supreme Court. He was educated at Georgetown University and the University of Fribourg, and received his law degree from Harvard University, where he was the note editor for the Harvard Law Review. He has served as general counsel for the Office of Telecommunications Policy in the Executive Office of the President, and as an assistant attorney general in the Office of Legal Counsel at the U.S. Department of Justice. He was a professor of law at the University of Virginia and the University of Chicago, a visiting professor at Georgetown University and Stanford University, and a scholar in residence at the American Enterprise Institute. He was nominated to the U.S. Court of Appeals in 1982, and took the oath of office for the Supreme Court in 1986. He is the author of *A Matter of Interpretation: Federal Courts and the Law* (1997).

I

The title of these lectures, as I assume those who are not here by accident have been advised, is "Common-Law Courts in a Civil-Law System: The Role of United States Federal Courts in Interpreting the Constitution and Laws." That title is a reflection of one of my concerns with modern American legal education, and one of the reasons I believe my philosophy of statutory construction in general (known loosely as textualism) and of constitutional construction in particular (known loosely as originalism) is repugnant to the first instincts of much of the legal profession. In this first day's lecture, I intend to describe generally the common-law system, and how it is taught, and to contrast it with the work of statutory construction that is the principal business of modern courts. In tomorrow's lecture I will discuss some of the techniques of textual interpretation, including those particularly applicable to the constitution.

It is difficult to convey to someone who has not attended law school the enormous impact of the first year of study. Many students remark upon the phenomenon: It is like a mental rebirth, the acquisition of what seems like a whole new mode of perceiving and thinking. Thereafter, even if one does not yet know much law, he — as the expression goes — "thinks like a lawyer."

The overwhelming majority of the courses taught in that first year of law school, and surely the ones that have the most impact, are courses that teach the substance, and the methodology, of the common law — torts, for example; contracts; property; criminal law. We lawyers cut our teeth upon the common law. To understand what an effect that must have, you must appreciate that the common law is not really common law, except insofar as judges can be regarded as common. That is to say, it is not "customary law," or a reflection of the people's practices, but is rather law developed by the judges. Perhaps in the very infancy of the common law it could have been thought that the courts were mere expositors of generally accepted social practices; and certainly, even in the full maturity of the common law, a well established commercial or social practice could form the basis for a court's decision. But from an early time — as early as the Year Books, which record English judicial decisions from the end of the thirteenth century to the beginning of the sixteenth — any equivalence between custom and common law had ceased to exist, except in the sense that the doctrine of *stare decisis* rendered prior judicial decisions "custom." The issues coming before the courts involved, more and more, refined questions that customary practice gave no answer to.

Oliver Wendell Holmes's inflential book *The Common Law* — which is still suggested reading for entering law students — talks a little bit about Germanic and early English custom. But mostly it talks about individual judicial decisions, and about the judges, famous and obscure, who wrote them: Chief Justice Choke, Doderidge, J., Lord Holt, Redfield, C.J., Rolle, C.J., Hankford, J., Baron Parke, Lord Ellenborough, Lord Holt, Peryam, C.B., Danby and Brian, Brett, J., Cockburn, C.J., Popham, C.J., Hyde, C.J., and on and on and on. Holmes's book is a paean to reason, and to the men who brought that faculty to bear in order to *create* Anglo-American law.

This is the image of the law — the common law — to which an aspiring lawyer is first exposed, even if he hasn't read Holmes over the previous summer as he was supposed to. You all know about the case-law method, brought to movies and TV by the famous Professor Kingsfield. The student is assigned to read a series of cases, set forth in a casebook, designed to show how the law developed. In the field of contracts, for example — to take a course I once taught — he reads, and discusses in class, the famous old case of *Hadley* v. *Baxendale*,[1] decided a century and a half ago by

[1] 9 Ex. 341, 156 Eng. Rep. 145 (1854).

the English Court of Exchequer: A mill in Gloucester ground to a halt (so to speak) because of a cracked crank-shaft. To get a new one made, it was necessary to send the old one, as a model, to the manufacturer of the mill's steam-engine, in Greenwich. The miller sent one of his workers to a carrier's office to see how long the delivery would take; the worker told the carrier's clerk that the mill was stopped, and that the shaft must be sent immediately. The clerk replied that if the shaft was received by noon it would be delivered the next day. The miller delivered the shaft to the carrier before noon the next day and paid the fee to have it transported; but because of the carrier's neglect it took several additional days to be delivered, with the result that the mill took several additional days to get back into service. The miller sought, as damages for breach of the shipping contract, his lost profits for those days, which were of course many times what the carrier had received as the shipping charge. The carrier said that he was not liable for such remote consequences.

Now this was a fairly subtle and refined point of law. As with most points that reached the stage of litigation, it could not really be said that there was a general practice which the court could impose as common, customary law. The court decided, essentially, that the carrier was right, and it laid down the very important rule, that in a suit for breach of contract not *all* damages suffered because of the breach can be recovered, but only those that "could have been fairly and reasonably contemplated by both the parties when they made [the] contract." The opinion contains some policy reasons for the result, citation of a few earlier opinions by English courts, and citation of not a single snippet of statutory law — though counsel arguing the case did bring to the court's attention the disposition set forth in the French Civil Code. For there *was* no relevant English statutory law; contract law was almost entirely the creation of English judges.

I must interject at this point (the old contracts professor in me compels it), that even assuming the new rule that only reasonably foreseeable damages are recoverable, the miller rather than the carrier should have won the case. The court's opinion simply overlooks the fact that the carrier was *informed* that the mill was stopped; it must have been quite clear to the carrier's clerk that restarting the mill was the reason for the haste; and that profits would be lost while the mill was idle. But if you think it is terribly important that the case came out wrong, you are not yet thinking like a lawyer — or at least not like a common lawyer. That is really secondary. Famous old cases are famous, you see, not because they came out right, but because the rule of law they announced was the intelligent one. Common-law courts performed two functions: One was to apply the law to the facts. All adjudicators — French judges, arbitrators, even baseball umpires and football referees — do that. But the second function, and the more important one, was to *make* the law.

If you were sitting in on Professor Kingsfield's class when *Hadley* v. *Baxendale* was the assigned reading, you would find that the class discussion would not end with the mere description and dissection of the opinion. Various "hypotheticals" would be proposed by the crusty (yet, under it all, good-hearted) old professor, testing the validity and the sufficiency of the "foreseeability" rule. What if, for example, you are a blacksmith, and a young knight rides up on a horse that has thrown a shoe. He tells you he is returning to his ancestral estate, Blackacre, where he must be that very evening to claim his inheritance, or else it will go to his wicked, no-good cousin, the Sheriff of Nottingham. You contract to put on a new shoe, for the going rate of three farthings. The shoe is defective, or is badly shod, and the knight reaches Blackacre too late. Are you really liable for the full amount of his inheritance? Is it reasonable to impose that degree of liability for three farthings? Wouldn't the parties have set a different price if liability of that amount had been contemplated? Ought there not be, in other words, some limiting principle to damages beyond mere foreseeability? Indeed, might not that principle — call it presumed assumption of risk — explain why *Hadley* v. *Baxendale* reached the right result after all, though not for the precise reason it assigned?

What intellectual fun all of this is! I describe it to you, not — please believe me — to induce those of you in the audience who are not yet lawyers to go to law school. But rather, to explain why first-year law school is so exhilarating: because it consists of playing common-law judge. Which in turn consists of playing king — devising, out of the brilliance of one's own mind, those laws that ought to govern mankind. What a thrill! And no wonder so many lawyers, having tasted this heady brew, aspire to be judges!

Besides learning how to think about, and devise, the "best" legal rule, there is another skill imparted in the first year of law school that is essential to the making of a good common-law judge. It is the technique of what is called "distinguishing" cases. It is a necessary skill, because an absolute prerequisite to common-law lawmaking is the doctrine of *stare decisis* — that is, the principle that a decision made in one case will be followed in the next. Quite obviously, without such a principle common-law courts would not be making any "law"; they would just be resolving the particular dispute before them. It is the requirement that future courts adhere to the principle underlying a judicial decision which causes that decision to be a legal rule. (There is no such requirement in the civil-law system, where it is the text of the law rather than any prior judicial interpretation of that text which is authoritative. Prior judicial opinions are consulted for their persuasive effect, much as academic commentary would be; but they are not *binding*.)

Within such a precedent-bound common-law system, it is obviously critical for the lawyer, or the judge, to establish whether the case at hand falls within a principle that has already been decided. Hence the technique — or the art, or the game — of "distinguishing" earlier cases. A whole series of lectures could be devoted to this subject, and I do not want to get into it too deeply here. Suffice to say that there is a good deal of wiggle-room as to what an earlier case "holds." In the strictest sense, the holding of a decision cannot go beyond the facts that were before the court. Assume, for example, that a painter contracts to paint my house green, and he paints it instead a god-awful puce. And assume that not I, but my *neighbor*, sues the painter for this breach of contract. The court would dismiss the suit on the ground that there was no "privity" of contract: the painter made his deal with *me*, and not my neighbor. Assume a later case in which a computer company contracts to fix my home computer, which has been malfunctioning; it does a bad job, and as a consequence my wife loses a whole series of valuable files that it takes many hours to replicate. *She* sues the computer company. Now the broad rationale of the earlier case (no suit will lie where there is no privity of contract) would dictate dismissal of this complaint as well. But a good common-law lawyer would argue (and some good common-law judges have held) that that rationale does not extend to this *new* fact situation, in which the breach of a contract relating to something used in the home harms a family member, though not the one who made the contract. The earlier case, in other words, is "distinguishable."

It should be apparent that, by reason of the doctrine of *stare decisis*, as limited by the principle I have just described, the common law grew in a peculiar fashion — rather like a scrabble-board. No word previously spoken could be erased, but you could add qualifications to it. The first case lays on the board: "No liability for breach of contractual duty without privity"; the next player adds "unless injured party is member of household." And the game continues.

As I have described, this system of making law by judicial opinion, and making law by distinguishing earlier cases, is what every American law student, what every newborn American lawyer, first sees when he opens his eyes. And the impression remains with him for life. His image of the great judge — the Holmes, the Cardozo — is the man (or woman) who has the intelligence to know what is the best rule of law to govern the case at hand, and then the skill to perform the broken-field running through earlier cases that leaves him free to impose that rule — distinguishing one prior case on his left, straight-arming another one on his right, high-stepping away from another precedent about to tackle him from the rear, until (bravo!) he reaches his goal: good law. That image of the great judge remains with the former law student when he himself becomes a judge, and thus the common-law tradition is passed on and on.

All of this would be an unqualified good, were it not for a trend in government that has developed in recent centuries, called democracy. In most countries, judges are no longer agents of the king, for there are no kings. In the English system, I suppose they can be regarded as in a sense agents of the legislature, since the Supreme Court of England is theoretically the House of Lords. That was once the system in the American colonies as well; the legislature of Massachusetts is still honorifically called the General Court of Massachusetts. But the highest body of Massachusetts judges is called the Supreme Judicial Court, because at about the time of the founding of our federal republic this country embraced the governmental principle of separation of powers. That doctrine is praised, as the cornerstone of the proposed federal Constitution, in *Federalist no. 47*. Consider the compatibility of what James Madison says in that number with the ancient system of lawmaking by judges. Madison quotes Montesquieu (approvingly) as follows: "Were the power of judging joined with the legislative, the life and liberty of the subject would be exposed to arbitrary control, for the *judge* would then be the legislator."[2] I do not suggest that Madison was saying that common-law lawmaking violated the separation of powers. He wrote in an era when the prevailing image of the common law was that of a preexisting body

---

[2] *The Federalist* no. 47, at 326 (James Madison) (ed. Jacob E. Cooke, 1961; emphasis in original). The reference is to Montesquieu, *The Spirit of Laws* (trans. Thomas Nugent, 1949), vol. 1, 152.

of rules, uniform throughout the nation (rather than different from state to state), that judges merely "discovered," rather than created. It is only in this century, with the rise of legal realism, that we came to acknowledge that judges in fact "make" the common law, and that each state has its own.

I do suggest, however, that once we have taken this realistic view of what common-law courts do, the uncomfortable relationship of common-law lawmaking to democracy (if not to the technical doctrine of the separation of powers) becomes apparent. Indeed, that was evident to many even before legal realism carried the day. It was one of the principal motivations behind the law-codification movement of the nineteenth century, associated most prominently with the name of David Dudley Field, but espoused by many other avid reformers as well. Consider what one of them, Robert Rantoul, had to say in a Fourth-of-July address in Scituate, Massachusetts, in 1836:

> Judge-made law is ex post facto law, and therefore unjust. An act is not forbidden by the statute law, but it becomes void by judicial construction. The legislature could not effect this, for the Constitution forbids it. The judiciary shall not usurp legislative power, says the Bill of Rights: yet it not only usurps, but runs riot beyond the confines of legislative power.
>
> Judge-made law is special legislation. The judge is human, and feels the bias which the coloring of the particular case gives. If he wishes to decide the next case differently, he has only to distinguish, and thereby make a new law. The legislature must act on general views, and prescribe at once for a whole class of cases.[3]

This is just by way of getting warmed up. Rantoul continues, after observing that the common law "has been called the perfection of human reason":

> The Common Law is the perfection of human reason, — just as alcohol is the perfection of sugar. The subtle spirit

[3] Robert Rantoul, Oration at Scituate (July 7, 1836), in Kermit L. Hall et al., *American Legal History* (1991), 317, 317–18.

of the Common Law is reason double distilled, till what was wholesome and nutritive becomes rank poison. Reason is sweet and pleasant to the unsophisticated intellect; but this sublimated perversion of reason bewilders, and perplexes, and plunges its victims into mazes of error.

The judge makes law, by extorting from precedents something which they do not contain. He extends his precedents, which were themselves the extension of others, till, by this accommodating principle, a whole system of law is built up without the authority or interference of the legislator.[4]

The nineteenth-century codification movement espoused by Rantoul and Field was, as you may know, generally opposed by the bar, and hence did not achieve substantial success, except in one field: civil procedure, the law governing the trial of civil cases. (I have always found it curious, by the way, that the only field in which lawyers and judges were willing to abandon judicial lawmaking was a field important to nobody except litigants, lawyers, and judges. Civil procedure used to be the *only* statutory course one studied in first-year law school.) Today, generally speaking, the old private-law fields — contracts, torts, property, trusts and estates, family law — remain firmly within the control of state common-law courts. Indeed, it is probably true that in these fields judicial lawmaking can be more freewheeling than ever, since the doctrine of *stare decisis* has appreciably eroded. Prior decisions that even the cleverest mind cannot distinguish can nowadays simply be overruled.

I have led you through this discussion not to urge that we scrape away the common law as a barnacle on the hull of democracy. I would be no more successful in that endeavor than David Dudley Field. No, I am content to leave the common law, and the process of developing the common law, where it is. It has proven to be a good method of developing the law in many fields — and

[4] Ibid., 318.

perhaps the very best method. An argument can be made that development of the bulk of private law by judges (an elite class "far removed from the people," as described by Madison)[5] is a desirable limitation upon popular democracy. Or as the point was more delicately put in the late nineteenth century by James C. Carter of New York, one of the ardent opponents of Field's codification projects: "the question is whether growth, development and improvement of the law" should "remain under the guidance of men selected by the people on account of their special qualifications for the work" (i.e., judges) or "be transferred to a numerous legislative body, disqualified by the nature of their duties for the discharge of this supreme function?"[6]

But though I have no quarrel with the common law and its process, I do question whether the *attitude* of the common-law judge — the mindset that asks, "What is the most desirable resolution of this case, and how can any impediments to the achievement of that result be evaded?" — is appropriate for most of the work that I do, and much of the work that state judges do. We live in an age of legislation, and most new law is statutory law. As one legal historian has put it, in modern times "the main business of government, and therefore of law, [is] legislative and executive. . . . Even private law, so-called, [has been] turning statutory. The lion's share of the norms and rules that actually govern[] the country [come] out of Congress and the legislatures. . . . The rules of the countless administrative agencies [are] themselves an important, even crucial, source of law."[7] This is particularly true in the federal courts, where, with a qualification so small it does not bear mentioning, there is no such thing as common law. Every issue of law I resolve as a federal judge is an interpretation of text — the text of a regulation, or of a statute, or of the Constitution. Let me put the Constitution to one side for the time being.

---

[5] *The Federalist* no. 49, at 341 (ed. Jacob E. Cooke, 1961).

[6] James C. Carter, *The Proposed Codification of Our Common Law* (1884), 87.

[7] Lawrence M. Friedman, *A History of American Law* (1973), 590.

There are many who believe that that document is in effect a charter for judges to develop an evolving common law of freedom of speech, of protections against unreasonable searches and seizures, etc. I think that is wrong — indeed, as I shall discuss later, I think it frustrates the whole purpose of a written constitution. But we need not pause to debate that point now, since constitutional adjudication forms a relatively small portion of most judges' work. Indeed, even in the Supreme Court of the United States, I would estimate that something less than a fifth of the issues we confront are constitutional issues — and probably less than a twentieth if one excludes criminal-law cases. The vast majority of what I do is to interpret the meaning of federal statutes and of federal agency regulations. Thus, the subject of statutory interpretation deserves study and attention in its own right, as the principal business of lawyers and judges. It will not do to treat the enterprise as simply an inconvenient modern add-on to the judges' primary role of common-law lawmaking. Indeed, attacking the enterprise with the Mr. Fix-it mentality of the common-law judge is a sure recipe for incompetence and usurpation.

The state of the science of statutory interpretation in American law is accurately described by Professors Henry Hart and Albert Sacks (or by Professors William Eskridge and Philip Frickey, editors of the famous often-taught-but-never-published Hart-Sachs materials on the legal process) as follows:

> Do not expect anybody's theory of statutory interpretation, whether it is your own or somebody else's, to be an accurate statement of what courts actually do with statutes. The hard truth of the matter is that American courts have no intelligible, generally accepted, and consistently applied theory of statutory interpretation.[8]

[8] Henry M. Hart, Jr., and Albert M. Sacks, *The Legal Process* (ed. William N. Eskridge, Jr., and Philip P. Frickey, 1994), 1169.

Surely this is a sad commentary: We American judges have no intelligible theory of what we do most.

Even sadder, however, is the fact that the American bar and American legal education, by and large, are unconcerned with the fact that we have no intelligible theory. Whereas legal scholarship has been at pains to rationalize the common law — to devise the *best* rules governing contracts, torts, and so forth — it has been seemingly agnostic as to whether there is even any such thing as good or bad rules of statutory interpretation. There are few law-school courses on the subject, and certainly no required ones; the science of interpretation (if it is a science) is left to be picked up piecemeal, by reading cases (good and bad) in substantive fields that are largely statutory, such as securities law, natural resources law, and employment law.

There is to my knowledge only one treatise on statutory interpretation that purports to treat that subject in a systematic and comprehensive fashion — compared with about six or so on the substantive field of contracts alone. That treatise is J. G. Sutherland's *Statutes and Statutory Construction*, first published in 1891, and updated by various editors since, now embracing some eight volumes. As its size alone indicates, it is one of those lawbooks that functions primarily not as a teacher or advisor, but as a litigator's research tool and expert witness — to say, and to lead you to cases that say, why the statute should be interpreted the way your client wants. Despite the fact that statutory interpretation has increased enormously in importance, it is one of the few fields where we have a drought rather than a glut of treatises — fewer than we had fifty years ago, and many fewer than a century ago. The last such treatise, other than Sutherland's, was Professor Earl T. Crawford's one-volume work, *The Construction of Statutes*, published more than half a century ago (1940). Compare that with what was available in the last quarter or so of the nineteenth century, which had, in addition to Sutherland's original 1891 treatise, *A Handbook on the Construction and Interpretation of the Laws* by Henry Campbell Black (author of *Black's Law Dictionary*), published in 1896; *A Commentary on the Interpretation of Statutes* by G. A. Endlich, published in 1888, an Americanized version of Sir Peter Maxwell's 1875 English treatise on the subject; the 1882 *Commentaries on the Written Laws and Their Interpretation* by Joel Prentiss Bishop; the 1874 second edition of Theodore Sedgwick's *A Treatise on the Rules Which Govern the Interpretation and Construction of Statutory and Constitutional Law*; and the 1871 Potter's *Dwarris on Statutes*, an Americanized edition by Platt Potter of Sir Fortunatus Dwarris's influential English work.

Statutory interpretation is such a broad subject that I do not expect to get very deeply into it in these lectures. But I do want to address a few aspects that are of particular interest to me, and I can begin at the most fundamental possible level. So utterly unformed is the American law of statutory interpretation that not only is its methodology unclear, but even its very *objective* is. So I put the basic question: What are we looking for when we construe a statute?

You will find it frequently said in judicial opinions of my court and others, that the judge's objective in interpreting a statute is to give effect to "the intent of the legislature." This principle, in one form or another, goes back at least as far as Blackstone. Unfortunately, it does not square with some of the (few) generally accepted concrete rules of statutory construction. One is the rule that when the text of a statute is clear, that is the end of the matter. Why should that be so, if what the legislature *intended*, rather than what it *said*, is the object of our inquiry? In selecting the words of the statute, the legislature might have misspoken. Why not permit that to be demonstrated from the floor debates? Or indeed, why not accept, as proper material for the court to consider, later explanations by the legislators — a sworn affidavit signed by the majority of each house, for example, as to what they *really* meant?

Another accepted rule of construction is that ambiguities in a newly enacted statute are to be resolved in such fashion as to make the statute not only internally consistent, but also compatible with previously enacted laws. We simply assume, for purposes of our search for "intent," that the enacting legislature was aware of all those other laws. Well of course that is a fiction, and if we were really looking for the subjective intent of the enacting legislature we would more likely find it by paying attention to the text (and legislative history) of the new statute in isolation.

We do not really look for subjective legislative intent. We look for a sort of "objectified" intent — the intent that a reasonable person would gather from the text of the law, placed alongside the remainder of the *corpus juris*. As Bishop's old treatise nicely put it, elaborating upon the usual formulation: "[T]he primary object of all rules for interpreting statutes is to ascertain the legislative intent; *or, exactly, the meaning which the subject is authorized to understand the legislature intended.*" [9] And the reason we adopt this objectified version is, I think, that it is simply incompatible with democratic government — or indeed, even with fair government — to have the meaning of a law determined by what the lawgiver meant, rather than by what the lawgiver promulgated. It was said of the tyrant Nero that he used to have his edicts posted high up on the pillars, so that they would be more difficult to read, thus entrapping some into inadvertent violation. A legal system that determines the meaning of laws on the basis of what was meant rather than what was said is similarly tyrannical. It is the *law* that governs, not the intent of the lawgiver. That seems to me the essence of the famous American ideal set forth in the Massachusetts constitution: A government of laws, not of men. Men may intend what they will; but it is only the laws that they enact that bind us.

---

[9] Joel Prentiss Bishop, *Commentaries on the Written Laws and Their Interpretation* (1882), 57–58 (emphasis added; citation omitted).

In reality, however, if one accepts the principle that the object of judicial interpretation is to determine the intent of the legislature, being bound by genuine but unexpressed legislative intent rather than the law is only the *theoretical* threat. The *practical* threat is that, under the guise or even the self-delusion of pursuing unexpressed legislative intents, common-law judges will in fact pursue their own objectives and desires, extending their lawmaking proclivities from the common law to the statutory field. When you are told to decide, not on the basis of what the legislature said, but on the basis of what it *meant*, and are assured that there is no necessary connection between the two, surely your best shot at figuring out what the legislature meant is to ask yourself what a wise and intelligent person *should* have meant; and that, of course, will bring you to the conclusion that the law means what you think it *ought* to mean — which is precisely how judges decide things under the common law. As Dean James Landis of Harvard Law School (a believer in the search for legislative intent) put it in a 1930 article:

> [T]he gravest sins are perpetrated in the name of the intent of the legislature. Judges are rarely willing to admit their role as actual lawgivers, and such admissions as are wrung from their unwilling lips lie in the field of common and not statute law. To condone in these instances the practice of talking in terms of the intent of the legislature, as if the legislature had attributed a particular meaning to certain words, when it is apparent that the intent is that of the judge, is to condone atavistic practices too reminiscent of the medicine man.[10]

Let me describe for you what I consider to be the prototypical case involving the triumph of supposed "legislative intent" (a handy cover for judicial intent) over the text of the law. It is called *Church of the Holy Trinity* v. *United States*,[11] and was

---

[10] James M. Landis, "A Note on 'Statutory Interpretation,'" *Harvard Law Review* 43 (1930): 886, 891.

[11] 143 U.S. 457 (1892).

decided by the Supreme Court of the United States in 1892. The Church of the Holy Trinity, in the city of New York, contracted with an Englishman to come over to be its rector and pastor. The United States claimed that this agreement violated a federal statute that made it unlawful for any person to "in any way assist or encourage the importation or migration of any alien . . . into the United States, . . . under contract or agreement . . . made previous to the importation or migration of such alien . . . , to perform labor or service of any kind in the United States . . . ." The Circuit Court for the Southern District of New York held the church liable for the fine that the statute provided. The Supreme Court reversed. The central portion of its reasoning was as follows:

> It must be conceded that the act of the [church] is within the letter of this section, for the relation of rector to his church is one of service, and implies labor on the one side with compensation on the other. Not only are the general words labor and service both used [in the statute], but also, as it were to guard against any narrow interpretation and emphasize a breadth of meaning, to them is added "of any kind;" and, further, . . . the fifth section [of the statute], which makes specific exceptions, among them professional actors, artists, lecturers, singers and domestic servants, strengthens the idea that every other kind of labor and service was intended to be reached by the first section. While there is great force to this reasoning, we cannot think Congress intended to denounce with penalties a transaction like that in the present case. It is a familiar rule, that a thing may be within the letter of the statute and yet not within the statute, because not within its spirit, nor within the intention of its makers.[12]

The Court proceeds to conclude from various extratextual indications, including even a snippet of legislative history (highly unusual in those days), that the statute was intended to apply only to *manual* labor — which of course renders the exceptions for actors, artists, lecturers, and singers utterly inexplicable. The Court

[12] Ibid., at 458–59.

then shifts gears and devotes the last seven pages of its opinion to a lengthy description of how and why we are a religious nation. That being so, it says, "[t]he construction invoked cannot be accepted as correct." It concludes:

> It is a case where there was presented a definite evil, in view of which the legislature used general terms with the purpose of reaching all phases of that evil, and thereafter, unexpectedly, it is developed that the general language thus employed is broad enough to reach cases and acts which the whole history and life of the country affirm could not have been intentionally legislated against. It is the duty of the courts, under those circumstances, to say that, however broad the language of the statute may be, the act, although within the letter, is not within the intention of the legislature, and therefore cannot be within the statute.[13]

Well of course I think that the act was within the letter of the statute, and was therefore within the statute, end of case. Congress can enact foolish statutes as well as wise ones, and it is not for the courts to decide which is which and rewrite the former. I acknowledge an interpretative doctrine of what the old writers call *lapsus linguae* (slip of the tongue), and what our modern cases call "scrivener's error," where on the very face of the statute it is clear to the reader that a mistake of expression (rather than of legislative wisdom) has been made. For example, a statute may say "defendant" when only "plaintiff" makes sense. The objective import of such a statute is clear enough, and I think it not contrary to sound principles of interpretation, in such extreme cases, to give the totality of context precedence over a single word. But to say that the legislature obviously misspoke is worlds away from saying that the legislature obviously overlegislated. *Church of the Holy Trinity* is cited to us whenever counsel wants us to ignore the narrow, deadening text of the statute and pay attention to the life-giving legislative intent. It is of course nothing but judicial law-making.

[13] Ibid.

There are more sophisticated routes to judicial lawmaking than reliance upon unexpressed legislative intent, but they will not often be found in judicial opinions because they are too obvious a usurpation. Calling the Court's desires "unexpressed legislative intent" makes it all seem OK. You will never, I promise, see in a judicial opinion the rationale for judicial lawmaking described in Guido Calabresi's book *A Common Law for the Age of Statutes*. It says:

> [B]ecause a statute is hard to revise once it is passed, laws are governing us that would not and could not be enacted today, and . . . *some* of these laws not only could not be reenacted but also do not fit, are in some sense inconsistent with, our whole legal landscape. . . .
>
> There is an alternate way of dealing with [this] problem of legal obsolescence: granting to courts the authority to determine whether a statute is obsolete, whether in one way or another it should be consciously reviewed. At times this doctrine would approach granting to courts the authority to treat statutes as if they were no more and no less than part of the common law.[14]

Indeed. Judge Calabresi says that the courts have already, "in a common law way, . . . come to the point of exercising [the law-revising authority he favors] through fictions, subterfuges, and indirection,"[15] and he is uncertain whether they should continue down that road or change course to a more forthright acknowledgment of what they are doing.

Another modern and forthright approach to according courts the power to revise statutes is set forth in Professor William Eskridge's recent book, *Dynamic Statutory Interpretation*. The essence of it is acceptance of the proposition that it is proper for the judge who applies a statute to consider " 'not only what the statute means abstractly, or even on the basis of legislative history, but also what

---

[14] Guido Calabresi, *A Common Law for the Age of Statutes* (1982), 2 (emphasis in original).

[15] Ibid., 117.

it ought to mean in terms of the needs and goals of our present day society.' "[16] The law means what it ought to mean.

I agree with Judge Calabresi (and Professor Eskridge makes the same point) that many decisions can be pointed to which, by subterfuge, accomplish precisely what Calabresi and Eskridge and other honest nontextualists propose. As I have said, "legislative intent" divorced from text is one of those subterfuges; and as I have described, *Church of the Holy Trinity* is one of those cases. What I think is needed, however, is not rationalization of this process but abandonment of it. It is simply not compatible with democratic theory that laws mean whatever they ought to mean, and that unelected judges decide what that is.

It may well be that the result reached by the Court in *Church of the Holy Trinity* was a desirable result; and it may even be (though I doubt it) that it was the unexpressed result actually intended by Congress, rather than merely the one desired by the Court. Regardless, the decision was wrong because it failed to follow the text. The text is the law, and it is the text that that must be observed. I agree with Justice Holmes's remark (quoted approvingly by Justice Frankfurter in his article on the construction of statutes) : "Only a day or two ago — when counsel talked of the intention of a legislature, I was indiscreet enough to say I don't care what their intention was. I only want to know what the words mean."[17] And I agree with Holmes's other remark, quoted approvingly by Justice Jackson: "We do not inquire what the legislature meant; we ask only what the statute means."[18]

Thinking this way makes me what I confessed to be at the outset of this talk: a textualist. I am aware that in some sophisticated

[16] William N. Eskridge, Jr., *Dynamic Statutory Interpretation* (1994), 50 (quoting Arthur Phelps, "Factors Influencing Judges in Interpreting Statutes," *Vanderbilt Law Review* 3 [1950]: 456, 469).

[17] Felix Frankfurter, "Some Reflections on the Reading of Statutes," *Columbia Law Review* 47 (1947): 527, 538.

[18] Oliver Wendell Holmes, *Collected Legal Papers* (1920), 207, quoted in *Schwegmann Bros. v. Calvert Distillers Corp.*, 341 U.S. 384, 397 (1951) (Jackson, J., concurring).

circles that is considered simple-minded; I think it is not. It does not mean that I am too dull to perceive the broader social purposes that a statute is designed, or could be designed, to serve; or that I am unaware that new times require new laws. It means only that I believe judges have no authority to pursue those broader purposes or write those new laws.

Textualism should not be confused with so-called strict constructionism, which is a degraded form of textualism that brings the whole philosophy into disrepute. I am not a strict constructionist, and no one ought to be — though better that, I suppose, than a nontextualist. A text should not be construed strictly, and it should not be construed leniently; it should be construed reasonably, to contain all that it fairly means. The difference between textualism and strict constructionism can be seen in a statutory case my Court decided last term.[19] The statute at issue provided for an increased jail term if, "during and in relation to . . . [a] drug trafficking crime," the defendant "uses . . . a firearm." The defendant in this case had sought to purchase a quantity of cocaine; and what he had offered to give in exchange for the cocaine was an unloaded firearm, which he showed to the drug-seller . The Court held, I regret to say, that the defendant was subject to the increased penalty, because he had "used a firearm during and in relation to a drug trafficking crime." The case was not even close (6–3). I dissented. Now I cannot say whether my colleagues in the majority voted the way they did because they are strict-construction textualists, or because they are not textualists at all. But a proper textualist, which is to say my kind of textualist, would surely have voted with me. The phrase "uses a gun" fairly connoted use of a gun for what guns are normally used for, that is, as a weapon. When you ask someone "Do you use a cane?" you are not inquiring whether he has hung his grandfather's antique cane as a decoration in the hallway.

[19] *Smith* v. *United States*, 508 U.S. 223 (1993).

But while the good textualist is not a literalist, neither is he a nihilist. Words do have a limited range of meaning, and no interpretation that goes beyond that range is permissible. My favorite example of a departure from text — and surely the departure that has enabled judges to do more freewheeling lawmaking than any other — pertains to the Due Process Clause found in the Fifth and Fourteenth Amendments of the United States Constitution. It says that no person shall "be deprived of life, liberty, or property without due process of law." It has been interpreted to prevent the government from taking away certain liberties beyond those, such as freedom of speech and of religion, that are specifically named in the Constitution. (The first Supreme Court case to make that extension, by the way, was *Dred Scott*[20]—not a desirable parentage.) Well, it may or may not be a good thing to guarantee additional liberties, but the Due Process Clause quite obviously does not bear that interpretation. By its inescapable terms, it guarantees only process. Property can be taken by the state; liberty can be taken; even life can be taken; but not without the *process* that our traditions require — notably, a validly enacted law and a fair trial. To say otherwise is to abandon textualism, and to render democratically adopted texts mere springboards for judicial lawmaking.

Besides being accused of being simple-minded, textualism is often accused of being "formalistic." The answer to that is, *of course it's formalistic!* The rule of law is *about* form. If, for example, a citizen performs an act — let us say the sale of certain technology to a foreign country — which is prohibited by a widely publicized bill proposed by the administration and passed by both Houses of Congress, *but not yet signed by the President*, that sale is lawful. It is of no consequence that everyone knows both Houses of Congress and the President wish to prevent that sale. Before the wish becomes a binding law, it must be embodied in a bill that passes both Houses and is signed by the President. Is that not formalism? A murderer has been caught with blood on his hands,

[20] *Dred Scott* v. *Sandford*, 60 U.S. (19 How.) 393, 450 (1857).

bending over the body of his victim; a neighbor with a home-video movie camera happens to have filmed the crime; and the murderer has confessed in writing and on videotape. We nonetheless insist that, before the state can punish this miscreant, it must conduct a full-dress criminal trial that results in a verdict of guilty. Is that not formalism? Long live formalism. It is what makes a government a government of laws and not of men.

II

I described yesterday the common-law system of judicial lawmaking that has acquired such a firm grip upon the American legal mind and discussed its unfortunate extension into the field of statutory interpretation, which has been accomplished principally by replacing a search for the meaning of the text with a supposed search for the unexpressed intent of the legislator. I described briefly what I consider to be the proper approach to statutory interpretation, which I am content to call textualism, and distinguished that from strict constructionism. Today I intend to discuss some of the techniques of statutory interpretation, good and bad, and to raise some special considerations applicable to the construction of constitutional texts.

Textualism is often associated with rules of interpretation called the canons of construction — which have generally been criticized, indeed even mocked, by the legal commentators. Many of the canons were originally in Latin, and I suppose that alone is enough to render them contemptible. One, for example, is *expressio unius est exclusio alterius*. Expression of the one is exclusion of the other. What it means is this: If you see a sign that says children under 12 may enter free, you should have no need to ask the proprietor whether your 13-year-old can come in free. The inclusion of the one class is an implicit exclusion of the other. Another frequently used canon is *noscitur a sociis*, which means, literally, "it is known by its companions." It stands for the principle that a word is given meaning by those around it. If you tell me "I took the boat out on the bay" I understand "bay" to mean one thing; if you tell me "I put the saddle on the bay" I understand it to mean something else. Another canon — perhaps representing only a more specific application of the last one — is *ejusdem generis*, which means "of the same sort." It stands for the proposition that when a text lists a series of items, a general term included in the list should be understood to be limited to items of the same sort. For instance, if someone speaks of using "tacks, staples, screws, nails, rivets, and other things" the general term "other things" surely refers to other fasteners.

All of this is so commensensical that, but for the fact it is Latin, you would find it hard to believe anyone could criticize it. But in fact, the canons have been attacked as a sham. As Karl Llewellyn put it in a derisive piece in the 1950 *Vanderbilt Law Review* that is much cited: "[T]here are two opposing canons on almost every point. An arranged selection is appended. Every lawyer must be familiar with them all: they are still needed tools of argument."[21] Llewellyn appends a list of canons in two columns, the left-hand column headed "Thrust," and the right-hand column "Parry." But if one examines the list, it becomes apparent that there really are not two opposite canons on "almost every point" — unless one enshrines as a canon whatever vapid statement has ever been made by a willful, law-bending judge. For example, the first canon he lists under "Thrust," supported by a citation of Sutherland, is "A statute cannot go beyond its text." Hooray for that. He shows as a "Parry," with no citation of either Sutherland or Black (his principal authorities throughout), the following: "To effect its purpose a statute may be implemented beyond its text." That is *not* a generally accepted canon, though I am sure some willful judges have used it, the judges in *Church of the Holy Trinity*, for example. And even if it were used more

[21] Karl N. Llewellyn, "Remarks on the Theory of Appellate Decision and the Rules or Canons about How Statutes Are to Be Construed," *Vanderbilt Law Review* 3 (1950): 395, 401.

than rarely, why not bring to the canons the same discernment that Llewellyn brought to the study of common-law decisions? Throw out the bad ones and retain the good. There are a number of other faux canons in Llewellyn's list, particularly in the "Parry" column. For example, Parry No. 8: "Courts have the power to inquire into real — as distinct from ostensible — purpose." Never heard of it.

Mostly, however, Llewellyn's "Parries" do not contradict the corresponding canon, but rather merely show that it is not absolute. For example, Thrust No. 13: "Words and phrases which have received judicial construction before enactment are to be understood according to that construction." Parry: "Not if the statute clearly requires them to have a different meaning." Well of course. Every canon is simply *one indication* of meaning; and if there are more contrary indications (perhaps supported by other canons) it must yield. But that does not render the entire enterprise a fraud — not, at least, unless the judge wishes to make it so.

Another aspect of textual interpretation that merits some discussion is the use of certain presumptions and rules of construction that load the dice for or against a particular result. For example, when courts construe criminal statutes, they apply — or should apply, or say they apply — what is known as the "rule of lenity," which says that any ambiguity in a criminal statute must be resolved in favor of the defendant. There is a rule which says that ambiguities in treaties and statutes dealing with Indian rights are to be resolved in favor of the Indians. And a rule, used to devastating effect in the conservative courts of the 1920s and 1930s, that statutes in derogation of the common law are to be narrowly construed. And another rule, used to equally devastating effect in the liberal courts of more recent years, that "remedial statutes" are to be liberally construed to achieve what is called their "intended purposes." There is a rule that waivers of sovereign immunity are to be narrowly construed. And a rule that it requires an "unmistakably clear" statement for a federal statute to eliminate state sovereign immunity.

To the honest textualist, all of these rules and presumptions are a lot of trouble. It is hard enough to provide a uniform, objective answer to the question whether a statute, on balance, more reasonably means one thing rather than another. But it is virtually impossible to expect uniformity and objectivity when there is added, on one side or another of the balance, a thumb of indeterminate weight. How "narrow" *is* the narrow construction that certain types of statute are to be accorded; how clear does a broader intent have to be in order to escape it? Every statute that comes into litigation is to some degree "ambiguous"; how ambiguous does ambiguity have to be before the rule of lenity or the rule in favor of Indians applies? How implausible an implausibility can be justified by the "liberal construction" that is supposed to be accorded remedial statutes? And how clear is an "unmistakably clear" statement? There are of course no answers to these questions, which is why these artificial rules increase the unpredictability, if not the arbitrariness, of judicial decisions. Perhaps for some of the rules that price is worth it. There are worse things than unpredictability and occasional arbitrariness. Perhaps they are a fair price to pay for preservation of the principle that one should not be held criminally liable for an act that is not clearly proscribed; or the principle that federal interference with state sovereign immunity is an extraordinary intrusion.

But whether these dice-loading rules are bad or good, there is also the question of where the courts get the authority to impose them. Can we really just decree that we will interpret the laws that Congress passes to mean less or more than what they fairly say? I doubt it. The rule of lenity is almost as old as the common law itself, so I suppose that is validated by sheer antiquity. The others I am more doubtful about. The rule that statutes in derogation of the common law will be narrowly construed seems like a sheer judicial power-grab. Some of the rules, I suppose, can be considered merely an exaggerated statement of what normal, no-thumb-on-the-scales interpretation would produce anyway. For example, since federal elimination of state sovereign immunity is such an extraordinary act, one would not normally find it to have been implied — so something like an "unmistakably clear" statement rule is merely normal interpretation. And the same, perhaps, with waiver of sovereignty immunity.

I want to say a few words — the time available will not allow me as much as I would like — about the use of legislative history in interpreting statutes. My view that the objective indication of the words, rather than the intent of the legislature, is what constitutes the law leads me, of course, to the conclusion that legislative history should not be used as an authoritative indication of the meaning of a statute. This was of course the traditional English, and the traditional American, practice. Chief Justice Taney wrote:

> In expounding this law, the judgment of the court cannot, in any degree, be influenced by the construction placed upon it by individual members of Congress in the debate which took place on its passage, nor by the motives or reasons assigned by them for supporting or opposing amendments that were offered. The law as it passed is the will of the majority of both houses, *and the only mode in which that will is spoken is in the act itself*; and we must gather their intention from the language there used, comparing it, when any ambiguity exists, with the laws upon the same subject, and looking, if necessary, to the public history of the times in which it was passed.[22]

That uncompromising view generally prevailed in this country until the present century. The movement to change it gained momentum in the late 1920s and 1930s, driven, believe it or not, by frustration with common-law judges' use of "legislative intent" and phonied-up maxims to impose their own views — in those days views opposed to progressive social legislation. I quoted yesterday from an article by Dean Landis inveighing against such judicial

[22] *Aldridge* v. *Williams*, 44 U.S. (3 How.) 9, 24 (1845) (emphasis added).

usurpation. The solution he proposed was not the banishment of legislative intent as an interpretive criterion, but rather the use of legislative history to place that intent beyond manipulation.

Extensive use of legislative history in this country dates only from about the 1940s. It was still being criticized by such respected Justices as Frankfurter and Jackson as recently as the 1950s. Jackson, for example, wrote in one concurrence:

> I should concur in this result more readily if the Court could reach it by analysis of the statute instead of by psychoanalysis of Congress. When we decide from legislative history, including statements of witnesses at hearings, what Congress probably had in mind, we must put ourselves in the place of a majority of Congressmen and act according to the impression we think this history should have made on them. Never having been a Congressman, I am handicapped in that weird endeavor. That process seems to me not interpretation of a statute but creation of a statute.[23]

In the past few decades, however, we have developed a legal culture in which lawyers routinely — and I do mean routinely — make no distinction between words in the text of a statute and words in its legislative history. I am frequently told, in briefs and in oral argument, that "Congress said thus-and-so" — when in fact what is being quoted is not the law promulgated by Congress, nor even any text endorsed by a single house of Congress, but rather the statement of a single committee of a single house, set forth in a committee report. I am sure some of you have heard the humorous quip that one should consult the text of the statute only when the legislative history is ambiguous. Well, that's no longer funny. Reality has overtaken parody. A few terms ago, I read a brief that *began* the legal argument with a discussion of legislative history, and then continued (I swear I am quoting it *verbatim*) : "Unfortunately, the legislative debates are not helpful. Thus, we turn

---

[23] *United States* v. *Public Utils. Comm'n of Cal.*, 345 U.S. 295, 319 (1953) (Jackson, J., concurring).

to the other guidepost in this difficult area, statutory language."[24]

As I have said, I object to the use of legislative history on principle, since I reject intent of the legislature as the proper criterion of the law. What is most exasperating about the use of legislative history, however, is that it does not even make sense for those who *accept* legislative intent as the criterion. It is much more likely to produce a false or contrived legislative intent than a genuine one. The first and most obvious reason this is true is that, with respect to 99.99 percent of the issues of construction reaching the courts, there *is* no legislative intent, so that any clues provided by the legislative history are bound to be false. Those issues almost invariably involve points of relative detail, compared with the major sweep of the statute in question. That a majority of both houses of Congress (never mind the President, if he signed rather than vetoed the bill) entertained *any* view with regard to such issues is utterly beyond belief. For a virtual certainty, the majority was blissfully unaware of the *existence* of the issue, much less had any preference as to how it should be resolved.

But assuming, contrary to all reality, that the search for "legislative intent" is a search for something that exists, that something is not likely to be found in the archives of legislative history. In earlier days, when Congress had much smaller staff and enacted much less legislation, it might have been possible to believe that a significant number of senators or representatives were present for the floor debate, or read the committee reports, and actually voted on the basis of what they heard or read. Those days, if they ever existed, are long gone. The floor is rarely crowded for a debate, the members generally being occupied with committee business and reporting to the floor only when a quorum call is demanded or a vote is to be taken. And as for committee reports, it is not even certain that the members of the issuing *committees* have found

[24] Brief for Petitioner at 21, *Jett* v. *Dallas Indep. Sch. Dist.*, 491 U.S. 701 (1989), quoted in *Green* v. *Bock Laundry Machine Co.*, 490 U.S. 504, 530 (1989) (Scalia, J., concurring).

time to read them, as demonstrated by the following Senate floor debate on a tax bill, which I had occasion to quote in an opinion written when I was on the Court of Appeals:

> Mr. ARMSTRONG. . . . My question, which may take [the chairman of the Committee on Finance] by surprise, is this: Is it the intention of the chairman that the Internal Revenue Service and the Tax Court and other courts take guidance as to the intention of Congress from the committee report which accompanies this bill?
>
> Mr. DOLE. I would certainly hope so. . . .
>
> Mr. ARMSTRONG. Mr. President, will the Senator tell me whether or not he wrote the committee report?
>
> Mr. DOLE. Did I write the committee report?
>
> Mr. ARMSTRONG. Yes.
>
> Mr. DOLE. No; the Senator from Kansas did not write the committee report.
>
> Mr. ARMSTRONG. Did any Senator write the committee report?
>
> Mr. DOLE. I have to check.
>
> Mr. ARMSTRONG. Does the Senator know of any Senator who wrote the committee report?
>
> Mr. DOLE. I might be able to identify one, but I would have to search. I was here all during the time it was written, I might say, and worked carefully with the staff as they worked. . . .
>
> Mr. ARMSTRONG. Mr. President, has the Senator from Kansas, the chairman of the Finance Committee, read the committee report in its entirety?
>
> Mr. DOLE. I am working on it. It is not a bestseller, but I am working on it.
>
> Mr. ARMSTRONG. Mr. President, did members of the Finance Committee vote on the committee report?
>
> Mr. DOLE. No.
>
> Mr. ARMSTRONG. Mr. President, the reason I raise the issue is not perhaps apparent on the surface, and let me just state

it. . . . The report itself is not considered by the Committee on Finance. It was not subject to amendment by the Committee on Finance. It is not subject to amendment now by the Senate. . . .
. . . If there were matter within this report which was disagreed to by the Senator from Colorado or even by a majority of all Senators, there would be no way for us to change the report. I could not offer an amendment tonight to amend the committee report.
. . . [F]or any jurist, administrator, bureaucrat, tax practitioner, or others who might chance upon the written record of this proceeding, let me just make the point that this is not the law, it was not voted on, it is not subject to amendment, and we should discipline ourselves to the task of expressing congressional intent in the statute.[25]

Ironically, but quite understandably, the more courts have relied upon legislative history, the less worthy of reliance it has become. In earlier days, it was at least genuine and not contrived — a real part of the legislation's *history,* in the sense that it was part of the *development* of the bill, part of the attempt to inform and persuade those who voted. Nowadays, however, when it is universally known and expected that judges will resort to floor debates and (especially) committee reports as authoritative expressions of "legislative intent," affecting the courts rather than informing the Congress has become the primary purpose of the exercise. It is less that the courts refer to legislative history because it exists, than that legislative history exists because the courts refer to it. One of the routine tasks of the Washington lawyer-lobbyist is to draft language that sympathetic legislators can recite in a prewritten "floor debate" — or, even better, insert into a committee report.

Now there are several common responses to some of the points I have just made. One is "So what, if most members of Congress do not themselves know what is in the committee report. Most of

[25] 128 Cong. Rec. 16918–19, 97th Cong., 2d Sess. (July 19, 1982), quoted in *Hirschey* v. *Federal Energy Regulatory Comm'n,* 777 F.2d 1, 7 n.1 (D.C. Cir. 1985) (Scalia, J., concurring).

them do not know the details of the legislation itself, either — but that is valid nonetheless. In fact, they are probably more likely to read and understand the committee report than to read and understand the text." That ignores the central point that genuine knowledge is a precondition for the supposed authoritativeness of a committee report, and not a precondition for the authoritativeness of a statute. The committee report has no claim to our attention except on the assumption that it was the *basis* for the house's vote, and thus represents the house's "intent," which we (presumably) are searching for. A statute, however, has a claim to our attention simply because Article I, section 7, of the Constitution provides that since it has been passed by the prescribed majority (*with or without adequate understanding*) it is a law.

Another response simply challenges head-on the proposition that legislative history must reflect congressional thinking: "Committee reports are *not* authoritative because the full house presumably knows and agrees with them, but rather because the full house *wants* them to be authoritative — that is, leaves to its committees the details of its legislation." It may or may not be true that the houses entertain such a desire; the sentiments of Senator Armstrong that I quoted earlier suggest that it is not. But if it is true, it is unconstitutional. "All legislative Powers herein granted," the Constitution says, "shall be vested in a Congress of the United States, which shall consist of a Senate and House of Representatives." [26] The legislative power is the power to make laws, not the power to make legislators. It is nondelegable. Congress can no more authorize one committee to "fill in the details" of a particular law in a binding fashion than it can authorize a committee to enact minor laws. Whatever Congress has not *itself* prescribed is left to be resolved by the executive or (ultimately) the judicial branch. That is the very essence of the separation of powers. The only conceivable basis for considering committee reports authoritative, therefore, is that they are a genuine indication of the will of the

[26] U.S. Const. art. I, §1.

entire house — which, as I have been at pains to explain, they assuredly are not.

I think that Dean Landis, and those who joined him in the prescription of legislative history as a cure for what he called "willful judges," would be aghast at the results a half century later. On balance, it has facilitated rather than deterred decisions that are based upon the courts' policy preferences, rather than neutral principles of law. Since there are no rules as to how much weight an element of legislative history is entitled to, it can usually be either relied upon or dismissed with equal plausibility. If the willful judge does not like the committee report, he will not follow it; he will call the statute not ambiguous enough, the committee report too ambiguous, or the legislative history (this is the favorite phrase) "as a whole, inconclusive." It is ordinarily very hard to demonstrate that this is false so convincingly as to produce embarrassment. To be sure, there are ambiguities involved, and hence opportunities for judicial willfulness, in other techniques of interpretation as well — the canons of construction, for example, which Dean Landis so thoroughly detested. But the manipulability of legislative history has not *replaced* the manipulabilities of these other techniques; it has *augmented* them. There are still the canons of construction to play with, *and in addition* legislative history. Legislative history provides, moreover, a uniquely broad playing field. In any major piece of legislation, the legislative history is extensive, and there is something for everybody. As Judge Harold Leventhal used to say, the trick is to look over the heads of the crowd and pick out your friends. The variety and specificity of result that legislative history can achieve is unparalleled.

I think it is time to call an end to a brief and failed experiment, if not for reasons of principle then for reasons of practicality. I have not used legislative history to decide a case for, I believe, the past seven Terms. Frankly, it has made very little difference (since it is ordinarily so inconclusive). In the only case I recall in which, had I followed legislative history, I *would* have come out the other way, the rest of my colleagues (who *did* use legislative history) did not come out the other way either.[27] The most immediate and tangible change the abandonment of legislative history would effect is this: Judges, lawyers, and clients will be saved an enormous amount of time and expense. When I was head of the Office of Legal Counsel in the Justice Department, I estimated that 60 percent of the time of the lawyers on my staff was expended finding, and poring over, the incunabula of legislative history. What a waste. We did not use to do it, and we should do it no more.

Finally, I want to say a few words about the distinctive problem of interpreting our Constitution. The problem is distinctive, not because special principles of interpretation apply, but because the usual principles are being applied to an unusual text. Chief Justice Marshall put the point as well as it can be put in *McCulloch* v. *Maryland*:

> A constitution, to contain an accurate detail of all the subdivisions of which its great powers will admit, and of all the means by which they may be carried into execution, would partake of the prolixity of a legal code, and could scarcely be embraced by the human mind. It would probably never be understood by the public. Its nature, therefore, requires, that only its great outlines should be marked, its important objects designated, and the minor ingredients which compose the objects be deduced from the nature of the objects themselves.[28]

In textual interpretation, context is everything, and the context of the Constitution tells us not to expect nit-picking detail, and to give words and phrases an expansive rather than narrow interpretation — though not, of course, an interpretation that the language will not bear.

---

[27] See *Wisconsin Publ. Intervenor* v. *Mortier*, 501 U.S. 597 (1991); *id.*, at 616 (Scalia, J., concurring).

[28] *McCulloch* v. *Maryland*, 17 U.S. (4 Wheat.) 316, 407 (1819).

Take, for example, the provision of the First Amendment that forbids abridgment of "the freedom of speech, or of the press." That phrase does not list the full range of communicative expression. Handwritten letters, for example, are neither speech nor press. Yet surely there is no doubt they cannot be censored. In this constitutional context, speech and press, the two most common forms of communication, stand as a sort of synecdoche for the whole. That is not strict construction, but it is reasonable construction.

It is curious that most of those who insist that the drafter's intent gives meaning to a statute reject the drafter's intent as the criterion for interpretation of the Constitution. I reject it for both. I will consult the writings of some men who happened to be Framers — Hamilton's and Madison's writings in the *Federalist*, for example. I do so, however, not because they were Framers and therefore their intent is authoritative and must be the law; but rather because their writings, like those of other intelligent and informed people of the time, display how the text of the Constitution was originally understood. Thus, I give equal weight to Jay's pieces in the *Federalist*, and to Jefferson's writings, even though neither of them was a Framer. What I look for in the Constitution is precisely what I look for in a statute: the original meaning of the text, not what the original draftsmen intended.

But the Great Divide with regard to constitutional interpretation is not that between Framers' intent and objective meaning; but rather that between *original* meaning (whether derived from Framers' intent or not) and *current* meaning. The ascendant school of constitutional interpretation affirms the existence of what is called the "living Constitution," a body of law that (unlike normal statutes) grows and changes from age to age, in order to meet the needs of a changing society. And it is the judges who determine those needs and "find" that changing law. Seems familiar, doesn't it? Yes, it is the common law returned, but infinitely more powerful than what the old common law ever pretended to be, for now it trumps even the statutes of democratic legislatures. Recall the words I quoted earlier from the Fourth-of-July speech of the avid codifier Robert Rantoul: "The judge makes law, by extorting from precedents something which they do not contain. He extends his precedents, which were themselves the extension of others, till, by this accommodating principle, a whole system of law is built up without the authority or interference of the legislator."[29] Substitute the word "people" for "legislator," and it is a perfect description of what modern American courts have done with the Constitution.

If you go into a constitutional law class, or study a constitutional-law casebook, or read a brief filed in a constitutional-law case, you will rarely find the discussion addressed to the text of the constitutional provision that is at issue, or to the question of what was the originally understood or even the originally intended meaning of that text. Judges simply ask themselves (as a good common-law judge would) what *ought* the result to be, and then proceed to the task of distinguishing (or, if necessary, overruling) any prior Supreme Court cases that stand in the way. Should there be (to take one of the less controversial examples) a constitutional right to die? If so, there is. Should there be a constitutional right to reclaim a biological child put out for adoption by the other parent? Again, if so, there is. If it is good, it is so. Never mind the text that we are supposedly construing; we will smuggle these in, if all else fails, under the Due Process Clause (which, as I have described, is textually incapable of containing them). Moreover, what the Constitution meant yesterday it does not necessarily mean today. As our opinions say in the context of our Eighth Amendment jurisprudence (the Cruel and Unusual Punishments Clause), its meaning changes to reflect "the evolving standards of decency that mark the progress of a maturing society."[30]

This is preeminently a common-law way of making law, and not the way of construing a democratically adopted text. I men-

[29] Rantoul, note 3 above, at 318.
[30] *Trop* v. *Dulles*, 356 U.S. 86, 101 (1958) (plurality opinion).

tioned earlier a famous English treatise on statutory construction called *Dwarris on Statutes*. The fourth of Dwarris's Maxims was as follows: "An act of Parliament cannot alter by reason of time; but the common law may, since *cessante ratione cessat lex*."[31] This remains (however much it may sometimes be evaded) the formally enunciated rule for statutory construction: statutes do not change. Proposals for "dynamic statutory construction," such as those of Judge Calabresi and Professor Eskridge that I discussed yesterday, are concededly avant-garde. The Constitution, however, even though a democratically adopted text, we formally treat like the common law. What, it is fair to ask, is our justification for doing so?

One would suppose that the rule that a text does not change would apply *a fortiori* to a constitution. If courts felt too much bound by the democratic process to tinker with statutes, when their tinkering could be adjusted by the legislature, how much more should they feel bound not to tinker with a constitution, when their tinkering is virtually irreparable. It surely cannot be said that a constitution naturally suggests changeability; to the contrary, its whole purpose is to prevent change — to embed certain rights in such a manner that future generations cannot take them away. A society that adopts a bill of rights is skeptical that "evolving standards of decency" always "mark progress," and that societies always "mature," as opposed to rot. Neither the text of such a document nor the intent of its framers (whichever you choose) can possibly lead to the conclusion that its only effect is to take the power of changing rights away from the legislature and give it to the courts.

The argument most frequently made in favor of The Living Constitution is a pragmatic one: Such an evolutionary approach is necessary in order to provide the "flexibility" that a changing society requires; the Constitution would have snapped, if it had not been permitted to bend and grow. This might be a persuasive

---

[31] *Rhodes* v. *Chapman*, 452 U.S. 337, 346 (1981), quoting from Fortunatus Dwarris, *A General Treatise on Statutes, with American Notes and Additions by Platt Potter* (1871), 122.

argument if most of the "growing" that the proponents of this approach have brought upon us in the past, and are determined to bring upon us in the future, were the *elimination* of restrictions upon democratic government. But just the opposite is true. Historically, and particularly in the past thirty-five years, the "evolving" Constitution has imposed a vast array of new constraints — new inflexibilities — upon administrative, judicial, and legislative action. To mention only a few things that formerly could be done or not done, as the society desired, but now can not be done:

- admitting in a state criminal trial evidence of guilt that was obtained by an unlawful search;

- permitting invocation of God at public-school graduations;

- electing one of the two houses of a state legislature the way the United States Senate is elected (i.e., on a basis that does not give all voters numerically equal representation);

- terminating welfare payments as soon as evidence of fraud is received, subject to restoration after hearing if the evidence is satisfactorily refuted;

- imposing property requirements as a condition of voting;

- prohibiting anonymous campaign literature;

- prohibiting pornography.

And the future agenda of constitutional evolutionists is mostly more of the same — the creation of *new* restrictions upon democratic government, rather than the elimination of old ones. *Less* flexibility in government, not *more*. As things now stand, the state and federal governments may either apply capital punishment or abolish it, permit suicide or forbid it — all as the changing times and the changing sentiments of society may demand. But when capital punishment is held to violate the Eighth Amendment, and suicide is held to be protected by the Fourteenth Amendment, all flexibility with regard to those matters will be gone. No, the reality of the matter is that, generally speaking, devotees of The Living Constitution do not seek to facilitate social change but to *prevent* it.

There are, I must admit, a few exceptions to that — a few instances in which, historically, greater flexibility *has been* the result of the process. But those exceptions only serve to refute another argument of the proponents of an evolving Constitution, that evolution will always be in the direction of greater personal liberty. (They consider that a great advantage, for reasons that I do not entirely understand. All government represents a balance between individual freedom and social order, and it is not true that every alteration of that balance in the direction of greater individual freedom is necessarily good.) But in any case, the record of history refutes the proposition that the evolving Constitution will invariably enlarge individual rights. The most obvious refutation is the modern Court's limitation of the constitutional protections afforded to property. The provision prohibiting impairment of the obligation of contracts, for example, has been gutted. I am sure that We the People agree with that development; we value property rights less than the Founders did. So also, we value the right to bear arms less than the Founders (who thought the right of self-defense to be absolutely fundamental), and there will be few tears shed if and when the Second Amendment is held to guarantee nothing more than the State National Guard. But this just shows that the Founders were right when they feared that some (in their view misguided) future generation might wish to abandon liberties that they considered essential, and so sought to protect those liberties in a Bill of Rights. We may *like* the abridgment of property rights, and *like* the elimination of the right to bear arms; but let us not pretend that these are not a *reduction* of *rights*.

Or if property rights are too cold to get your juices flowing, and the right to bear arms too dangerous, let me give another example: Several terms ago a case came before the Supreme Court involving a prosecution for sexual abuse of a young child. The trial court found that the child would be too frightened to testify in the presence of the (presumed) abuser, and so, pursuant to state law, she was permitted to testify with only the prosecutor and defense counsel present, the defendant, the judge, and the jury watching over closed-circuit television. A reasonable enough procedure, and it was held to be constitutional by my Court.[32] I dissented, because the Sixth Amendment provides that "[i]n *all* criminal prosecutions" (let me emhpasize the word "all") "the accused shall enjoy the right . . . to be confronted with the witnesses against him." There is no doubt what confrontation meant — or indeed means today. It means face-to-face, not watching from another room. And there is no doubt what one of the major purposes of that provision was: to induce *precisely* that pressure upon the witness which the little girl found it difficult to endure. It is difficult to accuse someone to his face, particularly when you are lying. Now no extrinsic factors have changed since that provision was adopted in 1791. Sexual abuse existed then, as it does now; little children were more easily upset than adults, then as now; a means of placing the defendant out of sight of the witness existed then as now (a screen could easily have been erected that would enable the defendant to see the witness, but not the witness the defendant). But the Sixth Amendment nonetheless gave *all* criminal defendants the right to *confront* the witnesses against them, because that was thought to be an important protection. The only significant thing that *has* changed, I think, is the society's sensitivity to so-called psychic trauma (which is what we are told the child witness in such a situation suffers) and the society's assessment of where the proper balance ought to be struck between the two extremes of a procedure that assures convicting 100 percent of all child abusers, and a procedure that assures acquitting 100 percent of those who have been falsely accused of child abuse. I have no doubt that the society is, as a whole, happy and pleased with what my Court decided. But we should not pretend that the decision did not *eliminate* a liberty that previously existed.

[32] See *Maryland* v. *Craig*, 497 U.S. 836 (1990).

My last remarks may have created the false impression that proponents of The Living Constitution follow the desires of the American people in determining how the Constitution should evolve. They follow nothing so precise; indeed, as a group they follow nothing at all. Perhaps the most glaring defect of Living Constitutionalism, next to its incompatibility with the whole antievolutionary purpose of a constitution, is that there is no agreement, and no chance of agreement, upon what is to be the guiding principle of the evolution. *Panta rei* is not a sufficiently informative principle of constitutional interpretation. What is it that the judge must consult to determine when, and in what direction, evolution has occurred? Is it the will of the majority, discerned from newspapers, radio talk shows, public opinion polls, and chats at the country club? Is it the philosophy of Hume, or of John Rawls, or of John Stuart Mill, or of Aristotle? As soon as the discussion goes beyond the issue of whether the Constitution is static, the evolutionists divide into as many camps as there are individual views of the good, the true, and the beautiful. I think that is inevitably so, which means that evolutionism is simply not a practicable constitutional philosophy.

I do not suggest, mind you, that originalists always agree upon their answer. There is plenty of room for disagreement as to what original meaning was, and even more as to how that original meaning applies to the situation before the court. But the originalist at least knows what he is looking for: the original meaning of the text. Often, indeed I dare say usually, that is easy to discern and simple to apply. Sometimes (though not very often) there will be disagreement regarding the original meaning; and sometimes there will be disagreement as to how that original meaning applies to new and unforeseen phenomena. How, for example, does the First Amendment guarantee of "the freedom of speech" apply to new technologies that did not exist when the guarantee was created — to sound trucks, or to government-licensed over-the-air television? In such new fields the Court must follow the trajectory of the First

Amendment, so to speak, to determine what it requires—and assuredly that enterprise is not entirely cut-and-dried, but requires the exercise of judgment.

But the difficulties and uncertainties of determining original meaning and applying it to modern circumstances are negligible compared with the difficulties and uncertainties of the philosophy which says that the Constitution *changes*; that the very act which it once prohibited it now permits, and which it once permitted it now forbids; and that the key to that change is unknown and unknowable. The originalist, if he does not have all the answers, has many of them. The Confrontation Clause, for example, requires confrontation. For the evolutionist, however, every question is an open question, every day a new day. No fewer than three of the Justices with whom I have served have maintained that the death penalty is unconstitutional, *even though its use is explicitly contemplated in the Constitution*. The Due Process Clause of the Fifth and Fourteenth Amendments says that no person shall be deprived of life without due process of law; and the Grand Jury Clause of the Fifth Amendment says that no person shall be held to answer for a capital crime without grand jury indictment. No matter. Under The Living Constitution the death penalty may have *become* unconstitutional. And it is up to each Justice to decide for himself (under no standard I can discern) when that occurs.

In the last analysis, however, it probably does not matter what principle, among the innumerable possibilities, the evolutionist proposes to determine in what direction The Living Constitution will grow. For unless the evolutionary dogma is kept a closely held secret among us judges and law professors, it will lead to the result that the Constitution evolves the way the majority wishes. The people will be willing to leave interpretation of the Constitution to a committee of nine lawyers so long as the people believe that it is (like the interpretation of a statute) lawyers' work—requiring a close examination of text, history of the text, traditional understanding of the text, judicial precedent, etc. But if the people come to believe that the Constitution is *not* a text like other texs; if it means, not what it says or what it was understood to mean, but what it *should* mean, in light of the "evolving standards of decency that mark the progress of a maturing society," well then, they will look for qualifications other than impartiality, judgment, and lawyerly acumen in those whom they select to interpret it. More specifically, they will look for people who agree with *them* as to what those evolving standards have evolved to; who agree with *them* as to what the Constitution *ought* to be.

It seems to me that that is where we are heading, or perhaps even where we have arrived. Seventy-five years ago, we believed firmly enough in a rock-solid, unchanging Constitution that we felt it necessary to adopt the Nineteenth Amendment to give women the vote. The battle was not fought in the courts, and few thought that it could be, despite the constitutional guarantee of Equal Protection of the Laws; that provision did not, when it was adopted, and hence did not in 1920, guarantee equal access to the ballot, but permitted distinctions on the basis not only of age, but of property and of sex. Who can doubt that, if the issue had been deferred until today, the Constitution would be (formally) unamended, and the courts would be the chosen instrumentality of change? The American people have been converted to belief in The Living Constitution, a "morphing" document that means, from age to age, what it ought to mean. And with that conversion has inevitably come the new phenomenon of selecting and confirming federal judges, at all levels, on the basis of their views regarding a whole series of proposals for constitutional evolution. If the courts are free to write the Constitution anew, they will, by God, write it the way the majority wants; the appointment and confirmation process will see to that. This, of course, is the end of the Bill of Rights, whose meaning will be committed to the very body it was meant to protect against: the majority. By trying to make the Constitution do everything that needs doing from age to age, we shall have caused it to do nothing at all.

As I said at the outset of these lectures, the interpretation and application of democratically adopted texts comprises virtually all the work of federal judges, and the vast majority of the work of state judges, in New Jersey and elsewhere. I have tried to explain why, in my view, we common lawyers come to the bench ill prepared for that task — indeed, even ill disposed towards that task. I have discussed a few principles of statutory interpretation that seem to me the most basic or the most currently in need of emphasis. That part was principally of interest to the lawyers among you. And finally, I have discussed the major issue of textual interpretation posed by that peculiar type of text known as a constitution. These last remarks were not distinctively lawyers' or judges' business, but the business of every intelligent citizen; for as I have explained, if the people misunderstand the nature of the Constitution, and the role of the courts in its enforcement, the enterprise cannot succeed.

On Lost Causes

EDWARD W. SAID

THE TANNER LECTURES ON HUMAN VALUES

Delivered at

University of Utah
October 16 and 17, 1995

EDWARD W. SAID, University Professor at Columbia University and Chair of the doctoral program in Comparative Literature, was born in West Jerusalem in 1935. A Palestinian, he fled with his family to Egypt in 1948. He was educated at Princeton and received his Ph.D. from Harvard University. He has been active in the struggle for Palestinian self-determination, having served as a member of the Palestine National Council from 1977 to 1991, and has also served as a consultant to the United Nations. He has been a visiting professor at Yale, Harvard, Johns Hopkins, and Toronto, and has given lectures at over 150 universities and institutes in North America, Europe, Africa, and Asia. He is well known as a cultural criitc, Middle East scholar, and as the author of numerous publications including *Orientalism* (1978), *Musical Elaborations* (1991), *Culture and Imperialism* (1993), *The Pen and the Sword: Conversations with David Barsamian* (1994), and *The Politics of Dispossession: The Struggle for Palestinian Self-Determination* (1994).

The phrase "a lost cause" appears with some frequency in political and social commentary: in recent accounts of the Bosnian agony, for example, the British writer Jeremy Harding uses the phrase in passing, as he refers to "the lost cause of Bosnian nationalism" in connection with an analysis of British politics. A lost cause is associated in the mind and in practice with a hopeless cause: that is, something you support or believe in that can no longer be believed in except as something without hope of achievement. The time for conviction and belief has passed, the cause no longer seems to contain any validity or promise, although it may once have possessed both. But are timeliness and conviction only matters of interpretation and feeling or do they derive from an objective situation? That I think is the crucial question. Many times we feel that the time is not right for a belief in the cause of native people's rights in Hawaii, or of gypsies or Australian aborigines, but that in the future, and given the right circumstances, the time may return, and the cause may revive. If, however, one is a strict determinist about the survival only of powerful nations and peoples, then the cause of native rights in Hawaii, or of gypsies or aborigines, is always necessarily a lost cause, something both predestined to lose out and because of belief in the overall narrative of power, required to lose.

But there is no getting round the fact that for a cause to seem or feel lost is the result of judgment, and this judgment entails either a loss of conviction or, if the sense of loss stimulates a new sense of hope and promise, a feeling that the time for it is not right, has passed, is over. Even a phrase like "a born loser" attaches to a person not because of something inherent in that person — which cannot be known anyway — but because a series of events results in the judgment. Narrative plays a central role here. When we say that Jim is a born loser the phrase is pronounced after Jim's sorry record is presented: he was born to poor parents, they were divorced, he lived in foster homes, he was lured into a life of crime at an early age, and so forth. A loser's narrative is implicitly contrasted with the story of someone who either surmounted all the obstacles (triumph in adversity) or was born in favorable circumstances, developed brilliantly, and won the Nobel prize in chemistry or physics. When the cause for something is associated with the narrative of a nation or a person we also employ narrative to present the evidence *seriatim*, and then we make the judgment.

Two other factors need to be stressed: one is the *time* of making the judgment, which usually occurs at an important juncture in the individual's life. I may be about to embark on my sixth marriage, and I have to decide whether I am unfit for wedded life or whether the institution of marriage itself is a lost cause, one that is so hopelessly inconvenient and complicated as never to result even in minimal success. Similarly one can imagine a great tennis player like John McEnroe at the beginning of the Grand Slam season, trying to decide whether another year of tournaments, an aging body, and a whole crop of new and hungry young players are likely to turn his campaign for more tournament victories into a lost cause. That predicament is more commonly encountered in the life of an individual as he or she nears the end of life, perhaps as the result of serious illness or a failure of capacity or energy due to age. Feeling that one's life is a lost cause as the possibility for cure or continued productivity appears more and more remote is one such instance: giving up on life, becoming withdrawn and dejected, and committing suicide are alternatives when the going gets rough and when we ask ourselves the question can I go on or is it hopeless, hence only despair is the answer. In these instances a cause is not momentous and public, like the survival of a nation or the struggle for national independence, but the sense of urgency may be greater and the stakes may appear to be higher. We are at the point now where genetics may soon make it possible to predict that a person is going to get Alzheimer's or a virulent form of cancer:

the bioethical question is whether in the absence of known cures to inform that person that he or she is doomed or to withhold information as a charitable form of letting things be.

The second factor is who makes the judgment, the believer or someone who stands outside the cause, perhaps an active opponent, a professional historian, philosopher, or social scientist, an indifferent onlooker? In the world of political causes a common psychological strategy is for opponents to try to undermine confidence in the cause that opposes them; a battle of wills ensues in which one side attempts to pile up one achievement or "actual fact" after another in the hope of discouraging people on the other side, demonstrating to them that they can have no hope of winning. In such a situation "hearts and minds" have to be won, or must be lost. Antonio Gramsci's political theory of the struggle for hegemony gave this contest a central place in modern politics and explains the motto (taken from Romain Rolland) that he affixed to his journal *L'Ordine nuovo*: "pessimism of the intelligence, optimism of the will." Yet no matter how fraught a situation is, it remains for the person whose cause it is to make the final determination, to keep the initiative, retain the prerogative.

Beginnings, endings, middles — these are the narrative periods or termini at which judgments of victory, success, failure, final loss, hopelessness are made. What I find particularly interesting for my purposes here is the interplay between the private and the public, between what appears to be the intensely subjective and overwhelmingly objective, between the emotional, intensely "gut" feeling and the portentously historical judgment, all of which are entailed in thinking about lost causes. Although we can use the phrase loosely to describe a highly circumscribed personal situation — as in "getting John to give up smoking is a lost cause" — I shall confine myself to situations in which the individual is representative of a more general condition. The word "cause" after all acquires its force and hearing from the sense we have that a cause is more than the individual; it has the significance of a project, quest, and effort that stand outside individuals and compel their energies, focus their efforts, inspire dedication. Serving the Grail is a cause; acquiring a new car or suit is not. A cause is not often exhausted by the people who serve it, whereas individuals can exhaust themselves in a cause, which is most normally characterized as ahead of one, something greater and nobler than oneself for which great striving and sacrifice is necessary. Alfred Tennyson's "Ulysses" catches this in its last, syntactically very awkward, lines; the aging hero reflects here on the persistence of his will in the service of a cause.

> We are not now and tho' that strength which in old days
> Moved earth and heaven, that which we are, we are —
> One equal temper of heroic hearts,
> Made weak by time and fate, but strong in will
> To strive, to seek, to find and not to yield.

So much of early education in school or family is informed by the need to make young people aware that life is more than self-satisfaction and doing as one likes. Every culture that I know of emphasizes explicitly as well as implicitly the idea that there is more to life than doing well: the "higher things" for which everyone is taught to strive are loyalty to the cause of nation, service to others, service to God, family, and tradition. All are components of the national identity. To rise in the world, that motif of self-help and personal betterment, is routinely attached to the good of the community and the improvement of one's people. As a child growing up in two British colonies and attending colonial schools during the dying days of the empire, I was soon made conscious of the internal contradiction in the stated, albeit divided, program of my education: on the one hand, I was a member of an elite class being educated to serve the cause of my people, to help raise them up and into the privileges of independence, and, on the other, I was not being educated in Arab but in British or European culture, the better to advance the cause of that alien yet more advanced and modern culture, to become intellectually more attached to it than to my own.

After independence the reemergence of euphoric nationalism, with its pantheon of founding fathers, texts, events strung together in a triumphalist story and contained in newly Arabized institutions, reached out and incorporated my generation. The new cause was Arabism itself, *al-'urûbah*; this came gradually to include the notion of a military-security state, the centrality of a strong army in national development, the idea of a one-party collective leadership (which favored the ideology of the great leader), a deeply critical, perhaps even paranoid suspicion of and obsession with the West as the source of most problems, and, so far as Israel was concerned, hostility combined with a will neither to know nor to have anything to do with the new society and its people. I mention these early causes not so much only as a way of criticizing them — they seemed inevitable at the time, for reasons I do not have the time to go into here — but as a way of marking the distance intellectual elites have travelled since. Today Arabism is supposed to be virtually dead, its place taken by a host of smaller, less causelike nationalisms; Arab leaders are largely drawn from unpopular and isolated minorities and oligarchies, and although there may be a residual anti-Western rhetoric in public discourse, both the state and its institutions have largely now been willingly incorporated into the American sphere. The emergence of an Islamic counter-discourse during the past two decades is due, I think, to the absence of a militant, secular, and independent political vision; hence reversion and regression, the desire to establish an Islamic state with its supposed roots in seventh-century Hijaz.

Another marker of how different things have become is supplied once we contrast Abdel Nasser (the twenty-fifth anniversary of whose death has just been very modestly observed in Egypt and elsewhere) with his arch-rivals King Hussein of the Hashemites and the reigning king of Saudi Arabia. Nasser was a family man, wildly popular, modest, personally incorruptible, culturally a representative of most average Egyptian Sunni Muslims with no property or class privileges to speak of; his rivals (who have outlived him by a quarter of a century) were heads of clans whose names, Hashemites and al-Saud, have been given to the countries they rule. They have come to represent both a feudal conception of rule and fealty to the United States. One of Nasser's most representative and unprecedented acts was to offer to resign on June 9, 1967, after his army's defeat by Israel: this is an unimaginable gesture for any Arab ruler to make today. In any event, it is difficult to discern the presence of a general cause like Arabism in today's Arab world, except for that of Islam. I shall return to this general subject a little later.

The passage from inculcated enthusiasm for higher causes in the young to the disillusionment of age is nevertheless not restricted to modern Middle Eastern history. The aesthetic form of this trajectory is the great realistic novel, one of whose most typical instances is Gustave Flaubert's *Education sentimentale*. Young Frederic Moreau comes to Paris with the ambitions of a provincial youth, determined to succeed in various vocations and causes. He and his friend Deslauriers entertain ideas of becoming prominent literary, intellectual, and political figures, Frederic as the Walter Scott of France, later as its greatest lawyer; Deslauriers has plans to preside over a vast metaphysical system, then to become an important politician. The events of the novel take place during the heady days of the 1848 revolution in Paris, in which upstarts, frauds, opportunists, bohemians, prostitutes, merchants, and, it appears, only one honest man, a humble idealistic worker, jostle each other in an unceasing whirl of dances, horse-races, insurrections, mob-scenes, auctions, parties.

By the end of the novel the revolution and France have been betrayed (Napoleon III, the cunning nephew of his magnificent imperial uncle, has taken over France) and the two young men have achieved none of their ambitions at all. Frederic "travelled. He came to know the melancholy of the steamboat, the cold awakening in the tent, the tedium of landscapes and ruins, the bitterness of interrupted friendships. He returned. He went into society and he had other loves. . . . His intellectual ambitions had also dwindled. Years went by; and he endured the idleness of his mind and the inertia of his heart" (411). Not a single cause is left. Frederic is visited by a woman he had once loved; he is filled with desire for her, yet restrained by the fear that he might feel disgusted later. He does nothing: *et ce fut tout*, Flaubert says. Deslauriers wanders from job to job and is dismissed from his one chance to serve his country. "After that," Flaubert says, "he had been director of colonization in Algeria, secretary to a pasha, manager of a newspaper, and an advertising agent; and at present he was employed as solicitor to an industrial company" (416).

In his *Theory of the Novel*, Georg Lukács calls *L'Education sentimentale* an instance of the romanticism of disillusion as embodied in the very form of the novel. According to Lukács the novel, unlike the epic, expresses the predicament of a world abandoned by God, in which time is felt as irony, and in which the individual hero strives for what he can never achieve, a correspondence between his idea and the world. In the novel of abstract idealism, which Lukács counterposes against the romanticism of disillusion, the hero is Don Quixote, a prototype of the soul that is narrower than the outside world, and whose main driving impulse is furnished by a demon pushing the individual towards the realization of an ideal or cause.

> The demonism of the narrowing of the soul is the demonism of abstract idealism. It is the mentality which chooses the direct, straight path towards the realisation of the ideal; which, dazzled by the demon, forgets the existence of any distance between ideal and idea, between psyche and soul; which, with the most authentic and unshakable faith, concludes that the idea, because it *should be*, necessarily *must be*, and because reality does not satisfy this *a priori* demand, thinks that reality is bewitched by evil demons and that the spell can be broken and reality be redeemed either by finding a magic password or by courageously fighting the evil forces. (97)

Although most readers would judge Quixote's cause to restore the age of chivalry as a completely lost one, Lukács takes the more audacious step of considering it a partial victory, because Quixote manages "to remain unblemished in the purity of his intent and is also able to transmit some of the radiance of [his] triumphant, though admittedly self-ironising, poetry to [his] victorious opponent" (104). Of course the Don is unsuccessful in restoring Amadis of Gaul and the age of chivalry, but the strength of his conviction is such as even to expose the sordid reality of this extremely unheroic world of ours — with its innkeepers, shepherds, itinerant rogues — to an idealism whose self-conviction and fervor look backward to an age that has disappeared.

> Thus the first great novel of world literature stands at the beginning of the time when the Christian God began to forsake the world; when man became lonely and could find meaning and substance only in his own soul, whose home was nowhere. . . . Cervantes lived in the period of the last, great and desperate mysticism, the period of a fanatical attempt to renew the dying religion from within; a period of a new view of the world rising up in mystical forms; the last period of truly lived by already disoriented, tentative, sophisticated, occult aspirations. (103-4)

The novel, according to Lukács, replaces the epic. Whereas the epic expresses the religious world of heroes and gods living on a par with each other, unproblematically and without a trace of self-consciousness, the novel expresses a fallen world, which God has abandoned. Heroes have been transformed into secular men and women, subject to the interior dislocations, lostness, and madness of what Lukács calls "transcendental homelessness." A rift has opened between Idea and actuality. That is why all the great novelistic figures, from Don Quixote to Frederic Moreau, cannot really adapt themselves to the secular, historical world because they are haunted by memories of what they have lost, searching in vain for self-realization and the success of a cause that cannot be maintained. In this, Lukács and Max Weber — friends, fellow-members of the Heidelberg circle, sociologists and aestheticians — chart the modern world as a place of disenchantment. Weber says that "the ultimate and most sublime values have retreated from public life either into the transcendental realm of mystic life or into the brotherliness of direct and personal human relations" ("The Vocation of Science," 155). Hence Don Quixote, whose cause has the efficacity of a private dream with no place to go, or Frederic Moreau and Deslauriers, failures in everything except in their friendship. Ours is not a happy, summertime world, but, as Weber says, "a polar night of icy darkness and hardness" ("The Vocation of Politics," 128).

Yet even in the religious world view that both Weber and Lukács lament and criticize there exists a patron saint of lost causes, Saint Jude. During the early years of the Christian era Jude or Judas was regularly described as Judas (*frater*) Jacobi, Judas the brother of James; along with John the Evangelist the three brothers were disciples of Jesus, although Jude had the misfortune of being confused with Judas Iscariot and was therefore known as Jude the Hidden. He and Saint Simon preached the gospel together in Mesopotamia and were martyred there. A book on modern pilgrimage says that after Peter and James — Santiago — Jude "ranks third among the apostles as a pilgrimage saint with at least nine European shrines to his credit. Saint Jude also has at least five shrines in North America. The cult of this apostle, who replaced Judas Iscariot among the original group, developed slowly and became important only in the twentieth century" (Nolan, 137). Even to someone like myself who is unpracticed in hagiography, Jude seems a required figure in the economy of the apostolic world. Surrounded as he is by larger-than-life figures — Peter the Rock, John the mystic and theologian, James the patron saint of pilgrims and killer of Moors (Santiago Matamoros) — and overshadowed by the great betrayer Judas Iscariot, Jude the Hidden comes to symbolize all those who have failed in distinction, whose promise has been unrealized, whose efforts and causes have not succeeded. And such a personality ultimately validates the Christian vision of charity and humility: there is a place for everyone, Jude seems to be saying, not just for those who have made it. Interestingly, however, Jude provides a last resort in a religion whose central figure is supposed to be the last resort; for even if one's faith in Christ falters, there is another opportunity afforded the believer by Jude.

It is as a savage attack on any such palliative that Thomas Hardy wrote his last and, in my opinion, his greatest novel, *Jude the Obscure*, first published in 1895. A mediocre young country boy of some sensitivity and admirable if inappropriate ambition, Jude Fawley aspires to better himself from the beginning to the last moment of his experience. We first see him at age ten, taking leave of his schoolmaster who is off to Christminster — a combination of Oxford and Cambridge—to complete his university studies. Jude is infected with the idea that he must try to do the same, and for the remainder of the novel he drifts in and out of Christminster, in search of learning, success, higher purpose. Yet all he encounters is setback, disappointment, and more and more entanglements that lead him into desperate degradation. Whenever he tries to improve his lot in as direct a way as possible he meets impossible resistance. When he acquires a set of Greek and Latin primers in order to teach himself the two classical languages he realizes that languages cannot be learned simply by reading a book; he then gives up. The two women who enter his life, Arabella and Sue Bridehead, exhaust him. He goes from job to job, getting poorer and poorer, as each disaster — the suicide of his children, Sue's relationship with Philotson, Jude's early schoolmaster model — humbles him further, especially after he and Sue discover an extraordinarily passionate love between them, for which they both risk and undergo social ostracism and even greater poverty. Jude's death occurs just as the "Remembrance games" take place outside his windows in his impoverished quarters in Christminster; the city and all its religious and educational institutions remain as impervious and insensitive to

Jude's basically harmless aspirations now during his final moments as they did when he began his unfortunate career. Hardy orchestrates the pathetic man's last moments by interweaving his singularly pertinent recollections from the Book of Job with the triumphant hurrahs and glorious music of the games:

'Throat — water — Sue — darling — drop of water — please — O please!'
No water came, and the organ notes, faint as a bee's hum, rolled in as before.
While he remained, his face changing, shouts and hurrahs came from somewhere in the direction of the river.
'Ah — yes! The Remembrance games,' he murmured. 'And I here. And Sue defiled!'
The hurrahs were repeated, drowning the faint organ notes. Jude's face changed more: he whispered slowly, his parched lips scarcely moving:
Let the day perish wherein I was born, and the night in which it was said, There is a man child conceived.'
('Hurrah!')
'Let that day be darkness; let not God regard it from above, neither let the light shine upon it. Lo, let that night be solitary, let no joyful voice come therein.'
('Hurrah!')
'Why died I not from the womb? Why did I not give up the ghost when I came out of the belly? . . . For now should I have lain still and been quiet. I should have slept: then had I been at rest!"
('Hurrah!')
'There the prisoners rest together; they hear not the voice of the oppressor. . . . The small and the great are there; and the servant is free from his master. Wherefore is light given to him that is in misery, and life unto the bitter in soul?' (*Jude*, 321)

The point of all this is to ram home the total hopelessness of Jude's condition, and at the same time — this is Hardy's hallmark as an unbeliever—to show that even St. Jude, patron of lost causes, is of no value whatever to Jude Fawley, his modern namesake.

The irony goes well beyond that of the novelists (Cervantes and Flaubert) that I spoke about earlier. Job has displaced Jude in the first place; whereas Don Quixote and Frederic Moreau might have been capable of some attainments, the one a knight, the other a relatively wealthy young man of good education, Jude is incapacitated from the start. Hardy sees to it that both circumstances and his own disabilities undermine everything he does. It is not only that by now God has abandoned the world entirely: it is also that whatever recollection or remnants of an earlier world persist, either they are obliviously mocking of the individual's misery (as when Jude quotes Job without any result of the sort that the biblical figure experiences after his travails; there is no Eliphaz the Temanite to do God's will, offer up seven bullocks and seven rams, and restore Job to happiness and justice) or they are deliberately unredemptive and untherapeutic, like the folk doctor Vilbert or the village wench Arabella, who first attracts Jude's attention by throwing a pig's pizzle at him.

But what Cervantes, Flaubert, and Hardy have in common is that their narratives are mature works, written near the end of their careers at precisely that moment when the individual feels the need for summing-up, making judgments, tallying up the evidence for and against the success of youthful ambitions and aspirations. That they do their summing-up in novels underscores more starkly than usual the underlying ironies and depressing exigencies of the novel form itself, conditioned by experience and the hidden god, to be a narrative in which time ironically exposes the disparity between reality and higher purpose, and in which the individual is really only afforded two on the whole dispiriting alternatives: either one conforms to the sordid practices of the world, thus sacrificing any hope of a noble cause, or one is killed off as Jude, Emma Bovary, and Quixote are killed off. What the novel offers therefore is a narrative without redemption. Its conclusion is not the rounded-off closure imputed to a contrite heart as, under the auspices of St. Jude, it re-accepts the final authority of God, but is rather the bitterness of defeat, ironized and given aesthetic form it is true, but conclusive nonetheless. So far as idealism is concerned, then, the novel is constitutively opposed. What remains are the ruins of lost causes and defeated ambition.

A lost cause is unimaginable without an adjoining or perhaps parallel victory to compare it with. There are always winners and losers, but what seems to count is how you look at things. A major part of most official culture is dedicated to proving that if, like Socrates, you are put to death for your virtues, which remain intact, you are the victor, your cause has won out, even though of course the obvious winners thrive on. "It depends on how you look at it" has something weasely about it, as if the real winner is only a winner in appearances or is so morally inferior as not to be a winner at all. The most devastating refutation of "hm . . . despite all our losses, we have really been the winners, and we live to fight on," is Jonathan Swift's *Gulliver's Travels*, a book that is certainly not a novel but a political satire with an extremely depressing end. Gulliver's voyage to Lilliput locates him in a tiny country where his strength is both an undeniable strength — as when he can entertain the queen's cavalry on his handkerchief — and a curious weakness when he is embroiled in Lilliputian politics and, through an act of quick-thinking rescue, he offends the queen when he urinates on her palace to put out a fire. He is so little a courtier that despite his size and strength he finds himself the victim of a palace plot, the net result of which he tells us is either to blind him or to starve him slowly and painfully to death. He goes to neighboring Blefescu seeking refuge there, but is then the object of an extradition request from Lilliput: he escapes, returns home, but is soon on the ocean again.

He ends up in Brobdingnag, as a tiny little humanoid in a country of giants, where once again neither his comparative agility nor his great experience is much of a help to him. He rather patronizingly tries to convince the king there that Europe is more advanced in both culture and practical politics, believing himself to be a representative of his own species and race as he does so. The king's answer is quite devastating and allows Gulliver not a whit of saving grace: everything noble or good seems, from the Brobdingnagian perspective, to be appallingly depraved:

> . . . you have made a most admirable Panegyrick upon your Country. You have clearly proved that Ignorance, Idleness, and Vice are the proper Ingredients for qualifying a Legislator. That Laws are best explained, interpreted, and applied by those whose Interest and Abilities lie in perverting, confounding, and eluding them. I observe among you some Lines of an Institution, which in its Original might have been tolerable; but these half erased, and the rest wholly blurred and blotted by Corruptions. It doth not appear from all you have said, how any one Perfection is required towards the Procurement of any one Station among you; much less that Men are ennobled on Account of their Virtue, that Priests are advanced for their Piety or Learning, Soldiers for their Conduct or Valour, Judges for their Integrity, Senators for the Love of their Country, or Counsellors for their Wisdom. As for yourself (continued the King) who have spent the greatest Part of your Life in travelling; I am well disposed to hope you may hitherto have escaped many Vices of your Country. But, by what I have gathered from your own Relation, and the Answers I have with much Pains wringed and extorted from you; I cannot but conclude the Bulk of your Natives, to be the most pernicious Race of little odious Vermin that Nature ever suffered to crawl upon the Surface of the Earth. (132)

Nor is Swift done with human illusion, especially of the sort that implies melioristically that a good cause might prevail if the perspective was correct. Having first let Gulliver seem too big, then too small for his context, he thus eliminates the possibility that hidden potential or latent goodness might develop and flourish if the individual was big and idealistic, or small and experienced, relative to the immediate environment. In the final voyage Gulliver becomes a Yahoo, that is, a degenerate savage programmed for lies, duplicity, mendacity, insincerity in a society entirely made up of horses, the Houyhnhnms, whose society produced neither letters nor knowledge of a traditional sort. The plain decency, bland goodness, and inoffensive (if somewhat boring) mores of the Houyhnhnms convince Gulliver that Yahoos — in other words, the human race — represent a totally lost cause, a realization that has no effect on the horses, whose assembly issues an Exhortation condemning Gulliver to exile and deportation. He finally returns to England mortified by his own being and more or less incapable even of enduring the presence of his wife and family. Swift's severity is so uncompromising, Gulliver's reduction in moral status so total, as to disallow any possible relief. There are no winners at all; there is no perspective, or right time, or final moment that permits any sort of redemptive cheer; the whole morass, good cause as well as lost cause, is condemned for the impossible congenital mess that it is. Even W. B. Yeats's "uncontrollable mystery on the bestial floor" is mild and indeed pious by comparison with Swift's strictures on social life in *Gulliver's Travels*.

The implication of Swift's satire is that when the moment for summing-up finally occurs we must be ready to say without the least fudging that human existence simply defeats all causes, good or bad. In the strictness with which he holds this view he belongs in the company of the novelists I have cited, except that he is unkinder and less charitable than they are. Swift, Flaubert, Cervantes, and Hardy allow us to discern how it is that good causes can be represented and defeated; I adduce them as opponents of a world view that is amply available in the Western tradition that claims that in the fullness of time good will prevail and evil will be overcome. I certainly do not have anything in mind that is so simple-mindedly optimistic as the deism lampooned by Voltaire in *Candide*, but rather great works of art written by poets and dramatists at the end of their career. The phenomenon of late style is something I have been studying for some years, since it concerns the way in which writers confront mortality in their last works, and how a separate, individualistically inflected *late style (Spätstil* or *style tardif*) emerges accordingly. A striking difference is to be observed between two types of late work: those like *The Tempest* and *The Winter's Tale*, or *Oedipus at Colonus*, in which resolution and reconciliation occur, and those like Henrik Ibsen's *When We Dead Awaken* and Euripides' *The Bacchae*, in which all the contradictions and unresolved antinomies of life are left standing, untouched by any sort of autumnal mellowness. According to Theodor Adorno, who is a sort of high priest of late-style gloom — he speaks here of Beethoven's third-period masterpieces — late works are the catastrophes.

What I have so far been discussing is a landscape charted by late works of the decidedly problematic and unreconciled second type, in which every decent intention and each admirable cause goes down to defeat and in effect loses, has no chance. Admittedly, I have been using the realm of the aesthetic to grapple with the nature and constitution of lost causes; these ultimately depend on how one represents the narrative course of a cause from intention to realization, but it is plain that the novel and drama, when they attempt to represent the full struggle between successful and lost causes, also tend to concede that good causes have little chance of success. As a student of literature I find this persuasive, in that a reflective and disabused consciousness is likely to render human reality as particularly hospitable to lost causes, and indeed to lost heroes and heroines. But it is essential to remind ourselves that in their sequentiality, originations, maturity, and death fiction and narrative mirror the process of human procreation and generation, which the novel mocks ironically through its attention to the biographies of its heroes and heroines, the continuity of their lives, and their subsequent maturity, marriage, and death.

But even the disillusionment and lost causes that form so essential a part of the Western narrative tradition seem like incidental things when compared with the Japanese tradition of what in a superb essay Marguerite Yourcenar alludes to as "the nobility of failure," which is the title of Ivan Morris's book on "heroic and violent aspects of the Japanese spirit." As befits the author of *The Memoirs of Hadrian*, Yourcenar elucidates the specific Japanese tradition of portraying and even of enacting the self-obliteration of a hero who is doomed to failure, the prototype for which goes back to the impoverished medieval *samurai*, whose last action is ritual suicide. Morris's book is a chronicle of lost causes, all of them Japanese, all of them represented by him (and fascinatingly by Yourcenar) as interesting "despite or possibly because of its complete uselessness"; the chronicle comes up to Yukio Mishima and the Kamikaze pilots of World War II, whose (to us) appalling self-sacrifice seems a representation of the ancient samurai's spirit, which "had lost its last effulgence there" (82). Yet Yourcenar adds (correctly I think):

> But, on the contrary, love of lost causes and respect for those who die for them seem to me to belong to all countries and all ages. Few escapades are as absurd as that of Gordon at Khartoum, but Gordon is a hero of nineteenth-century British history. Rochejacquelein and "le Garcs" in Balzac's *Les Chouans* are certainly defeated, and their cause with them, unless one considers the few years' reigns of Louis XVIII and Charles X as triumph: they speak no less forcefully to our imagination. The same is true of the Girondins and those sent to the guillotine on 9 Thermidor, whose political views one can hardly say triumphed but who count among the great human myths of the French Revolution. And it is probably much more Waterloo and Saint Helena than Wagram which made Napoleon such a beloved subject for the poets of the nineteenth century. I once caused a Roman emperor whose story I evoked to say that a moment comes when "life, for every man, is an accepted defeat." We all know that, and it is what makes us admire so much those who have consciously chosen defeat and who sometimes have achieved it early on. (83)

Still, there is a difference between the aesthetics of lost causes and the more personal, subjective experience for which no ritual form or ceremony exists. What if we try to grapple with lost causes in the public political world where efforts on behalf of causes actually take place? Is there the same ironized inevitability there, or do subjective hope and renewed effort make a lost cause something to be refused as defeatism? Here I can do no better than to offer my personal experiences as a politically active Palestinian as evidence, particularly as these have crystallized since the watershed Oslo agreement of September 1993.

One of the first things I noticed in the United States when I came here from the Middle East during the 1950s to attend school and university was the white southerner who would refer nostalgically to the Confederacy and speak romantically of the "lost cause" of southern independence, chivalry, nobility of sentiment. "We were defeated by the business ethic," one of them told me at Princeton, although little was ever said about the blacks whose slave labor and systematic oppression were essential to the southern cause. It took the Suez and June War of 1956 and 1967 respectively for me to be convinced that, as a young Palestinian who left Palestine in late 1947 and never returned there, the cause of our people in its effort to regain its land and rights was precariously close to being a lost one. But that realization lasted for only a relatively short time. By the time the Palestinian movement had re-emerged in 1968 from the ashes of all three Arab-Israeli wars that I had lived through I had become much more conscious than before of Palestinians as a people sharing a lot in common with the Vietnamese, Cubans, South Africans, Angolans, and others in the Third World struggling for national liberation. During those heady early years of the revived Palestinian national movement it seemed neither appropriate nor really possible to see ourselves in terms of other dispossessed and forgotten peoples like the Armenians, American Indians, Tasmanians, gypsies, and Australian aborigines. On the contrary we modelled ourselves on the Vietnamese people, whose resistance to U.S. intervention seemed exactly what we should undertake.

By the end of the decade, phrases like "people's war" and "armed struggle," with lots of passages from Frantz Fanon and Vo Nguyen Giap to back them up, proliferated everywhere in the region where Palestinians undertook their political activity. Yet as I look back on it now, the emphasis was on the symbols of struggle, rather than on organization and mobilization. None of this would have been possible without support from one or another Arab state; Yasir Arafat, who by that time had become the top leader, was a genius at maneuvering between rivals, and between Arab leaders who one day were with him, the next against him. Above all, this was also a period of amazingly plentiful — to call it bountiful would not be an overstatement — oil money; suddenly a whole cadre of individuals emerged who drank only Black Label Scotch whiskey, travelled first-class, drove fancy European cars, and were always surrounded by aides, bodyguards, and hangers-on. In the environment provided by Beirut between 1971 and 1982, when the Palestine Liberation Organization was driven out of the city by the Israeli army, and its leaders exiled to Tunisia, the real, as opposed to the illusory, parallels provided by Vietnam, Cuba, and South Africa were practically impossible to draw. Although only a tiny percentage of Palestinians actually engaged in armed struggle, and though the casualties sustained by Palestinians were multiples greater than those suffered by Israel, the great campaign for liberation, independence, and the like was pressed, regardless of cost or likelihood of victory.

Looking back over the history of organized Palestinian nationalism during the past several decades one can now distinguish within it that there were always losers and winners, although in the thick of an ongoing struggle it was difficult to make the distinction. Take as an instance a Palestinian friend and contemporary of mine who, having received an excellent education in the United States, with a Ph.D. from Harvard, got a good teaching job in a West Coast university, but then gave everything up in order to join the movement in Amman in 1968. I saw him regularly until his death in 1976. A man of great dedication and extraordinary principle, he rose in the movement by virtue of his selfless work and his demonstrated service to the ideals of commitment to the Palestinian dispossessed — refugees, camp-dwellers, workers, the disabled; in time he became widely known as a severe, albeit loyal critic of the leadership, its methods, and its dubious alliances. Retrospectively it now seems to me that he had become too much for that leadership, precisely because of his unsullied commitment to the cause, and, although I have no concrete proof of this, I believe that he was sent off on a futile mission in 1976, during the Lebanese Civil War, from which he never returned.

Every political theorist and analyst stresses the importance of hope in maintaining a movement. The world has forgotten that in 1948 Palestinians constituted almost 70 percent of the population of mandatory Palestine; in the years since Jewish immigration had begun on a serious scale, the incoming immigrants had managed to acquire only about 6 percent of the land of the country. Yet during the 1940s and especially after the Second World War — the years of my childhood — very little preparation for or understanding of the situation prevailed; I recall little sense of urgency or alarm at the presence of incoming foreigners from Europe, and little assessment of what their plans might be and how they would execute them. The War of 1948 — called Israel's War of Independence — was a catastrophe for Palestinians: two-thirds were driven out of their homes and country, many were killed, all their property was seized, and to all intents and purposes they ceased to exist as a people. I saw this directly in my own family on both my father's and mother's side, each member of which without a single exception became a refugee, was uprooted and totally disoriented, and still bears the scars of that terrible upheaval. To have lived as a member of a society (admittedly controlled by Britain) where it was possible to own property, maintain a profession or job, raise a family, go to school, pray, farm, and even die as a citizen, one day, and then suddenly on another day not to be able to do that, was for most people I knew a living death. This is the background to the period after the 1967 war that I have been discussing, during which hope for the people as a whole was aroused and seemed to make possible some restoration of Palestinian identity and of actual land.

Hope overrode the enormous obstacles that we faced as a people. Consider these obstacles now. We were the first people whose land had been colonized who were declared persona non grata, were dispossessed, and traces of whose national existence were systematically erased by the immigrants who replaced us. This was no exploitation Algerian-style, nor was it apartheid South African–style, nor was it mass extermination as in Tasmania. Rather we were made not to be there, invisible, and most were driven out and referred to as nonpeople; a small minority remained inside Israel and were dealt with juridically by calling them not "Palestinians" but "non-Jews." The rest officially ceased to exist, and where most of them went in the Arab world the majority were confined to refugee camps, special invidious laws were passed for them, and they became stateless refugees. Internationally and in the Arab world, our history and our national existence either were unrecognized or were treated as a local issue. To live through your own extinction, not permitted even the word "Palestine," while a successor state and people thrived with the world's attention focussed on them as pioneers, an island of democracy, miracle state, and so forth, had the programmatic effect of blanking out hope. It was quite ironic that after all the Arab armies were defeated by Israel in 1967 — Arab armies whose *raison d'être* was defense against and defeat of Israel — at that very moment there was a resurgence of hope in the idea not so much of restoring but of liberating Palestine as part of a worldwide process taking place in so many parts of the non-European and non-Atlantic world. The Palestinian cause as a universalist cause was thus born at a time when it was possible for us as a people to see ourselves in a different context than the bleak one provided by the defeated Arabs. We saw ourselves as a Third World people, subjected to colonialism and oppression, now undertaking our own self-liberation from domination as well as the liberation of our territory from our enemy.

Yet — to continue the litany of obstacles — we had no territorial base anywhere; where we tried to establish one (e.g., Jordan or Lebanon) we messily disrupted the local polity, came up against armed force, and were subsequently defeated. Moreover, without sovereignty we did not have a base or a haven; this emphasized the fact that most of our people were dispersed exiles, a condition in which geography became our main enemy. To make matters even worse, the Israelis were not the canonical white settlers of Algeria or South Africa. They were Jews — long the classical victims of Western society — with a history of oppression and genocidal attempts against them; they were mainly European, well connected in the countries from which they had emigrated, imbued with an ideological fervor that gave them both solidarity and resourcefulness. Compared to us, they were modern and disciplined, organized, fully capable of collective action. Unlike us, they always had a strategic partner in the greatest power of the day, which after 1967 was the United States. Their diaspora communities — unlike ours, who were mainly impoverished and unorganized refugees — were well established and could maintain a steady flow of support. The contrast between us and them was that between a developed and an underdeveloped people.

Nevertheless a nation and a movement concerned with something that came to be called the Palestinian cause did emerge with greater and greater definition. For the first time in our modern history we were recognized as a people at the United Nations in 1974. A whole network of institutions dealing with health, education, military training, social welfare, and women's and workers' rights administered by and for Palestinians took hold. In 1988 through the Palestine National Council, of which I was then a member — it was a parliament in exile — we recognized Israel and opted for partition in the land of historical Palestine. A national insurrection called the *intifada* had begun in late 1987 and was to last for four years: it attracted a great deal of attention, and even improved the international image of the Palestinians because of its courage, its willingness frontally to take on Israeli tanks and guns, its capacity for reorganizing society into small, self-sustaining, and independent units that circumvented some but by no means all the depredations of Israeli occupation. Yet during that whole time, Israel pressed on with the building of settlements, with an occupation that was extraordinarily brutal and expensive, with its refusal to recognize Palestinian nationalism. In the world's eyes, and thanks to major blunders of our own, we were known for a long time only as terrorists, although during the *intifada* that designation and Israel's quite favorable image were changed in our favor.

There was certainly an advance in Palestinian consciousness; there was a sense that although we were separated into three entirely discontinuous groups — Israeli Palestinians, inhabitants of the West Bank and Gaza, diaspora Palestinians who made up more than half the total number of our people — we were unified as a people, and regarded as such by an appreciable number of nations; we had now gained the status of a people with a real claim to a homeland. Those were all positive achievements. Nevertheless every change in the international system since 1982 was turned to advantage by Israel, a real disadvantage for us. The collapse of the Soviet Union and subsequent changes in Eastern Europe, as well as the victory of the U.S. coalition during the Gulf War (where our leadership had made a disastrous miscalculation by siding openly with Saddam Hussein), diminished Palestinian energies, as more people became refugees, and less support was available. Still it was possible to believe that the Palestinian cause continued to represent an idea of justice and equality around which many others could rally. By being for Palestinian rights we stood for nondiscrimination, for social justice and equality, for enlightened nationalism. Our aim was an independent sovereign state, of course. Even though we had lived through our loss, we were able to accept a compromise whereby what we lost in 1948 to Israel (contained within the prewar 1967 lines) would be lost forever, if in return we could have a state in the Occupied Territories. We had assumed (and I do not recall much discussion of this particular option for the future) that our state would have sovereignty, our refugees would have the right of some sort of repatriation or compensation, and our politics would be a distinct advance over those of the Arab states, with their oligarchies, military dictatorships, brutal police regimes.

During the period that was effectively terminated by the Oslo agreement of 1993 I recall quite distinctly that most of the intellectuals, professionals, political activists (leadership and nonleadership), and ordinary individuals that I knew well lived at least two parallel lives. The first was in varying degrees a difficult one: as Palestinians living under different jurisdictions, none of them Palestinian of course, with a general sense of powerlessness and drift. Second was a life that was sustained by the various promises of the Palestinian struggle, utopian and unrealistic perhaps, but based on solid principles of justice and, at least since the late 1980s, negotiated peace with Israel. The distorted view of us as a people single-mindedly bent on Israel's destruction that existed in the West bore no relationship at all to any reality I lived or knew of. Most of us, the overwhelming majority in fact, were most interested in the recognition and acknowledgment of our existence as a nation, and not in retribution; everyone I knew was flabbergasted and outraged that the Israelis, who had destroyed our society in 1948, took our land, occupied what remained of it since 1967, and who bombed, killed, and otherwise oppressed an enormous number of us, could appeal to the world as constantly afraid for their security, despite their immense power relative to ours. Few Westerners took seriously our insecurity and real deprivation: somehow Israel's obsession with its insecurity and need for assurance — with its soldiers beating up Palestinians every day after twenty-eight years of occupation — took precedence over our misery. I vividly recall the anger I felt when I learned that starting in the fall of

1992 under the auspices of the American Academy of Arts and Sciences, an organization of which I was a member, a group of privileged Palestinian intellectuals met with Israeli security officials in secret to begin a discussion of security for settlers and army personnel who would remain in the Occupied Territories should there be some form of Palestinian self-rule arrangement. This was a prelude to Oslo, but the fact that there was an acceptance of the Israeli agenda and a scanting of real Palestinian losses struck me as ominous, a sign that capitulation had already set in. Another sign of capitulation was the efflorescence of Islamic movements whose reactionary message (the aim of which was to establish an Islamic state in Palestine) testified to the secular desperation of the nationalist cause.

Let me skip directly to Oslo and after. The mystery there — indeed, from my viewpoint, the only interesting thing — is how a people that had struggled against the British and the Zionists for over a century (unevenly and without much success it is true) were persuaded — perhaps by the international and regional balance of power, the blandishments of their leaders, the fatigue of long and apparently fruitless struggle — to declare in effect that their hope of real national reconstruction and real self-determination was in effect a lost cause. One of the advantages of so extraordinary a *volte face* is that one can see what is happening against the immediate and also the more distant background. History of course is full of peoples who simply gave up and were persuaded to accept a life of servitude; they are all but forgotten, their voices barely heard, the traces of their life scarcely decipherable. History is not kind to them since even in the present they are seen as losers, even though it is sometimes possible, as Walter Benjamin says, to realize that "whoever has emerged victorious participates to this day in the triumphal procession in which the present rulers step over those who are lying prostrate" (*Illuminations*, 256).

How does the cause of a people, a culture, or an individual become hopeless? We had once believed as a people that there was room for us at the rendezvous of destiny. In the instance I have been discussing, it was certainly true that a collective sentiment developed that the time was no longer right, that now is the period of ascendancy of America and its allies, and that everyone else is required to go along with Washington's dictates. A gradual shift in perspective revealed to the collective consciousness that the cause of Palestinian nationalism, with its earlier yet long-standing and uncompromising position on sovereignty, justice, and self-determination, could no longer be fought for: there had to be a change of strategy whereby the nation now thought of its cause less as something won than as something conceded to it as a defeated people by its opponents and by the international authority. Certainly for Palestinians the growing sense of isolation among the other Arabs had been growing inexorably. What used to be *the great* Arab cause of Palestine was so diminished that it became a bargaining card in the hands of countries like Egypt and Jordan, who were desperately hard up for American patronage and largesse and therefore tried to position themselves as talking realistic sense to the Palestinians. Whereas in the past Palestinians gathered hope and optimism from the struggles of other peoples (e.g., the South African battle against apartheid), the opposite became true: *they* were successful because their circumstances were more favorable, and since we did not have the same conditions, we needed instead to become more accommodating. What had once been true for liberation movements was no longer applicable in our case. Soviet help was nonexistent, and besides the times had changed. Libertarian was no longer a timely cause — democracy and the free market were, and where better to make application for joining those campaigns than in Washington. The *intifada* had failed to end the occupation, and so a new strategy based on the conviction of loss had to be adopted swiftly and dramatically.

I must confess to you that since the Oslo agreement between Israel and the PLO was announced and then signed in the fall of 1993 I have been trying to understand how it is that a people and its leadership dramatically stepped down and away from the cause of Palestine, which at very least was to have achieved the recovery of land lost to Israel in 1967, the end of military occupation, annexation, and settlement, and, perhaps most important, the beginnings of a process of real democracy and real self-determination (resources, borders, sovereignty, repatriation, and unity of people in one territory). *That* cause also expressed itself as part of the universal struggle for freedom and equality.

Instead: 1. Our consent was given for the first time in liberation history to continued occupation.

2. Our population was redivided — refugees, residents of the West Bank and Gaza, Israeli Palestinians.

3. Israel retained borders and its settlements; it redeployed but kept the army in Gaza and the West Bank and it also held on to Jerusalem, resources, overall security control.

4. Arafat became responsible to Israel, as the local enforcer.

5. He established a dictatorial regime.

To me and every Palestinian I know these agreements signify defeat, not only militarily and territorially but, more important, morally. Our cause had been to refuse and struggle against the injustice inflicted on us as a people. Now we had conceded that we were prepared to exist not as a sovereign people on our land but as a scattered, dispossessed people, some of whom were given municipal authority by the Israelis, with very little to check further Israeli encroachments against us or to prevent violations of the ungenerous pettifogging agreements they tied us into. The American scholar Norman Finkelstein has recently drawn a harrowing portrait of the defeat of the Cherokee Indians and has suggested that a similar fate might now be befalling Palestinians. The sudden transformation of Arafat from freedom-fighter and "terrorist" into an Israeli enforcer and a (relatively welcome) guest at the White House has been difficult for Palestinians to absorb, but I am certain that despite the momentary euphoria and approving media attention that this former symbol of terrorism now benefited from — his strutting presence at the victory celebrations in Washington, his embraces of Yitzhak Rabin and Shimon Peres, John Major and Jacques Chirac, his vision and courage celebrated by pundits and Zionist lobbyists who had formerly dedicated their professional energies to defaming him and his people — despite all this, most Palestinians saw the new Arafat as the symbol of defeat, the very embodiment of a lost cause, now compelled to speak not of Palestinian self-determination but of Israeli security as his top priority.

Arafat also now represented the cancellation of a heritage of loss and sacrifice: his White House speches, for instance, were profuse with gratitude for Israeli and American recognition, and never once mentioned the land his people had permanently lost, the years of suffering under occupation and in the wilderness, the immense burdens assumed on behalf of the PLO by people who had thought of what they were doing as legitimate support for a just cause. All that was scratched from the record as irrelevant and embarrassing. And when the political failure of a people's cause is so publicly evident, the next best thing to do is to rally round the last remaining symbol of national authority and try to make the best of a bad bargain.

Lost causes can be abandoned causes, the debris of a battle swept aside by history and by the victor, with the losing army in full retreat. In such a situation the collective and the individual still act in concert, agreeing that hopelessness, loss, defeat argue the end of a cause, its historic defeat, the land taken away, the people dispossessed and dispersed, the leaders forced to serve another set of masters. And then the narratives consolidate that decision, tracing — as I have done here — how something that began in hope and optimism ended in the bitterness of disillusion and disappointment. One could argue that no cause is ever totally and irrevocably lost, that personal and collective will can be maintained, and that as, for instance, the Jews were once defeated and destroyed, they were able to return in triumph at a later date. But that I think is an extremely rare case. Do many people now believe that the gypsies or the Native Americans can get back what they lost?

But does the consciousness and even the actuality of a lost cause entail that sense of defeat and resignation that we associate with the abjections of capitulation and the dishonor of grinning or bowing survivors who opportunistically fawn on their conquerors and seek to ingratiate themselves with the new dispensation? Must it always result in the broken will and demoralized pessimism of the defeated? I think not, although the alternative is a difficult and extremely precarious one, at least on the level of the individual. In the best analysis of alternatives to the helpless resignation of a lost cause that I know, Adorno diagnoses the predicament as follows. At a moment of defeat.

> For the individual, life is made easier through capitulation to the collective with which he identifies. He is spared the cognition of his impotence; within the circle of their own company, the few become many. It is this act — not unconfused thinking — which is resignation. No transparent relation prevails between the interests of the ego and the collective to which it assigns itself. The ego must abrogate itself, if it is to share in the predestination of the collective. Explicitly a remnant of the Kantian categorical imperative manifests itself: your signature is required. The feeling of new security is purchased with the sacrifice of autonomous thinking. The consolation that thought within the context of collective actions is an improvement proves deceptive: thinking, employed only as the instrument of action, is blunted in the same manner as all instrumental reason. (167–68)

As opposed to this abrogation of consciousness, Adorno posits as an alternative to resigned capitulation of the lost cause the intransigence of the individual thinker whose power of expression is a power — however modest and circumscribed in its capacity for action or victory — that enacts a movement of vitality, a gesture of defiance, a statement of hope whose "unhappiness" and meager survival are better than silence or joining in the chorus of defeated activists.

In contrast, the uncompromisingly critical thinker, who neither superscribes his conscience nor permits himself to be terrorized into action, is in truth the one who does not give up. Furthermore, thinking is not the spiritual reproduction of that which exists. As long as thinking is not interrupted, it has a firm grasp upon possibility. Its insatiable quality, the resistance against petty satiety, rejects the foolish wisdom of resignation. (168)

I offer this in tentative conclusion as a means of affirming the individual intellectual vocation, which is neither disabled by a paralyzed sense of political defeat nor impelled by groundless optimism and illusory hope. Consciousness of the possibility of resistance can reside only in the individual will that is fortified by intellectual rigor and an unabated conviction in the need to begin again, with no guarantees except, as Adorno says, the confidence of even the loneliest and most impotent thought that "what has been cogently thought must be thought in some other place and by other people." In this way thinking might perhaps acquire and express the momentum of the general, thereby blunting the anguish and despondency of the lost cause, which its enemies have tried to induce.

We might well ask from this perspective if *any* lost cause can ever really be lost.

I. Shakespeare and the Value of Personality
II. Shakespeare and the Value of Love

HAROLD BLOOM

THE TANNER LECTURES ON HUMAN VALUES

Delivered at

Princeton University
November 15 and 16, 1995

HAROLD BLOOM is Sterling Professor of the Humanities at Yale University and Berg Professor of English at New York University. He was educated at Cornell University, Cambridge University, and Yale University, where he received his Ph.D. He also holds honorary degrees from Boston College, Yeshiva University, and the University of Bologne. A recipient of a MacArthur Fellowship, he is a member of the American Academy of Arts and Letters and the American Philosophical Society. Among his twenty-three published books are *The Visionary Company* (1961), *The Anxiety of Influence* (1973), *Ruin the Sacred Truths* (1988), *The American Religions* (1992), and *The Western Canon* (1994).

I. SHAKESPEARE AND THE VALUE OF PERSONALITY

1

Karl Marx, whose visions belong to the history of Christian heresy rather than of Jewish heresy, was enough of an apocalyptic to emulate Jesus in crying out: "Let the dead bury their dead!" Emile Durkheim famously remarked that Marxism was not a social science but a cry of pain. Our current, fashionable attitudes towards literary tradition, and towards Shakespeare in particular, blend Marx and Michel Foucault, yet are mostly a cry of pain, while purporting to be one historicism or another. Inauthentic victimization may have its pleasures, but its pains are unpersuasive. Walter Benjamin, an ironically authentic victim of the Nazis, persuades us, within his context, when he remarks that every monument of civilization is also a monument of barbarism. But our context is very different, and our cheerleaders of cultural resentment scarcely earn their Marxist cries of pain. *The* great monument of our canon, and so of our civilization, is Shakespeare, and I hasten to insist that by "our" I do not mean the Western world alone. Shakespeare is the universal center of the world canon: Christian European and American white males are only a fraction of his audience. Shakespeare, the canonical sublime, cannot be judged a monument of barbarism, not a statement I make at all easily, since I have to regard *The Merchant of Venice*, in one of its salient aspects, as a very barbaric work indeed, while *Titus Andronicus*, unless (as I suspect) it was a send-up of Christopher Marlowe, is the essence of barbarism. If there is a monument of human civilization it must be Shakespeare, who is not only the canon, as I have insisted elsewhere, but the canonical sublime, the outer limit of human cognitive and aesthetic power.

The Australian poet-critic Kevin Hart remarks of Dr. Samuel Johnson: "He is one of those writers — like Dante, Goethe, and

Shakespeare — whose monumentality exceeds his canonicity." Hart grants that the line between canonicity and monumentality is difficult to trace, and so he offers us a definition that is useful yet not altogether acceptable to me:

> A monument is the rallying point for a community; it must be the focus of a large and usually diffuse cultural will, the centre of a network of imaginary relationships and real desires.

I reflect, as I read this, that the United States has no such literary monument, not even in its greatest writer, Walt Whitman, whose hermetic nuances both assure his canonicity and prohibit his monumentality. Our national sage, Emerson, is a larger and wider influence upon our culture than Dr. Johnson is upon that of the English, but Emerson too is no monument. Perhaps there never have been high cultural personalities who are rallying points for us, because we have not been a community in the European sense since about 1800, when the American Religion came to its belated birth at Cane Ridge and other titanic revival meetings. Our authentic religion is not communal, but is based upon an idiosyncratic relationship between each American and the American Christ, who is a figure neither European nor ancient Jewish. Where religion is so profoundly eccentric, there can be no cultural monuments. Even an American Shakespeare could not have achieved such status in a society where nearly everyone has a perfect and private assurance that God loves her or him upon a personal and individual basis.

English Shakespeare, as opposed to French Shakespeare (the creation of the New Historicists, feminists, and allied lemmings), is now a multicultural monument, except in the United States and in France. Shakespeare's monumentalism seems to me rather less significant than his universal canonicity, East and West, because Shakespeare's worldwide effect reverses Kevin Hart's formula: the plays represent *real* relationships and *imaginary* desires, rather than the reverse, which would be more cinematic. We find it difficult as we begin to slide into the cosmos of virtual reality always to remember that Shakespeare's art is primarily auditory and not visual. I am so weary of badly directed Shakespeare that I would prefer to attend public readings rather than performances of the plays, if only such readings were available. The greatest of all writers addresses the inner and outer ear, as well as the inner eye, which explains how he had the audacity to compose dramas as visionary as *A Midsummer-Night's Dream* and *The Tempest* for a stage almost primitive in comparison to our theatrical craft, let alone to our cinema.

Are there, beyond language itself, any Shakespearean values? Do the inner and outer ear, and the inner eye, constitute adequate receptors for human value as such? The answer to these questions would help contribute to the defense of aesthetic value, somewhat to the exclusion of most societal demands. Plato's war against Homer is weakly echoed by all our contemporary politicizings of aesthetic concerns. If there is to be an aesthetic counterattack, Shakespeare ought to be the field of battle, since Shakespeare *is* the largest aesthetic value that we will ever know. Doubtless there are values aplenty in both human personality and human eros, and I do not pretend to know what Shakespeare's stance, as an actual human being, was towards most of those values. Pragmatically, though, personality and eros were for the poet-playwright Shakespeare primarily aesthetic values, and as such I wish to approach them. I begin here with Shakespeare as the canonical sublime in representing personalities, and I admit at the start that I am being absurdly naive. In relation to the current academic world, I am a dinosaur, and more of a Bloomian Brontosaurus than a Tyrannosaurus Rex. I have been accused of seeking to revive the nefarious A. C. Bradley, Hegelian Edwardian. But actually I am a disciple of the eighteenth-century British colonial bureaucrat Maurice Morgann, who reacted to the American Revolution, which cost him his job as secretary of the province of New Jersey, by turning to Shakespearean criticism. In 1777, he published *An Essay on the Dramatic Character of Sir John Falstaff*, an extended exercise I happily commend to whatever fellow dinosaurs still exist among us.

Morgann invested much of his essay in defending Falstaff from the charge of cowardice, an imputation incessantly urged upon Falstaff by Prince Hal. As Morgann demonstrates, Falstaff is anything but a coward, and I myself would venture that what Hal calls cowardice is actually freedom, freedom from the rapacities of what Freud (or rather his translator James Strachey) called the superego. The Freudian metaphor of the *überich*, that which is above the capital letter "I," essentially is a Punch-and-Judy puppet show, in which the censorious superego keeps beating up on the punchy ego, punishing him for supposed aggressivity, and as the wretched ego surrenders all drive, the superego hits him only the harder, while shouting even louder: "Stop being so aggressive!" Sir John Falstaff has less superego pummeling away at him than any other literary character I know, with the single exception of François Rabelais's demoniac Panurge. When Prince Hal constantly berates Falstaff for being "a natural coward without instinct," I learn something complex about the future King Henry V, but absolutely nothing about the finest comic character in all literature. Part of the value of the Shakespearean representation of personality is its incredible depth and complexity, which achieves a magnitude in Falstaff matched only by that of Hamlet. The late Sir William Empson, who was rather less in love with Falstaff than I am, gives an accurate sense of the ambiance of the role that seems to have been Shakespeare's greatest success with his own contemporaries:

> But to stretch one's mind round the whole character (as is generally admitted) one must take him, though as the supreme expression of the cult of mockery as strength and the comic idealisation of freedom, yet as both villainous and tragically ill-used.

I hardly know in what sense Falstaff can be judged "villainous" compared to absolutely everyone else in the two parts of *Henry IV*, including the hypocritical Prince Hal and the doom-eager Hotspur, not to mention the usurping King Henry IV, and all his supporters, and all his enemies. Empson derided those who view Falstaff as a "lovable old dear," but is that the only alternative to seeing the great wit and pragmatist as a villain? I hesitate to select any single power out of Shakespeare's infinite variety of powers as being foremost, but sometimes I would vote that eminence to his control of perspectivism. You identify your true self by your judgment of Shakespeare's characters: if you are either a whoremonger or a puritan, then Cleopatra is a whore; if you are even a touch more interesting, then she is the most vital woman in Shakespeare, surpassing Rosalind and Portia. Empson was a great critic, but his (rather exotic) Chinese Communist moralism made him see Falstaff as "villainous." Admittedly, if you thought that Mao was a great and good man, then you would not be happy with Sir John, who believed neither in men nor in causes, but only in the blessing of life itself, at the expense of all idealism or supposedly good works whatsoever.

Algernon Charles Swinburne, now absurdly undervalued both as poet and as critic, wrote a splendid book on Shakespeare (1880), in which he shrewdly compared Falstaff both to Rabelais's Panurge and to Cervantes's Sancho Panza, and awarded the palm to Falstaff, not just for his massive intellect but for his range of feeling and indeed even for his "possible moral elevation." Here Swinburne anticipated A. C. Bradley, who rightly remarked that all adverse moral judgments upon Falstaff are antithetical to the nature of Shakespearean comedy. Try to envision what Molière might have done with Falstaff, and you will go quite blank; in Molière's vision the consciousness of vice is secondary to the realization that consciousness is all but identical with vice. Molière, despite his debt to Montaigne, was not a vitalist; Shakespeare was everything and nothing, including a vitalist and a nihilist. Sir John Falstaff is the greatest vitalist in Shakespeare, but while he is certainly not the most intense of Shakespeare's nihilists, his strain of nihilism is extraordinarily virulent. Indeed, his nihilism seems to me Falstaff's version of Christianity, and helps account for the darkest element in the grand wit, his realistic obsession with rejection, massively to be realized at the end of *Henry IV Part Two*.

It is the image of rejection, rather than of damnation, that accounts for Falstaff's frequent allusions to the frightening parable of the purple-clad glutton, Dives, and poor Lazarus the beggar that Jesus tells in Luke 16:19–26:

> There was a certeine riche man, which was clothed in purple and fine linen, and fared wel and delicately euerie day.
> Also there was a certeine beger named Lazarus, which was laied at his gate ful of sores,
> And desired to be refreshed with the crommes that fell from the riche mans table: yea, and the dogs came and licked his sores.
> And it was so that the begger dyed, and was caryed by the Angels into Abrahams bosome. The riche man also dyed and was buryed.
> And being in hel in torments, he lift vp his eyes, and sawe Abraham a farre of, & Lazarus in his bosome.
> Then he cryed, and sais, Father Abraham, gaue mercie on me, and send Lazarus that he may dippe y typ of his finger in water, and coole my tongue: for I am tormented in this flame.
> But Abraham said, Sonne, remember that thou in thy life time recciuedft thy pleasures, and likewise Lazarus paines: now therefore is he comforted, and thou art tormented.
> Besides all this, betwene you and vs there is a great gulfe set, so that they which wolde go from hence to you, can not, nether can they come from thence to vs.
> (S. Luke Chap. 16:19–26 from the Geneva Bible)

Three times Falstaff alludes to this fierce parable; I will suggest that there is a fourth, concealed allusion when Falstaff kneels and is rejected by King Henry V, in his new royal purple, and manifestly there is a fifth when the Hostess, describing Falstaff's death in the play he is not permitted to enter, *Henry V*, assures us that Falstaff is "in Arthur's bosom," with the British Arthur substituting for Father Abraham. To be sure, Henry V allows that Falstaff is to be fed crumbs from the royal table, but the initial feeding is held in prison, by order of the Lord Chief Justice. If we are to credit his Sonnets, Shakespeare knew what it was to be rejected, though I certainly do not wish to suggest an affinity between the creator of Falstaff and Falstaff himself. I wonder though at the affinities between Prince Hal and the Earl of Southampton, neither of them candidates for Abraham's bosom. But the more interesting matter, as always, concerns Sir John Falstaff, who is not only witty beyond all others but who also possesses a cognitive power that nearly rivals Hamlet's. What is Sir John's implicit interpretation of the parable of the rich man and the beggar?

Falstaff's first allusion to the parable is the richest and most outrageous, beginning as a meditation upon Bardolph's fiery nose, that makes him "the Knight of the Burning Lamp." The hurt Bardolph complains: "Why, Sir John, my face does you no harm," to which Falstaff makes a massive reply:

> No, I'll be sworn, I make as good use of it as many a man doth of a death's-head or a *memento mori*. I never see thy face but I think upon hell-fire and Dives that liv'd in purple; for there he is in his robes, burning, burning. If thou wert any way given to virtue, I would swear by thy face; my oath should be "By this fire, that['s] God's angel." But thou art altogether given over, and wert indeed, but for the light in thy face, the son of utter darkness. When thou ran'st up Gadshill in the night to catch my horse, if I did not think thou hadst been an *ignis fatuus* or a ball of wildfire, there's no purchase in money. O, thou art a perpetual triumph, an everlasting bonfire light! Thou hast sav'd me a thousand marks in links and torches, walking with thee in the night betwixt tavern and tavern; but the sack that thou hast drunk me would have bought me lights as good cheap at the dearest chandler's in Europe. I have maintain'd that salamander of yours with fire any time this two and thirty years, God reward me for it!

"For there he is in his robes, burning, burning": of course we are to note that Falstaff is another glutton, but I do not believe we are to take seriously Falstaff's fear of hellfire, any more than we are to identify Bardolph with the Burning Bush. Sir John is at work subverting Scripture, even as he subverts everything else that would constrain him: time, the state, virtue, the chivalric concept of "honor," and all ideas of order whatsoever. The brilliant fantasia upon Bardolph's nose does not allow us much residual awe in relation to Jesus' rather uncharacteristic parable. What chance has the rhetorical threat of hellfire against the dazzling metamorphoses of Bardolph's nose, which goes from a *memento mori* to the Burning Bush to a will-of-the-wisp to fireworks to a torchlight procession to a bonfire to a fiery salamander, seven amiable variants that far outshine the burning in Jesus' parable. Falstaff, the greatest of Shakespeare's prose-poets, leaps from metaphor to metaphor so as to remind us implicitly that the parable's "burning, burning" is metaphor also, albeit a metaphor that Sir John cannot cease to empty out. He returns to it as he marches his wretched recruits on to the hellfire of the battle of Shrewsbury: "slaves as ragged as Lazarus in the painted cloth, where the glutton's dogs lick'd his sores." Why does the allusion recur in this context? Hal, staring at Falstaff's troop, observes: "I did never see such pitiful rascals," prompting Falstaff's grand rejoinder: "Tut, tut, good enough to toss, food for powder, food for powder; they'll fill a pit as well as better. Tush, man, mortal men, mortal men." Would it be more honorable if you tossed on a pike better-fed, better-clothed impressed men? How could one state it more tellingly: Falstaff's recruits have all the necessary qualities — food for powder, corpses to fill a pit, mortal men, who are there to be killed, only to be killed, like their betters, whose "grinning honor" Prince Hal will worship. Falstaff has drafted the poorest, like the beggar Lazarus, in contrast to the purple glutton he previously named as Dives, a name not to be found in the Geneva Bible or later in King James. It is not likely that either Shakespeare or Falstaff had read Luke in the Vulgate, where the "certain rich man" is a *dives*, Late Latin for a "rich man," but Dives by Shakespeare's day was already a name out of Chaucer and the common tongue. Sir John, after collecting the bribes of the affluent to release them from service, has put together a fine crew of Lazaruses, who will be stabbed and blown up to serve the Henrys, father and son. Yet, true to his charismatic personality, Falstaff, marching with a bottle of sack in his pistol-holster, observes: "I have led my ragamuffins where they are pepper'd; there's not three of my hundred and fifty left alive, and they are for the town's end, to beg during life." All we can ask of Falstaff he has done; a mortal man, he *led* his Lazaruses to their peppering, taking his chances with them where the fire was hottest. Sir John's cognitive contempt for the entire enterprise is his true offense against time and the state; Prince Hal is never less hypocritical than when he bellows at Falstaff: "What, is it a time to jest and dally now?" while throwing at Sir John the bottle of sack the Prince has just drawn from the holster, in attempting to borrow a pistol.

Falstaff's last explicit allusion to Dives omits any mention of Lazarus, since it is turned against a tailor who has denied him credit: "let him be damn'd like the glutton! Pray God his tongue be hotter!" Since Falstaff perpetually is in want of money, neither he nor we associate the fat knight with Dives. It is a fearful irony that Sir John must end like Lazarus, rejected by the newly crowned king, in order to win admission to "Arthur's bosom," but clearly Shakespeare was not much in agreement with nearly all of his modern critics, who unite in defending the rejection of Falstaff, that spirit of misrule. They mistake this great representation of a personality not less than wholly, and I return again to Jesus' parable, for a final time. Falstaff's implicit interpretation of the text is nihilistic: either one must be damned with Dives or else be saved with Lazarus, an antithesis that loses one either the world to come or this. Emerson once said: "other world? There is no other world; here or nowhere is the whole fact." Falstaff is more than pragmatic enough to agree with Emerson, and I find nothing in Shakespeare to indicate that he himself hoped to join Falstaff in Arthur's bosom, or Lazarus in Abraham's. Falstaff is the prose-poet of the whole fact, and I venture that for Sir John the whole fact is what we call "personality," as opposed to "character." Against time, the state, moral virtue, and the superego, Falstaff is the heroic poet of the ego, largely conscious, though necessarily in part repressed. As prime precursor, Sir John had Chaucer's Dame Alys, the Wife of Bath. The Panurge of Rabelais is an analogue, not a forerunner, while Sancho Panza is an exact contemporary. To call Panurge a personality is of course monstrously inadequate; Panurge, monster of desire, breaks beyond personality into the realm of William Blake's Giant Forms. But the Wife of Bath, Sancho Panza, and Falstaff are what we ought to mean by "personality," not so much in a dictionary sense, but as a cosmos of value, in literature as in life.

Sancho has no enemies, outside the pages of Cervantes, but Falstaff, more even than the Wife of Bath, abounds in scholarly detractors, who love Sir John rather less than they love moral virtue and its alliance with the nation-state. There are also a handful or so of literary enemies, but they are motivated by creative envy in regard to Shakespeare. George Bernard Shaw, who said that he felt only pity for the mind of Shakespeare when he compared it to his own, angrily called Falstaff "a besotted and disgusting old wretch." One might as accurately characterize Hamlet the Dane as "a murderous and solipsistic young wretch," if moral virtue is to be one's standard of value. The Shakespearean charismatic has little in common with the sociological charismatic of Max Weber, but shares rather more in Oscar Wilde's sense that comprehensiveness in consciousness is the sublime of value, when the representation of personality is at the center of one's concern. Shakespeare has other gorgeous triumphs: Rosalind, Iago, Cleopatra among them, but in circumference of consciousness there are no rivals for Falstaff and Hamlet. The Edmund of *King Lear* perhaps is as intelligent as Falstaff and Hamlet, yet he is all but void of affect until he sustains his death-wound, and must be judged as a negative charismatic in comparison to Sir John and the Prince of Denmark. Weber's sense of charisma, though derived from religion, has clear affinities with Carlyle's and Emerson's exaltation of heroic genius. Institution and routine, in Weber's vision, quickly absorb the effect of the charismatic individual upon his followers. But Caesarism and Calvinism are not aesthetic movements; Falstaff and Hamlet scarcely can be routinized or institutionalized. Falstaff disdains any task or mission, and Hamlet cannot tolerate being the protagonist of a revenge tragedy. In both figures, charisma goes back beyond the model of Jesus to his ancestor King David, who uniquely held the blessing of Yahweh. Falstaff, though derided by virtuous scholars and rejected by the newly virtuous King Henry V, nevertheless retains the blessing, in its truest sense: more life. Personality, even upon its deathbed, retains its unique value. When I was fifteen, half a century ago, I saw the late Sir Ralph Richardson play Falstaff in New York City. With the rest of the audience, I saw and heard only Richardson; to this day, I cannot recall who played Hal, and I know that I saw Laurence Olivier play Hotspur in the same production only because I have since come upon a photograph of Olivier in the part. Dramatic personality becomes charismatic when it embodies a power of thought that suggests a divinity at work rather than a human. I have known a number of intelligent philosophers and a vast multitude of poets, novelists, storytellers, playwrights. No one should expect them to talk as well as they write, yet even the best of them, on their best day, cannot equal those men made out of words, Falstaff and Hamlet. One wonders: just how does the representation of cognition, in Shakespeare, differ from cognition itself? Pragmatically, can we tell the difference? One wonders again: just how does the representation of charisma, in Shakespeare, differ from charisma itself? Charisma, by definition, is not a social energy; it originates outside society. Shakespeare's uniqueness, his greatest originality, can be described either as a charismatic cognition, which comes from without before it enters group thinking, or as a cognitive charisma, which cannot be routinized. We are on the path that takes us from the personality of

Falstaff, inexhaustible yet ending in grief, to the personality of Hamlet, also inexhaustible to contemplation and ending in something that looks very like a new kind of transcendence.

Charles Taylor, in his *Sources of the Self*, a comprehensive and trenchant study and defense of modern subjectivity, extensively cites Augustine, Luther, and Montaigne, and never once mentions Shakespeare. And yet I hear Shakespeare as an undersong throughout Taylor's book, another indication of one of the ways in which Shakespeare has assimilated us, without our quite knowing it. Shakespeare is so pervasive as the prime source of the self that it seems redundant even to notice him. I find a special fascination in Ludwig Wittgenstein's rather morose observations upon Shakespeare, now gathered together in the little volume called *Culture and Value*. Chagrined both by Shakespeare's power and by his pervasiveness, Wittgenstein finally makes the suggestion that we ought to consider Shakespeare not as a writer but as "a creator of language." I would urge, against Wittgenstein's palpable evasion, that we might more accurately regard Shakespeare as a creator of memory, particularly in that sense in which memory is crucial both for cognition and for a source of the self. I could return to Falstaff as my paradigm here but rather reluctantly I will forsake him for Hamlet, primarily because Falstaff never loses faith either in himself or in language, and so seems to emanate from a more primordial Shakespeare than Hamlet does. The Hamlet who tells us: "The readiness is all" echoes Jesus in the Geneva Bible, when poor Simon Peter falls asleep upon watch, and provokes the compassionate: "The spirit is readie but the flesh is weak." Hamlet's "readiness" has to do with our "willingness," and the Prince, like Jesus, understands that the spirit is willing and yet indeed the flesh is weak. Falstaff, acting a play-within-the-play with Hal, yields himself completely to the spirit's readiness, and then falls asleep in the manner of Simon Peter before him. We never will hear from Sir John: "Sir, in my heart there was a kind of fighting, that would not let me sleep." Think how strange it would sound to say of

Falstaff that he thinks too well! Yet that is Hamlet's greatest malady — he thinks much too well, as Friedrich Nietzsche saw when he remarked: "that is the doctrine of Hamlet, not that cheap wisdom of Jack the Dreamer who reflects too much and, as it were, from an excess of possibilities does not get around to action. Not reflection, no — true knowledge, an insight into the horrible truth." The horrible truth presumably includes Nietzsche's Hamlet-like realization that what we find words for is something already dead in our hearts, so that there is always a kind of contempt in the act of speaking. What Falstaff finds words for is still alive in his heart, and for him there is no contempt in the act of speaking. Falstaff possesses wit lest he perish of the truth; Hamlet's wit, thrown over by him in the transition to Act V, vanishes from the stage, and so Hamlet becomes the sublime personality whose fate must be to perish of the truth.

2

Falstaff, in Shakespeare's lifetime, seems to have been more popular even than Hamlet; the centuries since have preferred the prince not only to the fat knight, but to every other fictive being. Hamlet's universalism seems our largest clue to the enigma of his personality; the less he cares for anyone, including the audience, the more we care for him. It seems the world's oddest love affair; Jesus returns our love, and yet Hamlet cannot. His blocked affections, diagnosed by Dr. Freud as Oedipal, actually reflect a transcendental quietism for which, happily, we lack a label. Hamlet is *beyond* us, beyond indeed everyone else in Shakespeare or in literature, unless indeed you agree with me in finding the Yahweh of the J Writer and the Jesus of the Gospel of Mark to be literary characters. When we reach Lear, we understand that his beyondness has to do with the mystery of kingship, so dear to Shakespeare's patron, James I. But we have trouble seeing Hamlet as a potential king, and few playgoers and readers tend to agree with Fortinbras's judgment that the prince would have joined Hamlet

Senior and Fortinbras as another great royal basher of heads. Clearly, Hamlet's sublimity is a question of personality; four centuries have so understood it. August Wilhelm von Schlegel accurately observed in 1809 that "Hamlet has no firm belief either in himself or in anything else," including God and language, I would add. Of course there is Horatio, whom Hamlet notoriously overpraises, but Horatio seems to be there to represent the audience's love for Hamlet. Horatio is our bridge to the beyond, to that curious but unmistakable negative transcendence that concludes the tragedy.

Hamlet's linguistic skepticism coexists with a span and control of language greater even than Falstaff's, because its range is the widest we have ever encountered in a single work. It is always a shock to be reminded that Shakespeare used more than 21,000 separate words, while Racine used fewer than 2,000. Doubtless some German scholar has counted up just how many of the 21,000 words Hamlet had in his vocabulary, but we scarcely need to know the sum. The play is Shakespeare's longest because Hamlet speaks so much of it, and I frequently wish it even longer, so that Hamlet could have spoken on even more matters than he already covers. Falstaff, monarch of wit, nevertheless is something short of an authorial consciousness in his own right; Hamlet bursts through that barrier, and not just when he revises *The Murder of Gonzago* into *The Mousetrap*, but almost invariably as he comments upon all things between earth and heaven. G. Wilson Knight admirably characterized Hamlet as death's ambassador to us; no other literary character speaks with the authority of the undiscovered country, except for Mark's Jesus. Harry Levin pioneered in analyzing the *copiousness* of Hamlet's language, which utilizes the full and unique resources of English syntax and diction. Other critics have emphasized the mood-shifts of Hamlet's linguistic decorum, with its startling leaps from high to low, its mutability of cognition and of affect. I myself always am struck by the varied and perpetual ways in which Hamlet keeps *overhearing himself speak*. This is not just a question of rhetoricity or word-consciousness; it is the essence of Shakespeare's greatest originalities in the representation of character, of thinking, and of personality. Ethos, Logos, Pathos — the triple basis of rhetoric, psychology, and cosmology — all bewilder us in Hamlet, because he changes with every self-overhearing. It is a valuable commonplace that *The Tragedy of Hamlet, Prince of Denmark* is an overwhelmingly theatrical play. Hamlet himself is even more self-consciously theatrical than Falstaff tends to be. Falstaff is more consistently attentive to his audience, both onstage and off, and yet Falstaff, though he vastly amuses himself, plays less *to* himself than Hamlet does. This difference may stem from Falstaff's greater playfulness; like Don Quixote and Sancho Panza, Falstaff is *homo ludens*, while anxiety dominates in Hamlet's realm. Yet the difference seems still greater; the counter-Machiavel Hamlet could almost be called an anti-Marlovian character, whereas Falstaff simply renders Marlowe's mode irrelevant. My favorite Marlovian hero-villain, Barabas, Jew of Malta, is a self-delighting fantastic, but being a cartoon, like nearly all Marlovian protagonists, he frequently speaks as though his words were wrapped up in a cartoonist's balloon floating above him. Hamlet is something radically new, even for and in Shakespeare: his theatricality is dangerously nihilistic because it is so paradoxically *natural* to him. More even than his parody Hamm in Beckett's *Endgame*, Hamlet is a walking mousetrap, the anxious expectations that are incarnating the malaise of Elsinore. Iago may be nothing if not critical; Hamlet is criticism itself, at once a theatrical interpreter and the perspectivist of his own story. With a cunning subtler than any other dramatist's, before or since, Shakespeare does not let us be certain as to just which lines Hamlet himself has inserted in order to revise *The Murder of Gonzago* into *The Mousetrap*. Hamlet speaks of writing some twelve or sixteen lines, but we come to suspect that there are rather more, and that they include the extraordinary speech in which the Player-King tells us that ethos is not the daimon, that character is not fate but accident, and that eros is the purest accident. We know that Shakespeare acted the ghost of Hamlet's father; it would have been expedient if the same actor rendered the part of the Player-King, another representation of the dead father. There would be a marvelous twist to Shakespeare himself intoning lines that his Hamlet can be expected to have written:

> Purpose is but the slave to memory,
> Of violent birth, but poor validity
> Which now, the fruit unripe, sticks on the tree,
> But fall unshaken when they mellow be.
> Most necessary 'tis that we forget
> To pay ourselves what to ourselves is debt.
> What to ourselves in passion we propose,
> The passion ending, doth the purpose lose.
> The violence of either grief or joy
> Their own enactures with themselves destroy.
> Where joy most revels, grief doth most lament;
> Grief [joys], joy grieves, on slender accident.
> This world is not for aye, nor 'tis not strange
> That even our loves should with our fortunes change:
> For 'tis a question left us yet to prove,
> Whether love lead fortune, or else fortune love.
> The great man down, you mark his favorite flies,
> The poor advanc'd makes friends of enemies.
> And hitherto doth love on fortune tend,
> For who not needs shall never lack a friend,
> And who in want a hollow friend doth try,
> Directly seasons him his enemy.
> But orderly to end where I begun,
> Our wills and fates do so contrary run
> That our devices still are overthrown,
> Our thoughts are ours, their ends none of our own.

How any audience could take in these twenty-six closely packed lines of a psychologized metaphysic through the ear alone, I scarcely know. They are as dense and weighted as any passage in Shakespeare; the plot of *The Mousetrap* does not require them, and I assume that Hamlet composed them as his key signature, as what that other melancholy Dane, Søren Kierkegaard, called: "The Point of View of My Work as an Author." They center upon their final lines:

> Our wills and fates do so contrary run
> That our devices still are overthrown,
> Our thoughts are ours, their ends none of our own.

Our "devices" are our intended purposes, products of our wills, but our fates are antithetical to our characters, and what we think to do has no relation to our thoughts' "ends," where "ends" mean both conclusions and harvests. Desire and destiny are contraries, and all thought thus must undo itself. Hamlet's nihilism is indeed transcendent, surpassing what can exist in the personages of Fyodor Dostoevsky, or in Nietzsche's forebodings. What we can find words for must be already dead in our hearts, and so Hamlet rarely speaks without a kind of contempt for the act of speaking. Only what cannot be said is worth the saying; perhaps *that* is why Shakespeare bothered Wittgenstein so much. Rather oddly, Wittgenstein compared Shakespeare to dreams: all wrong, absurd, composite, things *aren't like that*, except by the law that belonged to Shakespeare alone, or to dreams alone. "He is *not* true to life," Wittgenstein insisted of Shakespeare, while evading the truth that Shakespeare had made us see and think what we could not have seen or thought without him. Hamlet emphatically is *not* true to life, but more than any other fictive being Hamlet makes us think what we could not think without him. Wittgenstein would have denied this, but that was his motive for so distrusting Shakespeare: Hamlet, more than any philosopher, actually makes us see the world in other ways, deeper ways, than we may want to see it. Wittgenstein wants to believe that Shakespeare, as a creator of language, made a heterocosm, a dream. But the truth is that Shakespeare's cosmos became Wittgenstein's and ours, and we cannot say of Hamlet's Elsinore or Falstaff's Eastcheap that things aren't like that. They *are* like that, but we need Hamlet or Falstaff to illuminate the "like that," to more than flesh out the similes. The question becomes rather: Is life true to Hamlet, or to Falstaff? At its worst, sometimes, and at its best, sometimes, life can or may be, so that the real question becomes: Is Wittgenstein true to Hamlet, or Bloom to Falstaff?

I grant that you don't need to be a formalist or a historicist to assert that being true to Hamlet or to Falstaff is a nonsensical quest. If you read or attend Shakespeare in order to improve your neighbor or your neighborhood, then doubtless I am being nonsensical, a kind of Don Quixote of literary criticism. The late Anthony Burgess, in his *Nothing like the Sun*, a wonderful novel about Shakespeare, has the Bard make a fine, somewhat Nietzschean remark: "Tragedy is a goat and comedy a village Priapus and *dying* is the word that links both." Hamlet and Falstaff would have said it better, but the sexual play on *dying* is redemptive of the prose, and we are well reminded that Shakespeare writ no genre, and used poor Polonius to scorn those who did. Tragedy, Aldous Huxley once essayed, must omit the whole truth, yet Shakespeare comes close to refuting Huxley. John Webster wrote revenge tragedy; Shakespeare wrote *Hamlet*. There are no personalities in Webster, though nearly everyone manages to die with something like Shakespearean eloquence. Life must be true to Shakespeare, if personality is to have value, is to be value. Value and pathos do not commune easily with one another, yet who but Shakespeare has reconciled them so incessantly? What after all is personality? A dictionary would say the quality that renders one a person, not a thing or an animal, or else an assemblage of characteristics that makes one somehow distinctive. That is not very helpful, particularly in regard to Hamlet or Falstaff, mere roles for actors, as formalists tell us, and perhaps players fall in love with roles, but do we, if we never mount a stage? What do we mean by "the personality of Jesus," whether we think of the Gospel of Mark or of the American Jesus? Or what might we mean by "the personality of God," whether we think of the Yahweh of the J Writer or of the American God, so notoriously fond of Republicans and of Neo-Conservatives? I submit that we know better what it is we mean when we speak of the personality of Hamlet as opposed to the personality of our best friend, or the personality of some favorite celebrity. Shakespeare persuades us that we know something in Hamlet that is the best and innermost part of him, something uncreated that goes back farther than our earliest memories of ourselves. There is a breath or spark to Hamlet that is his principle of individuation, a recognizable identity whose evidence is his singularity of language, and yet not so much language as diction, a cognitive choice between words, a choice whose drive always is towards freedom: from Elsinore, from the ghost, from the world. Like Falstaff, Hamlet implicitly defines personality as a mode of freedom, more of a matrix of freedom than a product of freedom. Falstaff, though, as I intimated, is largely free of the censorious superego, while Hamlet in the first four acts suffers very terribly from it. In the beautiful metamorphosis of purgation that is Act V, Hamlet almost is freed from what is over or above the ego, though at the price of dying well before his death.

In *The Great Gatsby*, Fitzgerald's Conradian narrator, Nick Carraway, observes that personality is a series of successful gestures. Walter Pater would have liked that description, but its limits are severe. Perhaps Jay Gatsby exemplifies Carraway's definition, but who could venture that Hamlet's personality comprises a series of successful gestures? William Hazlitt cast his own vote for inwardness: "it is we who are Hamlet." Hamlet's stage, Hazlitt implied, is the theatre of mind, and Hamlet's gestures therefore are of the inmost self, very nearly everyone's inmost self. Confronting this baffling representation, at once universal and solitary, T. S. Eliot opined that the play was an aesthetic failure, a judgment so astonishing as to make us wonder if any other work of literature possibly could be an aesthetic success. I assume that Eliot, with his own wounds, reacted to Hamlet's sickness of the spirit, certainly the most enigmatic malaise in all of Western literature. Hamlet's own poetic metaphysic, as we have seen, is that character and fate are antithetical, and yet, at the play's conclusion, we are likely to believe that the prince's character was his fate. Do we have a drama of the personality's freedom, or of the character's fate? The Player-King says that all is accident; Hamlet in Act V hints that there are no accidents. Whom are we to believe? The Hamlet of Act V appears to have cured himself, and affirms that the readiness or willingness is all. I interpret that as meaning: personality is all, once personality has purged itself into a second birth. And yet Hamlet has little desire to survive.

The canonical sublime depends upon a strangeness that assimilates us even as we largely fail to assimilate it. What is the stance towards life, the attitude, of the Hamlet who returns from the sea at the start of Act V? Skepticism, once dominant, has been displaced by what seems to be disinterestedness or even quietism. Quietism, half a century after *Hamlet*, meant a certain Spanish mode of religious mysticism, but Hamlet is no mystic, no stoic, and hardly a Christian at all. He goes into the final slaughter-scene in the spirit of a suicide, and prevents Horatio's suicide with a selfish awareness that Horatio's felicity is being postponed, in order that the prince's own story can be told and retold. And yet he cares for his reputation as he dies; his "wounded name," if Horatio does not live to clear it, is his final anxiety. Since he has murdered Polonius, driven Ophelia to madness and to suicide, and quite gratuitously sent the wretched Rosencrantz and Guildenstern off to execution, his anxiety would seem justified, except that in fact he has no consciousness of culpability. His fear of a "wounded name" is one more enigma, and hardly refers to the deaths of Claudius and of Laertes, let alone of his mother, for whom his parting salute is the shockingly cold "Wretched Queen, adieu!" His concern is properly theatrical; it is for us, the audience:

> You that look pale, and tremble at this chance,
> That are but mutes or audience to this act . . .

That seems to me a playwright's concern, proper to the revisionist author of *The Mousetrap*. Joyce's Stephen, in the Library scene of *Ulysses*, scarcely distinguishes between Shakespeare and Hamlet, and Richard Ellmann assured us that Stephen's fantasia remained always Joyce's serious reading of the play. Hamlet himself seems quite free of the audience's shock that so vast a consciousness should expire in so tangled and absurd a mesh of poisoned sword and poisoned cup. It outrages our sensibility that the Western hero of intellectual consciousness dies in this grossly inadequate context, yet it does not outrage Hamlet, who has lived through much too much already. We mourn a great personality, perhaps the greatest; Hamlet has ceased to mourn in the interval betwen Acts IV and V. The profoundest mysteries of his personality are involved in the nature of his universal mourning, and in his self-cure. I will not bother with Oedipal tropes here, even to dismiss them, having devoted a chapter to just such a dismissal in a book on the Western canon, where I gave a Shakespearean reading of Freud. Hamlet's spiritual despair transcends a father's murder, a mother's hasty remarriage, and all the miasma of Elsinore's corruption, even as his apotheosis in Act V far transcends any passing of the Oedipus complex. The crucial question becomes: how ought we to characterize Hamlet's melancholia in the first four acts, and how do we explain his escape from it into a high place in Act V, a place at last entirely his own, and something like a radically new mode of secular transcendence?

Dr. Johnson thought that the particular excellence of *Hamlet* as a play was its "variety," which seems to me truer of the prince than of the drama. What most distinguishes Hamlet's personality is its metamorphic nature: his changes are constant, and continue even after the great sea-change that precedes Act V. We have the perpetual puzzle that the most intensely theatrical personality in Shakespeare centers a play notorious for its anxious expectations, for its incessant delays that are more than parodies of an endlessly delayed revenge. Hamlet is a great player, like Falstaff and Cleopatra, but his director, the dramatist, seems to punish the protagonist for getting out of hand, for being Hobgoblin run off with the garland of Apollo, perhaps for having entertained even more doubts than his creator had. And if Hamlet is imaginatively sick, then so is everyone else in the play, with the possible exception of the audience's surrogate, Horatio. When we first encounter him, Hamlet is a university student who is not being permitted to return to his studies. He does not appear to be more than twenty years old, yet in Act V he is revealed to be at least thirty, after a passage of a few weeks at most. And yet none of this matters: he is always both the youngest and the oldest personality in the drama; in the deepest sense, he is older than Falstaff. Consciousness itself has aged him, the catastrophic consciousness of the spiritual disease of his world, which he has internalized, and which he does not wish to be called upon to remedy, if only because the true cause of his changeability is his drive towards freedom. Critics have agreed, for centuries now, that Hamlet's unique appeal is that no other protagonist of high tragedy still seems paradoxically so free. In Act V, he is barely still in the play; like Whitman's "real me" or "me myself" the final Hamlet is both in and out of the game while watching and wondering at it. But if his sea-change has cured him of the Elsinore illness, what drives him back to the court and to the final catastrophe? We feel that if the Ghost were to attempt a third appearance in Act V, Hamlet would thrust it aside; his obsession with the dead father is definitely over, and while he still regards his maligned mother as a whore, he has worn out his interest there also. Purged, he allows himself to be set up for Claudius's refined, Italianate version of *The Mousetrap*, on the stated principle of "Let be." Perhaps the best comment is Wallace Stevens's variation: "Let be be finale of seem." And yet once more, we must return to the Elsinore illness, and to the medicine of the sea-voyage.

Every student of the imagery of the play *Hamlet* has brooded on the imposthume or abscess, which Robert Browning was to pun on brilliantly with his "the imposthume I prick to relieve thee of, — Vanity." Hamlet himself, precursor of so many Browning *personae*, may be playing on the abscess as imposture:

> This is th' imposthume of much wealth and peace,
> That inward breaks, and shows no cause without
> Why the man dies.

Elsinore's disease is anywhere's, anytime's. Something is rotten in every state, and if your sensibility is like Hamlet's, then finally you will not tolerate it. Hamlet's tragedy is at last the tragedy of personality—the charismatic is compelled to a physician's authority despite himself: Claudius is merely an accident; Hamlet's only persuasive enemy is Hamlet himself. When Shakespeare broke away from Marlovian cartooning, and so became Shakespeare, he prepared the abyss of Hamlet for himself. Not less than everything himself, Hamlet also knows himself to be nothing in himself. He can and does repair to that nothing at sea, and returns disinterested, or nihilistic, or quietistic, whichever you may prefer. But he dies with great concern for his wounded name, as if reentering the maelstrom of Elsinore partly undoes his great change. But only in part: the transcendental music of cognition rises up again in a celebratory strain at the close of Hamlet's tragedy, achieving the secular triumph of "The rest is silence." What is not at rest, or what abides before the silence, is the idiosyncratic value of Hamlet's personality, for which another term is the canonical sublime.

II. SHAKESPEARE AND THE VALUE OF LOVE

1

Job's sufferings have been suggested as the paradigm for Lear's ordeal; I once gave credence to this critical commonplace, but now find it unpersuasive. Patient Job is actually not very patient, despite his theological reputation, and Lear is the pattern of all impatience, though he vows otherwise, and movingly urges patience upon the blinded Gloucester. The pragmatic disproportion between Job's afflictions and Lear's is rather considerable, at least until Cordelia is murdered. I suspect that a different biblical model was in Shakespeare's mind: King Solomon. I do not mean Solomon in all his glory, in Kings, Chronicles, and obliquely in the Song of Songs, but the aged monarch, at the end of his reign, wise yet exacerbated, the supposed preacher of Ecclesiastes, and of the Wisdom of Solomon in the Apocrypha, as well as the putative author of the Proverbs. Presumably Shakespeare was read aloud to from the Bishops Bible, in his youth, and later read the Geneva Bible for himself, in his maturity. Since he wrote *King Lear* as a servant of King James I, famed as the wisest fool in Christendom, perhaps Shakespeare's conception of Lear was influenced by James's particular admiration for Solomon, wisest of kings. I admit that not many among us instantly associate Solomon and Lear, but there is crucial textual evidence that Shakespeare himself made the association, by having Lear allude to a great passage in the Wisdom of Solomon:

> I Myself am also mortal and a man like all other, and am come of him that was first made of the earth.
> And in my mothers womb was I facioned to be flesh in ten moncths: I was broght together into blood of the sede of man, and by the pleasure that cometh with slepe.
> And when I was borne, I received the cõmune aire, and fel upon the earth, which is of like nature, crying & weping at the first as all other do.
> I was nourished in swadling clothes, and with cares.
> For there is no King that had anie other beginning of birth.
> All men then have one entrance unto life, and a like going out.

That is the unmistakable text echoed in Lear's shattering sermon to Gloucester:

> *Lear.* If thou wilt weep my fortunes, take my eyes.
> I know thee well enough, thy name is Gloucester.
> Thou must be patient; we came crying hither.

Thou know'st, the first time that we smell the air
We wawl and cry. I will preach to thee. Mark.
  [*Lear takes off his crown of weeds and flowers.*]
Glou. Alack, alack the day!
Lear. When we are born, we cry that we are come
To this great stage of fools.

After Solomon the kingdom was divided, as it was by Lear. Yet I don't think that Shakespeare partly founds Lear upon the aged Solomon, because of the catastrophes of kingdoms. Shakespeare sought what we tend now not to emphasize in our accounts of Lear: a paradigm for greatness. These days, in teaching the play I have to begin by insisting upon Lear's foregrounding in grandeur, because my students are unlikely at first to perceive it. Patriarchal sublimity is now not much in fashion. Lear is at once father, king, and a kind of mortal god: he is the image of male authority, perhaps the ultimate representation of the Dead White European Male. Solomon reigned for fifty years, and was James I's wished-for archetype: glorious, wise, wealthy, even if Solomon's passion for women was not exactly shared by the sexually ambiguous James. Lear is in no way a portrait of James; Shakespeare's royal patron was meant to sympathize but not to empathize with the kingdom-dividing Lear. But Lear's greatness would have mattered to James: he too considered himself every inch a king. I think he would have recognized, in the aged Lear, the aged Solomon, each in their eighties, each needing and wanting love, and each worthy of love. When I teach *King Lear*, I have to begin by reminding my students that Lear, however unlovable in the first two acts, is very much loved by Cordelia, the Fool, Albany, Kent, Gloucester, and Edgar, that is to say, by every benign character in the play, just as he is hated and feared by Goneril, Regan, Cornwall, and Oswald, the play's lesser villains. The play's great villain, the superb and uncanny Edmund, is ice-cold, indifferent to Lear as he is even to his own father Gloucester, his half-brother Edgar, and his lovers Goneril and Regan. It is part of Shakespeare's genius not to have

Edmund and Lear address even a single word to one another in the entire play, because they are apocalyptic antitheses: the king is all feeling, and Edmund is bare of all affect. The crucial foregrounding of the play, if we are to understand it at all, is that Lear is lovable, loving, and greatly loved, by anyone at all worthy of our own affection and approbation.

Of course, whoever you may be, you can be loved and loving, and still demand more. If you are King Lear, and have ever but slenderly known yourself, then you are almost apocalyptically needy in your demand for love, particularly from the child you truly love, Cordelia. The play's foreground comprehends not only Lear's benignity, and the resentment of Goneril and Regan, weary of their being passed over for their sister, but most crucially, Cordelia's recalcitrance in the face of incessant entreaties for a total love surpassing even her authentic regard for her violently emotional father. Cordelia's rugged personality is something of a reaction-formation to her father's overwhelming affection. It is one of the many peculiarities of Shakespeare's double-plot that Cordelia, despite her absolute importance to Lear himself, is much less central to the play than is her parallel, Edgar. Shakespeare leaps over several intervening reigns in order to have Edgar succeed Lear as king of Britain. Legend, still current in Shakespeare's time, assigned to King Edgar the melancholy distinction that he rid Britain of wolves, who overran the island after the death of Lear. There are four great roles in *The Tragedy of King Lear*, though you might not know that from most stagings of the play. Cordelia's, for all her pathos, is not one of them, nor are Goneril's and Regan's of the same order of dramatic eminence as the roles of Lear and of the Fool. Edmund and Edgar, antithetical half-brothers, require actors as skilled and powerful as Lear and the Fool must have. I have seen a few appropriate Edmunds, best of all Joseph Wiseman many years ago in New York City, saving an otherwise ghastly production in which Louis Calhern, as Lear, reminded me only of how much more adequate he had been as Ambassador

Trentino in the Marx Brothers' *Duck Soup*. Wiseman played Edmund as an amalgam of Leon Trotsky and Don Giovanni, but it worked quite brilliantly, and there is much in the play's text to sustain that curious blend.

Many readers and auditors of Shakespeare become as dangerously enthralled by Edmund as they are by Iago, yet Edgar, recalcitrant and repressed, actually is the larger enigma, and is so difficult to play that I have never once seen a passable Edgar. The title-page of the first Quarto edition of *King Lear* assigns a prominence to Edgar rarely afforded him in our critical studies:

> M. William Shak-speare: His True Chronicle Historie of the life and death of King Lear and his three Daughters. With the unfortunate life of Edgar, sonne and heire to the Earle of Gloster, and his sullen and assumed humor of Tom of Bedlam...

"Sullen" in Shakespeare has the strong meaning of melancholia or depression, a variety of madness, assumed by Edgar in his disguise as Tom of Bedlam. The Earl of Kent disguises himself as Caius, to serve Lear. Edgar, in parallel flight, abases himself, sinking below the bottom of the social scale. Why does Edgar assume the lowest possible disguise? Is he punishing himself for his own credulity, for sharing his father's inability to see through Edmund's brilliant deceptions? There is something so profoundly disproportionate in Edgar's self-abnegation, throughout the play, that we have to presume in him a recalcitrance akin to Cordelia's, but far in excess of hers. Whether as bedlamite or as poor peasant, Edgar refuses his own identity for more than pragmatic purposes. The most extraordinary manifestation of this refusal is his consistent unwillingness to reveal himself to Gloucester, his father, even as he rescues the blinded Earl from murder by the despicable Oswald, and from suicide, after the defeat of Lear and Cordelia. Only when he is on the verge of regaining his own rank, just before challenging Edmund to mortal combat, does Edgar identify himself to Gloucester, so as to ask a paternal blessing for the duel. The recognition-encounter, which kills Gloucester, is one of Shakespeare's great unwritten scenes, being confined as it is to Edgar's narrative account, delivered to Albany after Edmund has received his death-wound. Why did Shakespeare choose not to dramatize the event?

A theatrical answer might be that the intricacies of the double-plot already seemed so substantial that Shakespeare declined to risk yet more complexity. The Shakespearean audacity is so immense that I doubt such an answer. Lear wakes up sane to be reconciled with Cordelia, a scene in which we all delight. Edgar and Gloucester reconciling, even though the intense affect kills the blind sufferer, could have been nearly as poignant a staged vision. Though we tend to assign greater prominence to the Fool, or to the frighteningly seductive Edmund, the subtitle of the play rightly guides us to Edgar, who will inherit the ruined kingdom. Shakespeare's dramatic self-denial in not writing the scene of Edgar's self-revelation to Gloucester necessarily places the emphasis more upon Edgar, who tells the tale, than upon his father We learn even more about Edgar's personality and character than we would have known, though we know a great deal already about a role that exemplifies the pathos and value of filial love far more comprehensively than Cordelia's can, because of the necessities of Shakespeare's plot. I return therefore to the voluntary overimmersion in humiliation that Edgar compels himself to undergo.

If we could speak of a poetic rather than dramatic center to the tragedy, we might choose the meeting between the mad King Lear and blind Gloucester in Act IV, Scene VI, lines 80–183. Sir Frank Kermode rightly remarks that the meeting in no way advances the plot, though it may well be the summit of Shakespeare's art. As playgoers and readers, we concentrate upon Lear and Gloucester, yet Edgar is the interlude's chorus, and he has set the tonality of Act IV, in its opening lines, with their keynote: "The lamentable change is from the best, / The worst returns to laughter." The entry of the blinded Gloucester darkens that desperate comfort, compelling Edgar to the revision: "the worst is not / So long as we can say 'This is the worst.'" It will be the worst only when "the worst" is already dead in our hearts, so that we will find no diction appropriate for it. Gloucester, blinded and cast forth, is a paternal image suggestive enough to reilluminate even Lear's outcast madness. Madness and blindness become a doublet profoundly akin to tragedy and love, the doublet that binds together the entire play. Madness, blindness, love, and tragedy amalgamate in a giant bewilderment.

"But what if excess of love / Bewildered them until they died?" W. B. Yeats asks in his "Easter, 116." Whatever that meant in regard to MacDonagh and MacBride, and Connally and Pearse, Yeats's question is appropriate to Lear himself. Love, whether it be Lear's for Cordelia or Edgar's for his father Gloucester and for his godfather Lear, is pragmatically a waste in this most tragic of all tragedies. Lust does no better; when the dying Edmund muses that in spite of all, he was beloved, his sudden capacity for affect superbly surprises us, but we would choose another word rather than "beloved" for the murderous passion of Goneril and Regan. In Hamlet's play there is a central consciousness, as there is in Macbeth's. In Othello's play, there is at least a dominant nihilist, but Lear's play is strangely divided. Before he goes mad, Lear's consciousness is beyond ready understanding: his lack of self-knowledge, blended with his awesome authority, makes him unknowable by us. Bewildered and bewildering after that, Lear seems less a consciousness than a falling divinity, Solomonic in his sense of lost glory. Yahweh-like in his irascibility. The play's central consciousness perforce is Edgar's, who actually speaks more lines than anyone except Lear. Edmund, more brilliant even than Iago, less of an improviser and more a strategist of evil, is further into nihilism than Iago was, but no one — hero or villain — can be dominant in Lear's tragedy. Shakespeare, *contra* historicists old and new, burns through every context, and never more than in this play. The figure of excess or overthrow never abandons Shakespeare's text; except for Edmund, everyone either loves or hates too much. Edgar, whose pilgrimage of abnegation culminates in vengeance, ends overwhelmed by the helplessness of his love, a love progressiveley growing in range and intensity, with the pragmatic effect of yielding him, as the new king, only greater suffering. Edmund, desperately attempting to do some good, despite what he continues to insist is his own nature, is carried offstage to die, not knowing whether Cordelia has been saved or not. No formalist or historicist would be patient with my asking this, but in what state of self-knowledge does Edmund find himself as he dies? His sense of his own identity, powerful until Edgar overcomes him, wavers throughout the long scene of his dying. Lear and Edgar have shared enormous bewilderments of identity, which appear to be further manifestations of excessive love. Shakespeare's intimation is that the only authentic love is between parents and children, yet the prime consequence of such love is only devastation. Neither of the drama's two antithetical senses of nature, Lear's or Edmund's, is sustained by a close scrutiny of the changes the protagonists undergo in Acts IV and V. Edgar's "ripeness is all" is misconstrued if we interpret it as a stoic comfort, let alone somehow a Christian consolation. Shakespeare deliberately echoes Hamlet's "The readiness is all," itself an ironical reversal of Simon-Peter's sleepiness provoking Jesus' "The spirit is ready, but the flesh is weak." If we must endure our going hence even as our coming hither, then "Ripeness is all" warns us how little "all" is. Soon enough, as W. R. Elton observed, Edgar will tell us "that endurance and ripeness are *not* all." His final wisdom is to submit to "the weight of this sad time," a submission that involves his reluctant assumption of the crown, with the ghastly historical mission of clearing a Britain overrun by wolves.

Love, Dr. Samuel Johnson once remarked, is the wisdom of fools and the folly of the wise. The greatest critic in our tradition was not commenting upon Lear's tragedy, but he might as well have been, since his observation is both Shakespearean and prudential, and illuminates the limitations of love in the play. Edgar has become wise when the play ends, yet love is still his folly by engendering his inconsolable grief for his two fathers. The great stage of fools has only three survivors standing upon it at the end: Kent willingly soon will join his master, Lear, while the much shaken Albany abdicates his interest to Edgar. The marriage between Albany and Goneril would have been more than enough to exhaust a stronger character than Albany, and Kent is only just barely a survivor. Edgar is the center, and we can wonder why we are so slow to see that, except for Lear, it is, after all, Edgar's play. Lear's excessive love for Cordelia inevitably sought to be a controlling love, until the image of authority was broken, not redeemed, as Christianizers of this pagan play have argued. The serving love of Edgar prepares him to be an unstoppable revenger against Edmund, and a fit monarch for a time of troubles, but the play's design establishes that Edgar's is as catastrophic a love as Lear's. Love is no healer in *The Tragedy of King Lear*; indeed it starts all the trouble, and is a tragedy in itself. The gods in *King Lear* do not kill men and women for their sport; instead they afflict Lear and Edgar with an excess of love, and Goneril and Regan with the torments of lust and jealousy. Nature, invoked by Edmund as his goddess, destroys him through the natural vengeance of his brother, because Edmund is immune from love, and so has mistaken his deity.

Dr. Johnson said that he could not bear Act V of the play because it outraged divine justice and so offended his moral sense, but the great critic may have mistaken his own reaction. What the drama of *King Lear* truly outrages is our universal idealization of the value of familial love, that is to say, both love's personal and love's social value. The play manifests an intense anguish in regard to human sexuality, and a compassionate despair as to the mutually destructive nature of both paternal and filial love. Maternal love is kept out of the tragedy, as if natural love in its strongest form would be too much to bear, even for this negative sublimity. Lear's queen, unless she were a Job's wife, laconically suggesting that Lear curse the gods and die, would add an intolerable burden to a drama already harrowing in the extreme. William Hazlitt thought that it was equally impossible to give a description either of the play itself or of its effect upon the mind. Rather strikingly, for so superb a psychological critic, Hazlitt remarks: "All that we can say must fall far short of the subject; or even of what we ourselves conceive of it." Hazlitt touches on the uncanniest aspect of *Lear*: something that we conceive of it hovers outside our expressive range. I think this effect ensues from the universal wound the play deals to the value of familial love. Laboring this point is painful, but everything about the tragedy of *Lear* is painful. To borrow from Nietzsche, it is not that the pain is meaningful, but that meaning itself becomes painful in this play. We do them wrong to speak of Lear's own permutations as being redemptive; there can be no regeneration when love itself becomes identical with pain. Every attempt to mitigate the darkness of this work is an involuntary critical lie. When Edgar says of Lear: "He childed as I fathered," the tragedy is condensed into just five words. Unpack that gnomic condensation, and what do you receive? Not, I think, a parallel between two innocences — Lear's and Edgar's — and two guilts — Lear's elder daughters' and Gloucester's — because Edgar does not consider his father to be guilty. "He childed as I fathered" has in it no reference whatsoever to Goneril and Regan, but only to the parallel between Lear/Cordelia and Edgar/Gloucester. There is love, and only love, between those four, and yet there is tragedy, and only tragedy, between them. Subtly, Edgar indicates the link between his own rugged recalcitrance and Cordelia's. Without Cordelia's initial recalcitrance there would have been no tragedy, but then Cordelia would not have been Cordelia. Without Edgar's stubborn endurance and self-abnegation, the avenging angel who strikes down Edmund would not have been metamorphosed out of a gullible innocent. We can wonder at the depth and prolongation of the self-abasement, but then Edgar would not have been Edgar without it. And there is no recompense; Cordelia is murdered, and Edgar despairingly will resign himself to the burden of kingship.

Critics have taken a more hopeful stance, to argue for redemptive love, and for the rough justice visited upon every villain in the play. The monsters in the deep all achieve properly bad ends: Edgar cudgels Oswald to death; the servant, defending Gloucester, fatally wounds Cornwall; Goneril poisons Regan, and then stabs herself in the heart; Edgar cuts Edmund down, as the audience knows Edgar is fated to do. There is no satisfaction for us in this slaughter of the wicked. Except for Edmund, they are too barbaric to be tolerated, and even Edmund, fascinating as he is, would deserve, like the others, to be indicted for crimes against humanity. Their deaths are meaningless, again even Edmund's, since his belated change fails to save Cordelia. Cordelia's death, painful to us beyond description, nevertheless has only that pain to make it meaningful. Lear and Gloucester, startlingly, both die more of joy than of grief. The joy that kills Lear is delusional: he apparently hallucinates, and beholds Cordelia either as not having died or as being resurrected. Gloucester's joy is founded upon reality, but pragmatically the extremes of delight and of anguish that kill him are indistinguishable. "He childed as I fathered": Lear and Gloucester are slain by their paternal love; by the intensity and authenticity of that love. War between siblings; betrayal of fathers by daughters and by a natural son; tormented misunderstanding of a loyal son and a saintly daughter by noble patriarchs; a total dismissal of all sexual congress as lechery: what are we bequeathed by this tragedy that we endlessly moralize? There is one valid form of love and one only, that at the end between Lear and Cordelia, Gloucester and Edgar. Its value, casting aside irrelevant transcendental moralizings, is less than negative: it may be stronger than death, but it leads only to death, or to death-in-life for the extraordinary Edgar, Shakespeare's survivor-of-survivors.

No one would regard *The Tragedy of King Lear* as a Shakespearean aberration: the play develops out of aspects of *Hamlet*,

Troilus and Cressida, Measure for Measure, and *Othello,* and clearly is prelude to aspects of *Macbeth, Antony and Cleopatra,* and *Timon of Athens.* Only *Hamlet,* of all the plays, seems more central to Shakespeare's incessant concerns than *King Lear* is, and in their ultimate implications the two works interlock. Does Hamlet love anyone as he dies? The transcendental aura that his dying moments evoke, our sensation of his charismatic freedom, is precisely founded upon his having become free of every object attachment, whether to father, mother, Ophelia, or even poor Yorick. There is only one mention of the word "father" by Hamlet in all of Act V, and it is to his father's signet, employed to send Rosencrantz and Guildenstern to extinction. The only reference by Hamlet to the person is when he speaks of Claudius as having killed "my king" and whored my mother. Hamlet's farewell to her is the not very affectionate: "Wretched Queen, adieu!" There is of course Horatio, whose love for Hamlet brings him to the verge of suicide, from which Hamlet saves him, but solely for the purpose of having a survivor who will clear his wounded name. Nothing whatsoever that happens in the tragedy *Hamlet* gives love itself anything except a wounded name. Love, in any of its modes, familial or erotic or social, is transformed by Shakespeare, more than by any other writer, into the greatest of dramatic and aesthetic values, yet more than any other writer, Shakespeare divests love of any supposed values of its own. The implicit critique of love, by Shakespeare, hardly can be termed a mere skepticism. Literary criticism, as I have learned from Dr. Johnson, is the art of making the implicit finely explicit, and I accept the risk of apparently laboring what may be to many among us quite obvious, once we are asked to ponder it. I also have no quarrel with Stanley Cavell's reading of *Lear,* in which the king's desire not to be known by any other, Cordelia in particular, is interpreted as "the avoidance of love." "We cannot choose whom we are free to love," a celebrated line of W. H. Auden's, may have been influenced by Freud, but Sigmund Freud, as time's revenges will show, is nothing but belated

William Shakespeare, "the man from Stratford" as Freud bitterly liked to call him, in support of that defrauded genius, the Earl of Oxford. There is love that can be avoided, and there is a deeper love, unavoidable and terrible, far more central to Shakespeare's invention of the human. It seems more accurate to call it that, rather than reinvention, because the time before Shakespeare had his full influence upon us was also "before we were wholly human and knew ourselves," as Wallace Stevens phrased it. Irreparable love, destructive of every value distinct from it, was and is a Romantic obsession. But the representation of love, in and by Shakespeare, was the largest literary contamination that produced Romanticism.

A. D. Nuttall, more than any other twentieth-century critic, has clarified some of the central paradoxes of Shakespearean representation. Two of Nuttall's observations always abide with me: Shakespeare is out ahead of us, illuminating our latest intellectual fashions more sharply than they can illuminate him, and Shakespeare enables us to see realities that may already have been there but that we would not find possible to see without him. Historicists — old, new, and burgeoning — do not like it when I add to Nuttall the realization that the difference between what Shakespeare knew and what we know is, to an astonishing extent, just Shakespeare himself. He is what we know, because we are what he knew: he childed as we fathered. Even if Shakespeare, like all of his contemporaries and like all of ours, is only a socially inscribed entity, histrionic and fictive, and so not at all a self-contained author, all the better. Jorge Luis Borges may have intended a Chestertonian paradox, but he spoke a truth more literal than figurative: Shakespeare is everyone and no one. So are we, but Shakespeare is more so. If you want to argue that he was the most precariously self-fashioned of all the self-fashioned, I gladly will agree. But wisdom finally cannot be the product of social energies, whatever those are. Cognitive power and an understanding heart are individual endowments. Wittgenstein rather desperately wanted to see Shakespeare as a creator of language rather than as a creator of thought, yet

Shakespeare's own pragmatism renders that a distinction that makes no difference. Shakespeare's writing creates what holds together language and thought in a stance that neither affirms nor subverts Western tradition. What that stance is hovers still beyond the categories of our critiques. Social domination, the obsession of our School of Resentment, is only secondarily a Shakespearean concern. Domination maybe, but that mode of domination is more personal than social, more internal than outward. Shakespeare's greatest men and women are pragmatically doom-eager not because of their relation to state-power but because their inner lives are ravaged by all the ambivalences and ambiguities of familial love and its displacements. There is a drive in all of us, unless we are Edmund, to slay ourselves upon the stems of generation, in Blake's language. Edmund is free of that drive, but is caught in the closed circle that makes him another of the fools of time. Time, Falstaff's antagonist and MacBeth's nemesis, is antithetical to nature in Lear's play. Edmund, who cannot be destroyed by love, which he never feels, is destroyed by the wheel of change that he has set spinning for his victimized half-brother. Edgar, stubborn sufferer, cannot be defeated, and his timing becomes exquisite the moment he and Gloucester encounter the bullying Oswald. The best principle in reading Shakespeare is Emerson's: "Shakespeare is the only biographer of Shakespeare; and even he can tell nothing, except to the Shakespeare in us." I myself deviate a touch from Emerson, since I think only Shakespeare has placed the Shakespeare in us. I don't believe I am that horrid thing, much deprecated by our current pseudo-Marxist Shakespeareans, an "essentialist humanist." As a Gnostic sect of one, I blink at a supposed Shakespeare who is out to subvert Renaissance ideology, and who hints at revolutionary possibilities. Essentialist Marxists or feminists or Franco-Heideggerians ask me to accept a Shakespeare rather in their own image. The Shakespeare in me, however placed there, shows me a deeper and more ancient subversion at work: in much of Shakespeare, but in the four high tragedies or domestic tragedies of blood in particular. Dostoevsky founded Svidrigailov and Stavrogin upon Iago and Edmund, while Nietzsche and Kierkegaard discovered their Dionysiac forerunner in Hamlet, and Herman Melville came to his Captain Ahab through MacBeth. The nihilist questers emerge from the Shakespearean abyss, as Freud at his uncanniest emerged. I do not offer a nihilistic Shakespeare or a Gnostic one, but skepticism alone cannot be the origin of the cosmological degradation that contextualizes the tragedies *King Lear* and *Macbeth*. The more nihilistic Solomon of Ecclesiastes and the Wisdom of Solomon tells us, in the latter, Apocryphal work, that "we are borne at all adventure, and we shall be hereafter as though we had never been." The heretic John Milton did not believe that God had made the world out of nothing; we do not know what Shakespeare did not believe. Lear, as charted by W. R. Elton in *King Lear and the Gods*, is neither an Epicurean materialist nor a skeptic; rather he is, "in rejecting creation *ex nihilo* a pious pagan but a skeptical Christian," as befits a pagan play for a Christian audience. Lear, we always must remind ourselves, is well past eighty, and his world wears out to nothing with him. As in *Macbeth*, an end-time is suggested. The resurrection of the body, unknown to Solomon, is also unknown to Lear, who dies in his evident hallucination of Cordelia's revival from the dead.

King Lear is Lear's play, not Edmund's, but as I've continued to say, it is also Edgar's play, and ironically the later Edgar is Edmund's unintended creation. The sullen or assumed humor of Tom O' Bedlam is the central emblem of the play: philosopher, fool, madman, nihilist, dissembler — at once all of these and none of these. There is a horror of generation that intensifies as the tragedy grows starker, and Edgar, harsher as he proceeds, shares it with Lear. Nothing sweetens Edgar's imagination of sexuality, whereas Edmund, icy libertine, is deliciously indifferent: "Which of them shall I take? / Both? One? Or neither?" A double-date with Goneril and Regan might faze even King Richard III or Aaron the Moor, but is second nature to Edmund, who attributes his vivacity, freedom from hypocrisy, and power of plotting to his bastardy, at once provocation to his pride and to some uneasiness of spirit:

> Why brand they us
> With base? with baseness? bastardy? base, base?
> Who, in the lusty stealth of nature, take
> More composition, and fierce quality,
> Than doth within a dull, stale, tired bed
> Go to th' creating a whole tribe of fops,
> Got 'tween asleep and wake?

That is Edmund in his "fierce quality," not the mortally wounded man who has the continued accuracy to say, " 'Tis past, and so am I." Edgar, at that moment, takes an opposite view of that "lusty stealth of nature":

> The gods are just, and of our pleasant vices
> Make instruments to plague us:
> The dark and vicious place where thee he got
> Cost him his eyes.

The dying Edmund accepts this, but it can be judged very disconcerting, since that "dark and vicious place" does not appear to be an adulterous bed but is identical with what Lear stigmatized in his madness:

> Down from the waist they are Centaurs,
> Though women all above;
> But to the girdle do the gods inherit,
> Beneath is all the fiends': there's hell, there's darkness,
> There is the sulphurous pit, burning, scalding,
> Stench, consumption.

Admirable son of Gloucester and admirable godson of Lear, approved avenger and future king, Edgar nevertheless emerges impaired in many respects from his long ordeal of abnegation. Not least of these impairments is his evident horror of female sexuality, "the dark and vicious place." A high price has been exacted for the long descent into the sullen and assumed humor of Tom O' Bedlam. The cost of confirmation for Edgar is a savage wound in his psyche, but the entire play is more of a wound than the critical tradition has cared to acknowledge. Feminist critics, and those influenced by them, at least address themselves to the rhetoric of male trauma and hysteria that governs the apparent misogyny of Lear's drama. I say "apparent" because the revulsion from all sexuality by Lear and by Edgar is a mask for an even more profound alienation, not so much from excessive familial love, as from bewilderment by such love. Edmund is brilliant and resourceful, but his prime, initial advantage over everyone else in the play is his total freedom from all familial affect, a freedom that enhances his fatal fascination for Goneril and Regan.

Are Shakespeare's perspectives in *Lear* incurably male? The only woman in the play who is not a fiend is Cordelia, whom some recent feminist critics see as Lear's own victim, a child he seeks to enclose as much at the end as at the beginning. Such a view is certainly not Cordelia's perspective upon her relationship with her father, and I am inclined to credit her rather than her critics. Yet their sense of being troubled is an authentic and accurate reaction to a play that divests all of us, male and female auditors and readers alike, of not less than everything. Dr. Johnson's inability to sustain the murder of the virtuous Cordelia is another form of the same reaction. When Nietzsche said that we possessed art lest we perish of the truth, he gave a very equivocal homage to art, and yet his apothegm is emptied out by *King Lear*, where we do perish of the truth. The Freudian, witty oxymoron of "family romances" loses its wit in the context of *King Lear*, where familial love offers you only a choice between destructions. You can live and die as Gloucester, Lear, and Cordelia do, or as Goneril, Regan, and Edmund do, or you can survive as Edgar does, a fate darker than that of all the others.

The noun "value" in Shakespeare lacks our high-mindedness: it means either an *estimation* of worth or a more speculative *esti-*

mate, both being commercial terms rather bluntly carried over into human relations. Sometimes I think that our only certain knowledge of the man Shakespeare is that his commercial shrewdness rivaled or overtopped every other author's before or since. Economy in Shakespeare extends to the noun "love," which can mean "lover" but also means "friend," or a "kind act," and sometimes "for love's sake" means for "one's own sake." Johnson, still the best of all Shakespearean critics, wonderfully tells us that, unlike every other dramatist, Shakespeare refuses to make love a universal agent:

> but love is only one of many passions, and as it has no great influence upon the sum of life, it has little operation in the dramas of a poet, who caught his ideas from the living world, and exhibited only what he saw before him. He knew, that any other passion, as it was regular or exorbitant, was a cause of happiness or calamity.

Johnson speaks of sexual love, rather than familial love, a distinction that Shakespeare taught Freud partly to void. Repressed incestuous desire for Cordelia, according to Freud, causes Lear's madness. Cordelia, again according to Freud, is so darkly silent at the play's opening because of her continued desire for her father. Certainly the family romance of Sigmund and Anna Freud has its effect in these rather too interesting weak misreadings. Lear's excessive love transcends even his attachment to Cordelia: it comprehends the Fool and others. The worship of Lear by Kent, Gloucester, Albany, and most of all his godson Edgar is directed not only at the great image of authority but at the central emblem of familial love, or patriarchal love (if you would have it so). The exorbitant passion or drive of familial love, both in Lear and in Edgar, is the cause of calamity. Tragedy at its most exorbitant, whether in Athens or at the Globe, must be domestic tragedy, or tragedy of blood in both senses of blood. None of us want to come away from a reading or performance of *King Lear* murmuring to ourselves that the domestic is necessarily a tragedy, but that may be the ultimate nihilism of this play.

2

Cleopatra's is too large a role to be fitted comfortably into a coda, but I want to juxtapose the Shakespearean representation of heterosexual passion to the vision of familial love in *King Lear*. *Romeo and Juliet* is too early, being pre-*Hamlet*, and *Troilus and Cressida* is too magnificently rancid, even for my unsavory purposes. I don't know that it is at all useful to characterize the relationship between Cleopatra and Antony as mutually destructive, though Shakespeare certainly shows that it helps destroy them. Still, in their high-stakes cosmos of power and treachery, Octavian doubtless would have devoured them both anyway, at a perhaps more leisurely pace. *All for Love*, John Dryden's exuberant title, would not have done for Shakespeare's play; even *All for Lust* misses the mark. Antony and Cleopatra are, both of them, charismatic politicians, almost celebrities in our bad sense. Each of them has so great a passion for herself and himself that it becomes marvelous for them actually to apprehend one another's reality, in even the smallest degree. Both of them take up all the space; everyone else, even Octavian, is reduced to part of their audience. There is, to be sure, a ghost who never appears in this play: Julius Caesar, who alone ever reduced *them* to supporting cast, though never to mere audience. Perhaps it was from Shakespeare's *Julius Caesar*, play and character, that Shakespeare's Antony and Cleopatra learned their endearing trait of never listening to what anyone else says, including one another. Antony's death-scene is the most hilarious instance of this, where the dying hero, making a very good end indeed, nevertheless sincerely attempts to give her some good advice, while she keeps interrupting, at one point splendidly responding to his "let me speak a little" with her "No, let me speak." Since his advice is quite bad anyway, as it has been throughout the play, this makes little difference except that Antony, just this once, almost stops acting the part of Antony, Herculean hero, whereas Shakespeare wishes us to see that Cleopatra never stops acting the part of Cleopatra. That is why it is so wonderfully difficult a role for an actress, who must act the part of Cleopatra, and also portray Cleopatra acting the part of Cleopatra. I recall the young Helen Mirren doing better with that double assignment than any other Cleopatra that I have seen.

Are Antony and Cleopatra "in love with one another," to use our language, which for once is not at all Shakespearean? Are *we* in love with one another? It was Aldous Huxley, I think, in one of his essays, who remarked that we use the word "love" for the most amazing variety of relationships, ranging from what we feel for our mothers to what we feel for someone we beat up in a bordello, or its many equivalents. Juliet and Romeo indeed are in love with one another, but they are very young, and she is astonishingly good-natured, with a generosity of spirit unmatched in all of Shakespeare. We certainly can say that Cleopatra and Antony do not bore one another, and clearly they are bored, erotically and otherwise, by everyone else in their world. Mutual fascination may not be love, but it certainly is romance in the defining sense of imperfect or at least deferred knowledge. Cleopatra in particular always has her celebrated remedies for staleness, famously celebrated by Enobarbus. Antony, also a mortal god, has his aura, really a kind of astral body, that departs with the music of Hercules, the oboes under the stage. There is no replacement for him, as Cleopatra realizes, since with his death the age of Julius Caesar and Pompey is over, and even Cleopatra is very unlikely to seduce the first great Chief Executive Officer, the Emperor Augustus.

The question therefore becomes: What is the value of mutual fascination, or of romantic love, if you want to call it that? Certainly it is less of a bewilderment, less of a vastation, than the familial love that afflicts Lear and Edgar. With monstrous shrewdness, Shakespeare modified Plutarch by having Antony abandoned by the god Hercules, rather than by Bacchus. A Dionysiac hero cannot be consigned to the past, as Hamlet's more-than-Nietzschean career continues to demonstrate. A Herculean hero was not as archaic for Shakespeare's contemporaries as he is for us, but clearly Antony is already a belated figure. Lear and Edgar are not as exposed to the audience's perspectivism as are Cleopatra and Antony. Whore and her aging gull is a possible perspective upon them, if you yourself are a savage reductionist, but then why would you want to attend or read this play? A Dionysiac Antony would call every value, whether erotic or social, more into question than a Herculean Antony is capable of doing. If there is a critique of value in the play, it must be embodied in Cleopatra, who is raised to an apotheosis after Antony breaks apart. He ceases to be a god, and then she becomes one.

What are we to do with an Egyptian goddess, even if we are free enough of Roman reductiveness so that we do not fall into the operatic trap of seeing her as a gypsy whore? If my interpretation of *King Lear* has any imaginative accuracy, then familial love, far from being a value, is exposed as an apocalyptic nightmare. Romantic love can be said to have hastened Antony's Osiris-like dismantling, yet it would be difficult, as I have been intimating, to demonstrate it either as value or as catastrophe, on the basis of his decline and fall. But Cleopatra is altogether another story, and her story certainly involves an augmentation of value. Is it the value of love? That seems to me a most difficult question, and a true challenge to what we used to call *literary* criticism. You could argue not only that the Cleopatra of Act V is a greater actress than she was before, but also that she becomes a playwright, exercising a talent released in her by Antony's death. The part that she composes for herself is very complex, and one strand in it is that she was and still is in love with Antony, and so is more than bereft. Indeed, she marries him as she dies, which is sublimely poignant, though it may remind us of Edmund's reaction to beholding the corpses of Goneril and Regan: "All three / Now marry in an instant."

Existence, we cannot forget Nietzsche observing, is justified only as an aesthetic phenomenon. I would hesitate, wicked old aesthete though I be, to judge that love, for Shakespeare, is justified only as an aesthetic value, but that does seem (to me) to be the burden of *The Tragedy of Antony and Cleopatra*, at least as Cleopatra rewrites it in the act where she has no rival in usurping all the space. Her would-be competitive dramatist, George Bernard Shaw, who asserted that he felt only disdain for the mind of Shakespeare when he compared it to his own, is quite cutting but weirdly off-center in his preface to his own *Caesar and Cleopatra*:

> . . . I have a technical objection to making sexual infatuation a tragic theme. Experience proves that it is only effective in the comic spirit. We can bear to see Mrs. Quickly pawning her plate for love of Falstaff, but not Antony running away from the battle of Actium for love of Cleopatra.

One can grant that Shaw seizes upon one of the least persuasive episodes in Antony's degradation, but surely *Antony and Cleopatra* hardly is a tragedy as *King Lear* and *Othello* are tragedies. More even than the rest of Shakespeare, the play has no genre, and the comic spirit has a large share in it. Enobarbus gives the answer to Shaw when he calls Cleopatra a wonderful piece of work. He means Cleopatra's daemonic drive, her narcissistic exuberance, the vitality of which approaches Falstaff's. Shaw abominated Falstaff, and associated Shakespeare's Cleopatra with Falstaff, which is to make the right linkage for the wrong reason. Rosalie Colie, in her fine book *Shakespeare's Living Art*, points out that Shakespeare never once shows Antony and Cleopatra alone onstage together. Whatever it is that they share is not revealed to us: we wonder whether they would cease to be theatrical, but Shakespeare does not tell us. This cannot be a question of tact, since Othello and Desdemona, Macbeth and Lady Macbeth, Juliet and Romeo, and so many others are left alone with one another and ourselves. It is rather an indication of Shakespeare's anxiety that by overrepresenting the relationship he might lessen its cosmological suggestiveness. What we are not allowed to see, we must imagine. Cleopatra, essentially an ironic humorist, even a parodist, presumably educated Antony in laughter even as Falstaff educated Hal, with the difference that Falstaff does not trade in sexual love, and Cleopatra does.

That returns me to the matter of value, and to Cleopatra's art as dramatist in Act V. She is Antony's elegist, but not in a personal way: her lament is for lost greatness, for the agonistic sublime, for her public passion:

> The crown o' th' earth doth melt. My lord!
> O, withered is the garland of the war,
> The soldier's pole is fall'n: young boys and girls
> Are level now with men. The odds is gone,
> And there is nothing left remarkable
> Beneath the visiting moon.

"The odds is gone" means that value, which depends upon distinctions, has been lost, the fallen soldier's pole having been the standard of measurement. Cleopatra's longing for a lost sublime does not mean that we have a new transcendental woman replacing the histrionic masterwork we have known. Dr. Johnson, to our initial surprise, complained that in *Antony and Cleopatra* "no character is very strongly discriminated." What could Johnson have meant, since that is not at all our experience of the play? John Bayley thinks that Johnson is right, and attributes this lack of distinctiveness to our sense that Antony is down and out from the start and to Shakespeare's supposed refusal to explore Cleopatra's inwardness. Shakespeare, I think, knew exactly what he did, and Dr. Johnson and Bayley may be victimized by the play's perspectivism. Antony certainly is past his earlier glory almost throughout the play, except for sudden revivals or epiphanies, but Shakespeare was improving upon the model of decline he had established with his own Julius Caesar. And with Cleopatra, how can we, or even Cleopatra herself, ever establish the demarcation between her inwardness and her outwardness? She is surely the most theatrical character in stage history, far surpassing Luigi Pirandello's experiments in the same mode. We need not ask if her love for Antony ever is love indeed, even as she dies, because the lack of distinctiveness in the play is between the histrionic and the passionate. The value of familial love in Shakespeare is overwhelming but negative; the value of passionate love in the most mature Shakespeare depends upon a fusion of theatricality and narcissistic self-regard. The art itself is nature, and the value of love becomes wholly artful.

The summit of this magnificent play comes in the interlude with the clown just before the apotheosis of Cleopatra's suicide, an interlude that sustains Janet Adelman's contention in *The Common Liar* that Shakespeare's "insistence upon scope, upon the infinite variety of the world, militates against the tragic experience." Uncanny perspectives abound throughout *Antony and Cleopatra*, but the clown's is the most unnerving. He dominates the interchange with Cleopatra, as her charm first melts his misogyny and then resolidifies it when he fails to persuade her against her resolve. Few exchanges in the world's literature are as poignant and as subtle as this:

> *Clown.* Very good. Give it nothing, I pray you, for it is not worth the feeding.
> *Cleopatra.* Will it eat me?

How difficult it is to categorize that childlike "Will it eat me?"; perhaps Cleopatra, before mounting into death and divine transfiguration, needs a final return to the playful element in her self that is her Falstaffian essence, the secret to her seductiveness. In the clown's repetition of "I wish you joy o' th' worm," we hear something beyond his phallic misogyny, a prophecy perhaps of Cleopatra's conversion of the painful ecstasy of her dying into an erotic epiphany of nursing both Antony and her children by her Roman conquerors. Her artfulness and Shakespeare's fuse together in a blaze of value that surmounts the equivocations of every mode of love in Shakespeare, equivocations that are true lies.

I. Jazz: A Historical Perspective
II. Duke Ellington
III. Charles Mingus

GUNTHER SCHULLER

THE TANNER LECTURES ON HUMAN VALUES

Delivered at

Cambridge University
February 5–7, 1996

GUNTHER SCHULLER has developed a musical career that ranges from composing and conducting to his extensive work as an educator, Jazz historian, administrator, music publisher, record producer, and author. By age seventeen he was principal French horn with the Cincinnati Symphony, and later held the same position with the Metropolitan Opera Orchestra. He gave up performing to devote himself primarily to composition, although he still conducts around the world. He has taught at the Manhattan School of Music, Yale University, and at the New England Conservatory of Music, Boston, where he was president for ten years. He has also been artistic director for the Berkshire Music Center at Tanglewood and for the Festival at Sandpoint, Idaho. He has been awarded the Pulitzer Prize and two Guggenheim Fellowships, and in 1991 he received a MacArthur Fellowship. He has written dozens of essays and four books, including *Early Jazz* (1986), *The Swing Era: The Development of Jazz, 1930–1945* (1989), and *The Compleat Conductor* (1997), and his collaborative album *Rush Hour* was selected as *Downbeat Magazine's* Record of the Year for 1995.

I. Jazz: A Historical Perspective

It must be self-evident to everyone in this room that one cannot deal in any significant detail with the history of jazz in a *one-hour* lecture. Such a task could take several days, not hours; and therefore I would like to clarify that the title of this talk, "Jazz: A Historical Perspective," with the emphasis on the final word, signifies a look at jazz history from a very *general* perspective and painted with a very large and broad brush — but aided and abetted by a few specially selected musical illustrations and personal points of view.

Since jazz is a musical language and since music is an aural art, it would be the happiest of options if we could now embark on a three-day listening marathon, with me acting as a kind of super disc jockey, presenting for your pleasure the great classics of jazz, past and present.

In that connection, I trust that you can all attend the listening session Professor Malcolm Longair has so kindly arranged on Wednesday afternoon. It might just be the most rewarding of all the planned Tanner events, as — I suspect — the discussant session earlier that day will also be. Now to the subject at hand!

The beginnings of jazz lie in obscurity somewhere in the past, say, about a hundred years ago, or perhaps somewhat later, one's dating depending on what one wants to call — *properly* — jazz, as a clearly definable musical style or language. Historians have, of course, used a certain day in early 1917 as the beginnings of jazz, when a group calling themselves the Original Dixieland Jass Band — mostly spelled *jass* in those days — made a series of recordings in New York. Whether those recordings really represent jazz, or, at least, jazz at its purest and best, is highly debatable. But some form of jazz music making *was* taking place long before that chance recording event in various parts of the United States, notably in New Orleans and the surrounding deep South, but also in the Midwest, around St. Louis and Kansas City, and very probably even in the far West, in places like Los Angeles and San Francisco. Several early tributaries to the eventual mainstream of jazz, such as the blues or ragtime or various kinds of popular dance musics, were, we know, practiced in many of these regions as early as the 1880s and 1890s. When all of this rich musical bouillabaisse coalesced into a more-or-less distinctive style and musical expression is shrouded in the past, and we shall probably never be able to date the actual beginnings of jazz in the precise way that we can now, for example, date the discovery of prehuman or animal skeletons millions of years ago, or the invention of the telephone, or the first visit to the South Pole. An art form does not lend itself to that kind of precise dating and defining.

The *origins* of jazz are a little easier to deal with, at least in relatively broad terms. There is little argument that the essential elements of jazz—those elements that make jazz jazz and separate it linguistically, stylistically, from any other forms of music-making—are of African, specifically West African, origin. Those elements are, above all, three primary ones: (1) a certain form of syncopation, rarely if ever heard in European music before, (2) that specific rhythmic pulse, which in jazz is called swing, and (3) the concept of improvisatory music making. However, those African elements, brought to America by the slaves, were fused in jazz with distinctly European elements, such as the European classical harmonic language (as it had developed into a relatively chromatic language around the turn of the century) and, of course, also a basically European instrumentarium.

Jazz is essentially an ensemble music, although admittedly it has, in its long evolution, also embraced the "solo," as both a composed element and an improvised one. Certainly in its early stages it was almost entirely an ensemble music, best exemplified by the great collective ensemble playing of the so-called New Orleans style, as epitomized by, let's say, King Oliver's Creole Jazz Band [brief excerpt from "Dippermouth Blues"]. I would add that it was almost inevitable, given its primary West African sources, that jazz be an ensemble music, since West African tribal, ritual, and dance musics are also all performed in collective ensembles. Now, one of the immediate historical forerunners of jazz was ragtime, despite its pianistic origins soon to develop also into an ensemble music, involving a great deal of syncopation and a good deal — if played right — of swing. But ragtime was a composed, written-down, notated music — *not* improvised — to be played and performed more or less in a particular predefined way, very much in the same sense that classical music was defined and to be performed as notated by the composer. Other tributary sources, such as the white European-based dance and popular musics of the late nineteenth century and the light semiclassical fare that flourished in America, were a mixture of composition and improvisation, mostly composed, notated, published, but often played in a semi-memorized loosely and spontaneously re-created manner that one cannot quite call improvisation, but at the same time quite removed from the strictures and performance practices of "serious" classical music.

But the blues, the other important predecessor of jazz, *was* primarily an improvised, handed-down (not written-down) kind of music. It was sung and played by ordinary folks, not necessarily trained or professional musicians, existing in an infinite, spontaneously created plethora of forms and personal interpretations.

One can thus see that, in its various component source influences, jazz was from the outset a musical hybrid. On both its African and European sides, it was the result of an unpremeditated, spontaneous coming-together of musical expressions and styles that ranged, in greatly varying degrees, from fixed, notated to loosely, spontaneously semi-improvised forms.

I say "semi-improvised" — and here I come to perhaps the first possibly controversial point of view in my talk — because, although jazz historians and jazz musicians have long perpetuated, either implicitly or explicitly, the notion that jazz always was an "improvised music," a spontaneously, instantaneously created, off-the-cuff kind of music, the facts are that, at least in the first three or four decades of jazz, the music was *not* improvised, certainly not in the pure and simple sense of that term. I say "at least in the first three or four decades of jazz," because it is true that eventually jazz — jazz musicians — *did* learn to improvise, to create truly spontaneously.

Indeed, today everybody in jazz worth even talking about improvises, *can* improvise, feels he or she *must* be able to improvise. How well, how creatively, is perhaps another matter. But if we could casually claim in the past that improvisation "is the heart and soul of jazz," then that is only technically accurate and true in recent decades, say, since the 1940s and 1950s, and a rather inaccurate and imprecise claim as regards earlier jazz forms.

For the fact is — and this is now easily confirmed by the issuance of hundreds of second and third takes of recorded pieces in the 1920s and 1930s as well as by the existence of archival manuscript evidence of countless written-out "solos," formerly thought to have been "improvised" — that the full flowering of truly spontaneous jazz improvisation did not, *could* not, occur until the technical virtuosic abilities of the players had reached a certain level of total command. Before that players prepared their "solos" — in a great variety of ways: everything from writing out to memorization and varying degrees of mental, musical, practical preparation. Some "soloists" *always* played previously premeditated "solos," memorized — but, let's say, in the case of the great Ellington trombonist, Lawrence Brown, so magically rendered, every time, that they sounded as if they were spontaneously created that moment. In the archives of the Duke Ellington collection at the Smithsonian Institution in Washington there are dozens of "solos" written in Duke Ellington's hand, which were then rendered by a Johnny Hodges or Harry Carney or Cootie Williams. To qualify that statement a little, let me add that, as the various players' abilities and technical command became more sophisticated and secure, they would in varying but increasing degrees ornament, embellish, loosen up the preconceived solo — be it their own or Duke's or someone else's — thus making it more personalized and more spontaneous. But more often than not the actual notes, the notated pitches, were the bare-bones basis of the solo passages. A given player may then have varied or freed up the solo, for example, rhythmically, or with certain embellishments, scoops, pitch bends, glissandos, articulations, phrasings, and the like to make the solo even more "personal."

May I remind us all that in classical music, which is often maligned by jazz fans for not featuring improvisation, the ideal performance of a "solo" — say in a concerto or a major solo in a work by Johannes Brahms or Pyotr Tchaikovsky or Igor Stravinsky (or whoever) — is one that sounds *as if it had just been created*. That is, of course — and alas — a very rare occasion indeed, given the general state of classical performance and performance practices. But every once in a while one does hear a remarkable performer re-create, realize, a composed solo passage in such a way — and, incidentally, without distorting or recomposing it (that also happens, unfortunately much too often) — that one feels one has heard it for the first time and that the performer just made it up at that moment.

There is also the clear case in jazz of many so-called solos that were composed themes, deemed so central, so integral, to the piece and its performance that they were considered immutable. For example, Bubber Miley's so-called solos in some of Ellington's earliest compositions, such as "Black and Tan Fantasy," "East St. Louis Toodle-oo," and "The Mooche" — these themes were mostly composed by Miley or co-composed with Ellington — were played almost exactly the same way for nearly sixty years, even unto today. When Cootie Williams took over Miley's trumpet chair, he played the same solos the same way for ten years; and when Ray Nance succeeded Williams, he then played the same solo, as did later incumbents, such as "Money" Johnson, Clark Terry, Cat Anderson, and several others.

Furthermore, some of the truly great creative solos of the period were kept intact, *precisely* because they were so great, whether they had originally been improvised or partially prepared or not; they were considered so integral and perfect for the piece that they were retained in their original form. The feeling was that they could not be improved upon.

I am emphasizing this point to some extent because it was misunderstood and misused for *so* many years by jazz historians, jazz critics, and jazz fans that it will take considerable effort to correct this bit of jazz mythology. It is also disturbing to me that there is in that version of jazz history an assumption, either implied or sometimes explicit, that the "solo" in jazz is everything — that the composition and/or the arrangement are somehow inferior or secondary aspects of jazz. Countless books on jazz have been written that completely ignore the element — the very existence — of composition, of arrangement, of ensemble playing in jazz, also thereby ignoring the reality that thousands of jazz solos were — and are — not great or memorable, indeed very often inferior to the composition and/or arrangement in which they are enclosed.

The meaningful, stylistically and compositionally cogent integration of solos into compositions and arrangements was in fact one of Ellington's primary concerns. He, as a real composer — a sitting-down, writing-out composer, not a mere arranger or tunesmith — held from the outset that a performance of his pieces should be above all a unified, fully integrated, fully thought-through effort, in which stylistic or compositional breaks should not occur, where the personality and individualism of the improviser should not disturb or override the basic conception of the total work. And that is why Duke for many years — admittedly less and less in later years — felt the need, with but a few exceptions, to control the "solos" in his pieces, even to the extent of most often writing them out for his soloists, at least in skeletal form.

The fact remains that all the early jazz musicians — even the great innovative creators, such as Louis Armstrong or Earl Hines or

Coleman Hawkins or Johnny Hodges — were involved to a high degree in prior preparation in advance of the event at which they produced their so-called solos. And why should we try to deny this, or regard it as a negative? I don't care how a solo was created or how long it took to create it; and I don't care whether it was improvised or not. All that matters in the end is whether it was any good or not, whether it fitted into the frame of the piece, whether it was an inspired, meaningful addition to the piece — or not.

There is another way to clarify this point. The very earliest jazz players — again with the historians' implication that this meant improvisers — weren't jazz players in the true sense at all. And most of them, if asked, would disclaim this. Bunk Johnson, one of the earliest of the renowned New Orleans trumpeters, was only one of many who claimed he was just "an old ragtime player." Quite so. Others called what they played merely "syncopated" music, with no implication of improvisation. In this connection it is well to recall the statement of Buster Bailey, the famous clarinetist who played from about 1915 into the 1960s and who, in commenting on his playing around 1917–18, said — and I quote — "I was embellishing around the melody. At that time I wouldn't have known what they meant by improvisation. But embellishment was a phrase I understood." And Buster Bailey was certainly not alone in making that admission; it was variously echoed by many other musicians.

The early players in the teens and twenties of the century all played the popular ragtime hits and syncopated dance tunes of the period. Ragtime was, after all, *the* popular music of the United States — and then, soon, in England and Europe as well — from about 1900 to 1918. And ragtime was, as I've mentioned, a composed, written-down, fixed music that was not meant to be improvised upon. Indeed, the idea of improvisation hardly occurred to anybody until the later years of that period. And the way that came about was a quite natural part of the transition from ragtime to jazz. Most of the players of that era, especially among the blacks and Creoles, were *not* professional musicians. They played music as a hobby or a part-time avocation, and certainly were not schooled or conservatory-trained musicians; as such, very few of them, including some of the best and most famous ones, could read music. Someone like Bunk Johnson, for example, a contemporary of Armstrong, could not really read music; he hadn't been taught to read music, and in his kind of work, playing for dances and in nightclubs, he was never required to read music. But he and others like him had terrific ears: they could *hear* the music they couldn't read. They simply picked up tunes by ear, including the basic popular ragtime pieces of that time, such as "Maple Leaf Rag," "High Society," and "Tiger Rag," and, having more or less memorized those tunes, played them, but not exactly as written — embellished, ornamented, changed a little, thereby creating a more spontaneous, almost improvised effect. That is certainly what the earliest New Orleans trumpet players did, such as Bunk Johnson, King Oliver, and Freddie Keppard. Gradually, as the players' technical skills developed and as they became more versed in the new dance and blues repertory, they, of course, gradually became freer in their ornamentations and personal versions of tunes. And that practice eventually slid into something one could begin to call improvisation, at first rather tune-bound (i.e., merely embellishing the tune), until through the next decade or two the variations began to be done on the chord changes, not necessarily the melodies or themes, thus inventing their own melodies, imposed on the old chord changes. Clarinet players and trombone players, whose role was to provide obbligato or counter-lines to the main tune, were obliged to be a little more inventive. But they too did not, in an absolute sense, always improvise those obbligato passages, but worked them out beforehand, prepared them some way or another, and, as recorded evidence shows, played them, apart from occasionally adding a little new twist here and there, more or less the same way each time.

Of course, improvisation in jazz did eventually become a highly disciplined and technically extraordinarily demanding performing art. But make no mistake about it: it first had to be learned, and that took several decades. A few very gifted musicians, such as Louis Armstrong, Earl Hines, Coleman Hawkins, and Sidney Bechet, developed some forms of improvisatory abilities earlier than most others. But even in those cases there is plentiful evidence that what appeared on a given recording to have been improvised had in most cases been prepared, worked on, thought about, wholly or partially predetermined, in some way or other. As late as 1934 Hawkins, in an article he wrote for the English popular music magazine the *Melody Maker*, warned against prematurely trying to "play hot," the term that was coming into usage as a synonym for improvising a solo. He wrote: "Until a player has advanced himself to such a stage that he has more or less lost consciousness of the manual side of his instrument, it is wrong and foolish for him to worry about playing hot. Hot playing requires perfect control of one's instrument, so that musical thoughts can be automatically and unhesitatingly translated into notes." He added that "it required a complete knowledge of chords and harmonies, a super sense of rhythm and" — most importantly — "the gift of inventiveness." Highest musical discipline indeed!

Thus one can describe the transition from ragtime to jazz as (1) a transition from a composed notated music to a memorized and more loosely reinterpreted music, and/or (2), if you like, a transition from reading musicians to nonreading musicians who through their ears and creative imagination — very sharp among the great, the best ones — develop a whole new way of playing, of creating, of inventing and reinventing.

Once the transformation of ragtime into jazz had taken place — with, to be sure, a healthy infusion of the blues, around 1919–20 (when the first blues recordings with the great blues singers such as Bessie Smith and Mamie Smith began to be made) — the advances in jazz, both technically and stylistically, came in rapid succession. By the end of the decade, a high degree of instrumental sophistication, of technical skill and virtuosity, and, above all, of compositional creativity had taken over. It was in those years — say, 1924 to 1927 — that we witness the first great flowering of Louis Armstrong's art, both as a trumpeter and as a singer. One does not know where it came from — we cover such phenomena with terms like "innate talent" or "genius" or "the mystery of creativity" — but Armstrong discovered in his playing, as he was working with King Oliver (in Chicago) and Fletcher Henderson (in New York), a way to make the music swing [excerpt from "Big Butter and Egg Man" after Armstrong's vocal chorus to end]. That was a whole new way of playing never heard before in Western music. Swing is not just playing something rhythmically well or accurately. It is something beyond that; it is a feeling — an infectious, irresistible feeling — and a way of articulating and timing notes that is unique to jazz, as descended from its African roots. It is painfully conspicuous in its absence, but delightfully captivating when it is present.

Before Armstrong no one swung, no one knew what swing was — except perhaps Jelly Roll Morton (to some extent) and Earl Hines. It is not an exaggeration to say that Armstrong taught the world to swing, taught jazz to swing. Even a greater player such as Hawkins, at first, in his early recordings before, say, 1925 and 1926, did not, could not, play with swing. His playing was initially very stiff — energetic, yes, but primitive and inexpressive, made all the worse by his (and all saxophone players' of the time) penchant for "slap tongue." Hawkins learned to play with swing from Armstrong, when Louis was for one year the star soloist of the Fletcher Henderson orchestra. He taught the rest of the band to swing as well, and by extension all the other then burgeoning jazz players and jazz orchestras in New York and Chicago.

Armstrong also, along with Earl Hines, was the prime mover in bringing into jazz the concept of the jazz "solo." It was during those years, in the late 1920s, that jazz changed irreversibly from a collective ensemble music (with perhaps a few incidental solos here and there) into a music where the solo and the soloist became the new, exciting featured attraction [excerpts from "Potato Blues" and "Muggles" and then "Mahogany Hall Stomp"].

This required a certain level of technical skill — also a compositional, creative talent — that then developed in the jazz world in the 1930s like wildfire. Due to the tremendous influx of young talented musicians to the field — jazz was, after all, a new, relatively attractive field economically — the resultant intense competition among musicians generated an artistic/professional climate in which the technical and creative skills spiraled upward at a tremendous rate. Once an Armstrong had achieved some technical breakthrough — an extension of the upper range, an exciting new way of swinging, a new double-time effect, some new ways of articulating and phrasing on his instrument — other players not only could no longer say "that can't be done," but actually had to shape up and learn those new skills and deal with those new ideas, if they wanted to stay professionally competitive.

In the midst of all this creative ferment, there arrived on the scene an extraordinary genius, Edward Ellington — known soon as "the Duke" or "Duke Ellington." His talent lay in many directions: as pianist, as band leader, as arranger, but above all, as composer. Prodigiously creative — Ellington composed virtually day and night all his life — he produced nearly fifteen hundred compositions, many of them absolute masterpieces of the genre. He was innovative on many fronts, especially in regard to form and structure, but also in his harmonic explorations (years ahead of anyone else) and his sense, his ear, for instrumental/orchestral color. I will deal in more detail with Ellington the composer in tomorrow's talk.

Ellington, because of these unique talents, was always a bit of an outsider in the jazz world. Greatly admired and respected, even revered, he nevertheless was not as much of a major influence in jazz as one might think, precisely because he was somewhat apart from everyone else and so far in advance of the rest of the field that many musicians (and audiences) found his music too sophisticated, too subtle, too rich — some even too incomprehensible.

The mainstream of jazz developed along rather different lines. These can be exemplified by, on the one hand, the early 1930s bands of Fletcher Henderson and Chick Webb, playing exuberant, free-wheeling jazz, loosely arranged, featuring a collection of soloist stars, a bit rough in style but tremendously exciting; and, on the other hand, the more disciplined, rehearsed-to-the-nines approach of the band of Jimmy Lunceford, a well-educated and trained musician who sought to combine technical ensemble perfection and a great "two-beat" swing with a high level of elegant showmanship.

That was in New York. Another line developed in Kansas City, in the American Midwest, first through the bands of Bennie Moten and Walter Page's Blue Devils, both with Count Basie as pianist. Hear now the incredible virtuosity, arranging brilliance, and excitement of the Moten band as of December 1932! [Moten: "Toby"].

When Moten died in 1935, William Basie took over the band. That band had a tremendous aggregation of soloists: three outstanding trumpet players and two great saxophonists, Hershal Evans and Lester Young, and an incomparable rhythm section, which included the aforementioned Walter Page, as well as the greatest rhythm guitarist of all time, Freddie Green, and, of course, Count Basie himself, who had in the intervening years reduced his former exuberantly virtuosic stride-piano style to a highly economic, aphoristic manner. Eventually, by the 1950s, this became a formulaic mannerism, but in the early days it represented a completely original, refreshingly new style, soon to be much imitated [Lester Young/Basie: "Lady Be Good," small group].

What seems astonishing now in retrospect, when we consider how many great jazz orchestras flourished in those years, is the fact that all this occurred during the great American Depression. This was due, in part, to the enormous influx of new young talent, both black and white, but especially blacks, who saw in jazz a whole new world of enticing artistic and economic opportunities. The competition among all this young talent was fierce, and thus the technical, artistic, and creative standards rose precipitously.

Some orchestras, to be sure, went under in the Depression: Fletcher Henderson's, for example. But in a very interesting way Henderson's legacy was perpetuated in the orchestra and style (although somewhat modified) of Benny Goodman, when Goodman took over Henderson's compositions and arrangements and hired him as staff arranger

Although the leading black orchestras had long ago learned to swing and to develop strong soloists as well as virtuoso ensembles, all this was more or less unknown to most of the white population until 1935, when "swing" was discovered by all America in the person of the Benny Goodman band. Jazz was renamed "swing" and hundreds of white swing bands came into being, both good and bad, ranging from truly creative, innovative ensembles such as Red Norvo's, Teddy Wilson's, and Billie Holiday's, to fairly dismal, more or less commercial dance bands. As the country went swing crazy with Goodman, the Dorseys, Harry James, Ben Pollack, the Casa Loma Band, Artie Shaw, Charlie Barnet, and dozens of others, the great black bands — of Ellington, Basie, Webb, Lunceford, Cab Calloway, Hines — struggled along, gradually playing more to white audiences but in general appreciated primarily by their black audiences. I can attest to this fact personally, because I began to hear and see those orchestras in the early forties, during the war years, and for me there is no question that the black bands, when they played in the black sections of the big cities, the ghettos, at the dance emporia of the time (the various Savoy Ballrooms, Cotton Clubs, Rhumboogies), and, of course, in the black theatres, played to a more understanding, appreciative audience, played a different (better) repertory, and played it better.

Feeding talent into the black bands were the numerous so-called territory bands of the Midwest — roaming through the entire region from Texas to North Dakota, from Colorado to Ohio, living impossible lives, constantly traveling in broken-down buses and cars, sometimes not being paid by unscrupulous dancehall and nightclub operators, but making great music nonetheless, almost more as a hobby than as a profession. I'll name a few of these remarkable orchestras: Alphonse Trent, Troy Floyd, Boots and his Buddies out of Dallas; Nat Towles (perhaps the greatest) out of Omaha, Nebraska; Zach Whyte in Ohio (with Sy Oliver); Jay McShan (with the young Charlie Parker), Jesse Stone, and Harlan Leonard in Kansas City; and Jeter Pillars out of St. Louis. These bands were in effect traveling jazz conservatories, long before jazz musicians ever thought of going to music schools to study. You learned your craft in those territory bands, and if you were really good, the big name bands of Ellington, Lunceford, Calloway, etc., would soon hear about you in that wonderful, totally honest, black musical underground, and you'd be hired into the big time.

A tremendous center of jazz activity was Kansas City, a "wide open" city in the 1930s where "anything went," and jazz in this highly competitive, lucrative setting really flourished.

All this musical ferment, both black and white, grew into a gigantic stream during the years of World War II, in a country economically on the mend — wars strangely enough do that to countries — and eager for, indeed intensely craving, entertainment as relief from the war work.

With the arrival of such talents as Charlie Parker (from Kansas City), Dizzy Gillespie (originally from South Carolina, but later from Philadelphia and New York), Thelonious Monk, Bud Powell, Kenny Clark, and J. J. Johnson, and writer-arrangers such as Eddie Sauter, Ralph Burns, Neal Hefti, Gil Evans, Gil Fuller, and Gerry Valentine, a new brand of jazz developed and a new breed of jazz musicians suddenly appeared everywhere [Gillespie/Parker: "Shaw Nuff"]. From small combos — dozens of quartets and quintets and piano trios (Nat King Cole, Lennie Tristano, Monk, Bud Powell, etc.) — to big bands (such as Stan Kenton, Woody Herman, Boyd Raeburn, Claude Thornhill), they experimented in a wide range of styles and conceptions, collectively known as "bebop," or just plain "modern jazz" [Tristano: "I Can't Get Started," Herman: "Apple Honey," Monk: "Misterioso"]. These were musicians who were creating music — more often than not for smaller and singerless ensembles — to which they wanted you to listen, not to dance or drink to. This was "serious" music, beyond mere entertainment, music of increasing harmonic, melodic/thematic, rhythmic, formal complexity, which fairly soon, as it forged stylistically ahead into new musical territories, lost most of its audience. To what? — well, to the popular singers of the day — the Sinatras, Bing Crosbys, Billy Eckstines, and Ella Fitzgeralds and in the black communities to rhythm and blues and to so-called soul music. By the mid-1950s, when rock and roll started to come in — and even successful bands, such as Basie and Goodman, had to downsize in various ways — most of the great swing and modern jazz bands had disappeared. Jazz, on the one hand — real creative, innovative jazz — had found a smaller, younger, new and loyal audience; on the other hand, jazz was no longer America's popular music, as it had been from 1935 to 1945, and as ragtime had been from 1900 to around 1920.

Nonetheless, great talents — both white and black — began to pour in from all corners of the country — hundreds, if not thousands of them: Ray Brown, Milt Jackson, Miles Davis, John Lewis, Roy Eldridge, Stan Getz, Bill Harris, Fats Navarro, Serge Chaloff, Gerry Mulligan, Lee Konitz, Dave Brubeck, Vic Dickenson, Charles Mingus, Max Roach, Dodo Marmarosa, Sid Catlett, Lennie Tristano, Joe Mooney — the listing could go on for another three pages — creating a whole new universe of jazz styles and conceptions. That generation in turn spawned a new crop of musicians — here one would want to include Sonny Rollins, John Coltrane, Ornette Coleman, Eric Dolphy, George Russell, Jimmy Giuffre, Thad Jones, Miles Davis of course, by then already a veteran, and so many more — too many even to mention, let alone discuss their varied and marvelous achievements.

Into these developments — in the late 1950s and early 1960s — came a new movement, called Third Stream, which sought a closer rapprochement between jazz and classical music, a true fusion of the two musics in their contemporary manifestations: not a mere occasional or casual encounter, but fusion in such a way that a meaningful, balanced cross-fertilization could take place, music that would be performed (ideally) by musicians who would be equally versant in both musical mainstreams and skillful in both the written and the improvisatory traditions.

A rapprochement between classical music and jazz was, of course, not an entirely new idea. There had been various tentative attempts to bring some aspects of the two musics together — as early as Claude Debussy's "Golliwog's Cakewalk" (and some of his other ragtime-influenced pieces) or Charles Ives's and Stravinsky's encounters with ragtime; and, of course, a little later in the 1920s, there were fusionary experiments by Darius Milhaud, Aaron Copland, John Alden Carpenter, Louis Gruenberg, Kurt Weill, Ernst Krenek, Erwin Schulhoff, and many others.

Of these experiments, surely Milhaud's "Création du Monde" from 1923 is the most successful and important work of this category. But there was always one critical element missing in these pre–Third Stream liaisons: the element of swing and improvisation, of spontaneous extemporized creation. Those works were all written for classically trained musicians, who could neither swing nor improvise. And it was this lack that Third Stream attempted to correct, in order to achieve, however specifically it might be done, a more coherent and valid balance in the fusing of the two mainstreams. The real point was that now musical works could be created and produced that, but for the coming together of the two traditions in a deep and aesthetically equivalent fusion, *could not have existed before.*

Increasingly, musicians on both sides of the musical fence crossed over, learned from each others' traditions and techniques. Increasingly, jazz musicians learned to cope with complex forms and structures, with complex musical notation; and, conversely, more and more classical musicians (although primarily wind and brass players) learned to assimilate such elements as syncopated rhythms and swing, learned to free themselves from the written page and to improvise. Perhaps we can listen to an effort of mine from 1960, in which a certain type of fusion of classical and jazz techniques occurred. The piece is *Variants on a Theme of Thelonious Monk*, which features many superb jazz musicians of the time, including Ornette Coleman, Eric Dolphy, Bill Evans, and Scott LaFaro, to name but a few [Schuller: *Variants on a Theme of Thelonious Monk*].

With the breakthrough of jazz into harmonic atonality in the 1960s — some isolated attempts at this had occurred even in the 1930s and 1940s — and the freeing-up of various rhythmic and structural constraints and conventions, the stage was set for a new kind of music and music-making, where the boundaries between classical and jazz eventually became quite blurred and indistinguishable; as a result, the former easy labeling of music as either "jazz" or "classical" became impossible and pointless. Indeed, that again was the idea of Third Stream: not to create Third Stream *jazz* or Third Stream *classical music*, but just Third Stream — a new amalgam made up of potentially equal and no longer separable parts of what used to be previously completely distinct traditions.

What is rather astonishing as we look back over the last eighty to one hundred years of jazz developments is that jazz, as a musical language, accomplished in that short time span more or less what had taken classical music about *eight hundred* years! Minor divergences apart, jazz more or less followed a course similar to that of classical music. If we pinpoint the beginnings of classical music with Perotin, around 1150, and the beginnings of jazz, say, with Buddy Bolden or Scott Joplin around 1900, then we can see that, although the one started conceptually as a sacred, religious music, the other as a secular entertainment music, linguistically jazz developed from its primitive melodic, harmonic (almost aharmonic) beginnings and its simple early forms and structures to about the same point where classical music landed late in our century — only jazz did it about ten times faster.

Another parallel way of describing the history of jazz is to say that it developed from a folk music (in its earliest predawn beginnings) to an entertainment music in the teens and twenties and thence to an art music.

Except for a few cosmetic or technical wrinkles that have been added since the 1960s, things are more or less where they left off at that time. Of course, brilliant new players have come along — both in Europe and in America and Japan — well-trained in all manner of styles and conceptions, allowing now for an extraordinarily broad spectrum of musical expressions and fusions. Into this already vast mix have come tremendous infusions of ethnic, folk, vernacular musical traditions, all jostling with jazz and classical concepts, not for priority, but for some form of integration and fusion. Gone are the days when one had to hunt far and wide for someone in jazz who could read and understand something in Schönbergian atonality, or a musician who could read and improvise in any style or tradition (see Wynton Marsalis and hundreds like him — more or less). This opens up a remarkably broad-based future, at least potentially/ideally — and it is impossible to predict any specific direction or directions.

I am *not* saying that a musical utopia has now arrived and that all these fusions and merging streams will automatically create a nirvana of great music. Far from it; but the scene today simply presents some remarkable new opportunities, options, choices, influences that potentially, given the required *creative* talent, offer possibilities never dreamt of before. For, as always, it is not a technique or a system or a tradition that produces great music; it is only a creative individual who creates something new, vital, important, inspiring, moving.

Leaving aside the broader musical arena for the moment — and coming back to the jazz scene itself — we find ourselves in a brand new terrain. Something fundamental and unprecedented has happened in jazz, to jazz, in the last twenty or so years. There has been a remarkable tradeoff between the first sixty years of jazz and the last twenty. Whereas the first period was dominated by highly creative, original, innovative, distinctive musical voices — most of them representing in their respective times unique, unquestioned leadership — today the scene is devoid of such single or distinctive leadership. There's a different type of talent today; and the trade-off is that, whereas Louis Armstrong or Ben Webster or Lester Young was uniquely himself, instantly recognizable, but *not* capable of stylistical flexibility, diversity, versatility, the best musicians of today can play any kind of jazz — indeed any kind of *music*. However, they are, with an occasional rare exception, not distinctively, stylistically unique, rarely instantly recognizable, shrouded in a kind of amorphous anonymity, but — and this is a big and very important *but* — incredibly versatile, linguistically flexible, technically adept. We have traded off the distinctive leadership voices of the past for a remarkable stylistic and technical diversity and versatility, where, by the way, the emphasis is more and more on composition and the integration of improvisation into composition: Ellington's dream coming to be increasingly realized and demanded.

As a result of this new versatility, an exciting new option in the present jazz scene is the development of the concept of jazz repertory. It is something I have personally been pursuing and doing for about forty years, and it is now beginning to catch on — modestly perhaps — everywhere. It is a concept resisted by some as Eurocentric, rather than Afrocentric, or even as antijazz, but in other quarters recognized as another serious, rewarding, educational, and entertaining option in jazz performance. The fact is that, as a result of the remarkable efforts of hundreds (if not thousands) of gifted jazz musicians, composers, and arrangers over the last six or seven decades, there exists now — and has existed for some time — a huge repertory of jazz masterpieces, a jazz canon, if you will, that is not only worthy of loving, authentic re-creation, but literally cries out for it. For if a music is not kept alive in live performance, if it exists only on recordings or in other archival forms — as wonderful as all those thousands of recordings are — such a music will eventually atrophy and die.

There is much more to be said on the subject of jazz repertory, but I see that I must bring this talk to a close. I hope that I've been able to present to you an overview, with a few tantalizing musical glimpses, of the history and development of jazz in this shamefully short hour and a quarter. I also hope that I may have succeeded in providing some stimulating thoughts here and there that may lead to some lively discussions later on.

II. Duke Ellington

I don't think there can be much argument that Duke Ellington was — or is (however you want to put it) — the greatest, the most important composer in jazz. One can measure that fact in both qualitative and quantitative terms. Ellington composed an enormous amount of music in his lifetime; no one has yet been able to count the number of his works. The estimates are anywhere from over 1,000 to nearly 2,000; probably the former is more realistic. That has Ellington competing, on the quantity front, with Johann Sebastian Bach and Georg Philip Telemann — and Heitor Villa-Lobos. But mere quantity of production is certainly not the relevant issue when it comes to artistic creativity; it is the *quality* of the work that counts, and there Ellington ranks supreme in jazz history thus far. (The only possible other contender being Charles Mingus, whose work I will discuss in the third lecture in this series.) For among those many hundreds of Ellington compositions, many of them multimovement suites, there are, especially in the early period (say, from 1927 to about 1947), a vast number of what one can rightly call masterpieces, masterworks, compositions totally original in conception and realization — often original and unique not only in jazz, but in music in general — and, beyond that, *in* their originality almost always some ten to twenty years ahead of anyone else in the field of jazz.

Ellington was that rarity in jazz: a true composer. He was not merely an arranger or a tunesmith, a composer of popular songs (although he wrote a fair share of those too: "Sophisticated Lady," "Solitude," "Satin Doll"). From the outset, even in his earliest composition in the mid-to-late 1920s, one can hear his ability to create wholly original ideas and forms that went way beyond the idea of a mere functional dance music: rather, his music was coherent and through-composed and meant to be listened to. *If* it could serve several functions — as composition, as music to be danced to, as music accompanying dramatic tableaux or skits — so much the better; but his real interest from the outset lay in the direction of pure composition.

There was very little precedent for that in the mid-1920s: Jelly Roll Morton, perhaps, on the jazz side (as in his ragtime-inspired pieces), and George Gershwin on the more classical side (as in his *Rhapsody in Blue* of 1924). There was in those works and in Ellington's early works (many of them co-composed with his trumpet player, Bubber Miley) an exploration of musical ideas that went beyond the basic 32-bar standard song and the 12-bar blues forms of the day, including new phrase structurings, new, more advanced harmonies, structural, dynamic, and orchestrational, sonoric contrasts, and early, very simple, attempts at varying or developing the musical or thematic materials.

Bubber Miley was already an accomplished and quite famous blues player at the time and in some of those early co-authored pieces, such as "Black and Tan Fantasy," "East St. Louis Toodle-oo," and "The Mooche," one can hear the quite different approaches to musical creativity that Miley and Ellington represented. Ellington came from a piano ragtime and Broadway Musical show background, whereas Miley came from a by then already venerable blues and brass playing tradition. While one can readily hear and separate the two men's contributions in those early pieces—Miley's music earthy, harmonically simple yet saturated with blue notes; Ellington's music "smart," more harmonically sophisticated, rather removed from any blues or collective ensemble conceptions, as in New Orleans jazz. And yet somehow these pieces have a high degree of coherence and unity. Some of that derives from the integrity of the performance, the way the various members of Ellington's ten-piece band listened to each other, reaching out sonorically to each other, bridging the gaps between the diverse stylistic elements of the pieces.

I might as well mention right now at the outset that when one speaks of Ellington's music, one has to include as co-creators the musicians in his orchestra, as unique and yet as varied a collection of players as has ever been assembled in music — music of *any* kind. There are several points to be made in this respect. First, the players in Ellington's band — especially from the early 1930s on, when the orchestra's size grew to fourteen with the addition of the great trombonist Lawrence Brown — were each highly individual, totally distinctive musical voices, creative artists in their own rights, in respect to both their individual sound and their styling and phrasing. You could not mistake one player for another, yet — and this is point two — when these players were required to play ensemble in sections or various orchestrational groupings, they would sound as one, so perfectly blended that often you couldn't — you still can't — tell who is playing what part.

This feature of the Ellington canon — what Billy Strayhorn, his longtime composing partner, called the "Ellington effect" — is so endemic to the character of his music that it is worth dwelling upon for a moment or two. A prime example of this chameleonlike ability to change colors, to subjugate their individual sounds and styles to a larger unity, was the trombone section of "Tricky Sam" Nanton, Juan Tizol, and Lawrence Brown. Never have there been three more divergent playing styles than those of these three players. "Tricky Sam" played with a rough, countrified, blues style and sound, including a complete mastery of the so-called plunger/growl technique, using the simple bathroom plunger as a mute and using a throat flutter to produce the growl. Nanton could literally talk on his trombone; hence his name, "Tricky Sam." You had the definite sense that he was speaking words on his trombone, much in the manner, incidentally, in which a lot of West African music is speechified music or musicalized speech, a tradition that is also perpetuated in scat singing. Nanton played with a full rich — almost thick — baritonal sound and tone, with no vibrato. He also had a limited range, barely more than an octave, and curiously — unlike any jazz trombonist of his day — that octave was positioned in the very upper range of his instrument, from middle B♭ to high D and E♭. Furthermore, it was as if that octave-plus register was permanently nailed or screwed into his embouchure, because the man in some twenty years of playing with Ellington almost never missed or cracked a note. And it is in the high range where a brass player is most likely to miss notes. Well, not Nanton! He could play for hours in the upper range and never tire — again the upper range is, apart from being treacherous, physically very tiring. But not for Nanton!

So here we have this stentorian, rough-hewn colossus, Nanton, but next to him Juan Tizol, totally different, a Puerto Rican who played, as in Italian town bands, a valve trombone. Indeed, Tizol had grown up in the Italian band tradition and style of playing that had been imported from Italy to all Latin and South America and was prevalent in the entire region. A striking feature of that style, in total contrast to "Tricky Sam," was a light, thinnish tone, a great deal of agility on the instrument, and — again in total contrast to Nanton — a pronounced, vivid, fast vibrato. When I first started playing the horn as a teenager, I used to play in the Italian parades in "Little Italy" in downtown Manhattan, and we non-Italian musicians from uptown used to call the Italian wind players' vibrato a "nanny goat" vibrato. That should give you an idea of that sound and style, and the manner in which Tizol played, although he did this with great elegance and sensitivity, unlike some of those Manhattanite Italians of my youth. Furthermore, with his valve trombone Tizol could do things that you simply cannot do on a slide trombone. And did Ellington ever exploit that special capacity, even to the extent of setting certain pieces in certain keys that were perfect for fast runs and technical manipulation on a valve trombone but either horrendous or downright impossible on the slide trombone! (The famous "Koko" from 1940 is a case in point. It is in E♭ minor and the main theme contains a low C♭ which is easy to negotiate on the valve trombone, cumbersome or virtually impossible to negotiate on the slide trombone.) Ellington also often used Tizol as a third or fourth saxophone, so perfectly blended that it takes a really keen ear to note that there is a trombone in the midst of those saxophones.

The third member of that stellar trombone section and the last one to join to make it a trio — in 1932 — was Lawrence Brown. Here again, one cannot imagine a player and personality more different from Tizol or Nanton. Brown was ultimately the most all-around talent of the three. He was the lead trombone, he was a great lyric player — the only comparison that might be made in that respect would be with Tommy Dorsey — but he could also, as the occasion demanded, be a "hot" player, with technical virtuosity to burn, and was almost as good with mutes and plungers as Nanton, although that was not his preference. As a youngster, Brown had wanted to play the cello. But that meant playing in a symphony orchestra or a classical group of some kind, and in the 1920s and 1930s that was simply a social and professional impossibility. Black musicians definitely were not allowed to enter those sacred white musical precincts.

Lawrence Brown, out of his own innate talents and in answer to his repressed cellistic ambitions, simply turned to one of the nearest sonoric neighbors to the cello, the trombone, and in his playing it virtually became a cello. He loved to play the trombone with a singing, lyric style and sound, an elegance of phrasing and articulation, that was clearly derived from the concept of the cello — or a string instrument in any case — and he brought into jazz a unique voice that had never been heard there before. In the

1920s and early 1930s trombonists had to be "hot" players: loud, boisterous, mostly rough, at times technically virtuosic, but never elegant, songful, romantic. Even Tommy Dorsey played "hot" trombone well into the mid-1930s and wasn't, by the way, very good at it. He later *did* become one of the greatest lyric players of all time, but Brown was there some time before him.

So here you have these three totally divergent and distinct musical personalities, whose uniqueness Ellington certainly exploited time and time again — and let me add that no other band in the land had anything remotely comparable — and yet, when called upon to blend together into a refined, balanced ensemble trio, these three could do so instantaneously. Apart from occasional intonational problems, their ensemble playing over a period of ten years or so was as perfect as any in any symphony orchestra; indeed, I would say better.

The same could be said about the two other sections in Ellington's orchestra: the trumpets and saxophones — again unique, distinctive personalities who nonetheless could be instantly integrated into perfect ensembles. Ellington's four-man rhythm section took a little longer to homogenize and integrate. That didn't really occur until Billy Taylor and Jimmy Blanton (especially the latter), both bass players, came along in the late 1930s.

The point to be made here — and this is my third point regarding the Ellington band and the symbiotic relationship between Ellington and his musicians — is that this aggregation of players did not come about by chance or accident. These players were individually *chosen* by Ellington — and chosen *for* their diversity. Any other band leader would have chosen — and did choose — section players of *like* style, of *like* sound, of *like* musical conceptions. Not Ellington. As a potentially gifted visual artist — in his youth he had shown a great talent for painting and design — he carried over into his music an extraordinary sense for the tone colors, the specific sonorities, of instruments. And to enrich that coloristic orchestral palette, Ellington with unerring acuity picked his players precisely to give him the sonoric range that his musical imagination demanded.

The fourth point about Ellington and his orchestra is that, although he was a pianist — and a remarkable one — his real instrument was his orchestra. By hook or crook, in good times and bad times, he kept his orchestra going, often at his own personal financial expense. When there was no work for the orchestra, he paid his musicians out of his own pocket, realizing that if he didn't do so, sooner or later the musicians would be tempted to seek work elsewhere and he would lose them forever.

Ellington maintained an orchestra for nearly fifty years, right up to his death in 1974. This was unique in the history of jazz and can be compared with only a few situations in classical music, such as the relationship between Joseph Haydn and his Esterhazy orchestra, or Johann Sebastian Bach and his St. Thomas church musical forces in Leipzig. This longevity of relationship allowed Ellington to build, to experiment, to explore musical ideas and concepts on a virtually daily basis. In effect, anything he would write during the night, or on a given day, he could hear rehearsed the next morning. Not only that: his players would bring *their* creative input to the work — with Ellington, to be sure, the final arbiter in accepting, rejecting, or modifying such input. So from the outset there was an artistic, creative, collective collaboration at the basis of Ellington's compositional efforts, from which both sides learned and profited reciprocally. Of course, as Ellington's own creative powers grew, the direct influence on him from some of his players — such as Bubber Miley or Barney Bigard in the early days — waned, and Ellington certainly became increasingly the dominant creative force.

In 1927, by a fluke, Ellington and his band were hired by the Cotton Club in Harlem, the biggest and most successful club of its kind featuring black musical talent. They were so successful that they stayed on not for one week, but for three *years*. I have often referred to this engagement as a gigantic workshop period for Ellington. The financial and physical stability — no constant traveling was necessary — and the consistent daily opportunity to practice, rehearse, compose, experiment, hone and refine, all while being gainfully employed, represented a tremendous opportunity for Ellington. There is no question that this long-term engagement played a significant role in Ellington's and the band's development and allowed his genius to flower steadily, to flourish in an unprecedented way.

As one sifts through the more than two hundred recordings Ellington made in that Cotton Club period, one sees — hears — Ellington *the composer* emerge increasingly. Little by little, piece by piece, phrase by phrase, he assembled, as it were, an original musical language, style, orchestrational skills, explorations in form and continuity, that led to ideas and concepts never heard before in jazz — or for that matter in any kind of music — and he soon began to reach beyond the then-known confines and category of jazz.

It is a little bit absurd to try to deal with the immensity and quality and importance of Ellington's output in one simple hour. One just has to leave out too many great pieces, moments — leave too many things unsaid. But if we begin now to hop around a bit through Ellington's huge catalogue, we will very early come upon a now famous piece that represents a major musical breakthrough and, in fact, turned out to be Ellington's first big hit, financial and popular. That composition is "Mood Indigo" (from 1930).

At the Cotton Club Ellington had begun to create and work in five categories of pieces, some virtually forced upon him by the nature of the shows that the Cotton Club presented. There were numbers for dancing, that is, for the club's customers' dancing; then the *de rigueur* performance (and therefore orchestral arrangement, often "recomposition") of the constantly changing popular songs of the day, most coming from Broadway musical shows; third, there were the club's production numbers, for the chorus line and other entertainment acts (dancers, jugglers, fire eaters, etc.). The Cotton Club presented tableaux and skits that were intended to reflect life back in "darkest Africa," in the jungle, of tribal rituals and dances — all for the entertainment and, I assume they thought, edification of the *white* clientele that frequented the club. Slumming in Harlem was the most exciting entertainment you could find in those days, and only whites were allowed into this gangster-owned club; blacks were allowed only as hired help, including Ellington and his musicians and the beautiful leggy dancers. So Ellington, with the incalculable help of Bubber Miley and "Tricky Sam" Nanton, the two "plunger/growl" experts, developed a whole new musical genre, which soon came to be known as the "jungle style."

As a fourth category, there were the "mood" or "blue" pieces, written mostly for the quieter choreographic tableaux or displays; and fifth — Ellington's own vision — straightforward, "absolute" compositions that may have had a functional role at the club but that were meant to be primarily instrumental compositions, to be heard and listened to for their *musical* content, musical "tone poems," as it were.

To this latter category belongs "Mood Indigo." Apart from its utter simplicity, economy, stylistic integrity, and perfection — no foreign elements intruding here (as in some earlier Ellington pieces) — the most remarkable thing about the piece — and the reason I call it an innovative breakthrough — is that here Ellington took a venerable, almost ancient and worn-out musical convention and turned it into a wholly fresh, new idea and sound. For several decades in jazz the traditional New Orleans formation had featured a so-called frontline of trumpet, clarinet, and trombone. In this constellation, unalterably maintained, the trumpet played the tune, occasionally slightly embellished, but always recognizable as the main melody; the clarinet played high-register obbligatos, descant lines, above and around the trumpet; and the trombone gave off with baritone-register asides and commentaries, in part responding to the trumpet.

In "Mood Indigo" Ellington took that formation and in effect turned it upside down, putting the clarinet in its rich earthy *chalumeau* register on the bottom, keeping the trumpet where it was in

New Orleans jazz, but putting the trombone high up near the trumpet — here Nanton's high-register abilities come to the fore — and putting plungers or cup mutes on the brass, thus creating a brand new velvety, lyrical sound and instrumental color that had never before been heard in jazz and, beyond that, in any music whatsoever. A small radical breakthrough — and musical miracle. Later, soft brass, a low-register clarinet "solo," and three-part clarinet harmonizations complete the tone picture. Let us listen to "Mood Indigo" [Ellington: "Mood Indigo"].

This mood piece — "blue" piece — the Germans called such things *Character stücke* — became the first of a whole series of similar Ellington works — dozens of them — with names such as "Blue Tune," "Blue Light," "Subtle Lament," "Dusk," "On a Turquoise Cloud." Another such work, from 1937, is called "Azure" — note always the reference to the color blue. Here, seven years after "Mood Indigo," Ellington has expanded and enriched his orchestral palette and, even more importantly, has passed through harmonic bitonality and polytonality to the very edge of atonality. In "Azure," you hear combined Ellington's most unique gifts: his ear for sonority (tone color) and his fantastic ear for harmony [Ellington: "Azure"].

Another type of composition is represented by "Daybreak Express," dating from 1933, an extraordinarily early date, as you will hear, for such an outstanding jazz composition, not only remarkable *as* a composition but as a virtuosic performance *tour de force*. It is, again, a tone poem, depicting in sometimes very vivid, realistic sounds an express train ride in the early 1930s, in the days of steam engines (long before diesels), ingeniously capturing the train whistle sounds, the clickety-clack of the tracks, as the train hurtles through the countryside, the acceleration of the train as it leaves the station and slowing down when arriving at the next station, the strange wheezing sounds that locomotives used to make in those days, sixty years ago, and in the midst of all this a spectacular virtuosic four-way saxophone ensemble-chorus.

Another interesting aspect of the piece is that once the train has gathered full speed — after the introduction — Ellington builds his composition, very modern for its time, on *another* piece and chord progression, one as venerable as you could find in jazz — namely, the famous "Tiger Rag." Thus a brand new composition is built on the harmonic skeleton of a very old one [Ellington: "Daybreak Express"].

One cannot speak about Ellington's many wondrous achievements without mentioning the fact that from his very early days onward, he felt the constraints and artistic restrictions of the ten-inch 78 RPM disk to which jazz was relegated, permitting only three minutes of music per side, as very confining and limiting. (Classical music had the twelve-inch disk, with four minutes and twenty seconds of music available on each side.) Ellington soon overcame this limitation to become in time the greatest composer of three-minute miniature forms. But, at other times, he rebelled against this (as he saw it) limitation and stigmatization and soon found ways to expand and extend the forms and durations of his pieces. The first simple steps in this direction were taken in the recording of "Tiger Rag" (in 1929) and his "Creole Rhapsody" (in 1931), both presented on two sides of a ten-inch disk, thus comprising some six minutes of music — although you still had to turn the record over, of course, causing an unavoidable interruption of the music.

In 1935 we come to two major Ellington breakthroughs in extended form: a fifteen-minute film music, called *Symphony in Black*, and the fourteen-minute *Reminiscing in Tempo*, which was presented on *four* ten-inch sides. Whereas *Symphony in Black* was still a loosely strung-together sequence of separate musical episodes, geared, of course, to the film that it accompanied, *Reminiscing in Tempo* was a completely through-composed fourteen-minute work, which, remarkably, featured *no* improvisation. (Ironically and ludicrously, the executives at Columbia Records insisted on calling the piece a "Fox-Trot," printing as much on the label on each of the four sides.) Moreover, unlike any other extended Ellington works, it is a single movement work built as a series of variations on a main theme and two lesser transitional episodes. It is to be noted that thematic variation was something unheard of in jazz in those days — it didn't begin to make a really serious appearance in jazz until some twenty to twenty-five years later with players like Lester Young and Sonny Rollins. Ellington varies not only the main theme and its side motives, but some of the integral accompanimental material and countermelodies, and does so with a thoroughness almost comparable to that of Brahms — of whose work I am sure, by the way, Ellington knew nothing at the time.

There are fourteen variations in *Reminiscing in Tempo*, which are played without interruption and which (as one can readily imagine) cause the piece to undergo many tonal modulations, reaching into keys like D major and A major, keys that were unheard of in jazz at the time and that, incidentally, gave his musicians considerable trouble, especially in intonation, causing a kind of subtle discomfort being removed from the safe, tried-and-true keys of B♭, F, and E♭. Indeed, the highpoint and structural and emotional climax of the piece is in A major, but just barely, because it is polytonal, a powerful mixture of three keys—A major, C major, and F♯ major. But even in its less-than-perfect performance, *Reminiscing* exudes a powerful, deep, even weighty, tragic emotional quality, which was simply light-years removed from what anyone else was doing in jazz, not only at that time but for years and decades to come.

Ellington found in *Reminiscing in Tempo*, written in mourning after the death of his mother, to whom he was *very* close, a depth and power of expression that went way beyond the conventions and short-term entertainment values of the jazz of that time [Ellington: *Reminiscing in Tempo*].

Now a masterpiece from 1940, called "Cotton Tail," again a new composition built on an earlier piece, in this case — like hundreds if not several thousand pieces in the evolution of jazz, not just by Ellington but hundreds of other arrangers and composers — superimposed on the famous changes of Gershwin's "I Got Rhythm." Here we have a totally matured integration of "solo" and composition, the solo in this case by the great tenor saxophonist Ben Webster, for a year or so a member of Ellington's band. Also one must mention the perfect integration of the rhythm section here, featuring the then newly acquired nineteen-year-old bass player, Jimmy Blanton. He and Webster, both from the Southwest, brought a new kind of deeper, earthier swing and drive to the Ellington band, exemplified here at its best. In fact, because of the tremendous impact these two players had on the Ellington band and Ellington's compositions, that orchestra has often been referred to in this 1940 period as the "Webster/Blanton band" — high and just praise, indeed.

Among the many musical wonders of this piece and its performance, you might note that the original theme Ellington composes here, heard right at the outset, seems to be in C minor, when actually the piece turns out to be in B♭ major. It is just one of many such melodic/harmonic sleight-of-hand tricks Ellington played so often [Ellington: "Cotton Tail"].

And some people said the Ellington band didn't/couldn't swing. What a laugh!

I'd like to jump now another seven years to 1947 and have us listen to a most remarkable Ellington piece, "The Clothed Woman." It is primarily a piano-solo vehicle for Ellington, the composer-pianist (or pianist-composer), in a simple ABA form, the contents of which are, however, anything but simple, ordinary, or conventional. The A sections, played mostly on the piano alone, venture into the modern land of atonality (or in any case post-tonal music) *and* into free rhythm, free meter, unrhymed music, as it were. The B section, by the wildest of contrasts, harks back to ragtime and a simple, bouncy, early piano jazz that Ellington had learned in his youth from Willie "The Lion" Smith and Fats Waller. But even in its elderly style, this B section somehow receives a modern touch from Ellington, an elegant sophistication, and, more amazingly, seems to integrate at a certain high level with the modern, free-association A sections that enclose it [Ellington: "The Clothed Woman"].

The final work I would like to present — and leave you with — goes back to another form or genre that Ellington helped to develop, as did his players: the small group, sextet, or septet — the combo, as it is often known. Ellington and some of his men began in 1937 and 1938 to record in small groups, primarily to feature some of his great players, like Hodges or Williams, in a kind of chamber setting. At various times in the long career of the band (with its changing personnel) Ellington returned to this small format — here in a piece curiously titled "Where's the Music," dating from 1958. It features Clark Terry on trumpet, John Sanders on valve trombone, Jimmy Hamilton on clarinet, Johnny Hodges on alto, and Ellington's at the time guitarless rhythm section.

I think I would like to have Ellington's wonderful, soulful, bluesish music have the last word [Ellington: "Where's the Music"].

III. CHARLES MINGUS

If Ellington is, as I suggested earlier, the greatest and most important composer in jazz — "composer" in the full traditional sense of the word — then the nearest contender, at least in my view, is Charles Mingus. Again, as with Ellington, there is extraordinary creative quality and originality as well as quantity, the latter not of the magnitude of Ellington, but still representing remarkably rich oeuvre and full catalogue.

I want to concentrate initially in this talk on Mingus the composer, but later also on Mingus the brilliant bass player and performer/band leader. But a few details about his life might still be in order — a life as varied and complicated as any one can think of in the realm of music, except perhaps for Carlo Gesualdo. Although one cannot necessarily believe everything contained in

Mingus's autobiography — which is in any case an incomplete and expurgated version of the complete Urtext — his life was, to say the least, a colorful, hectic, problematic one, which ran a wide gamut of human activities, from the noblest to the most degrading. Mingus became embroiled, like one of his idols, Jelly Roll Morton, in many of the seedier sides of life, everything from pimping and gambling, drug pushing, and street pugilism to joining street gangs — mostly as a kind of self-defense for surviving in Watts (the Los Angeles ghetto) — all the way to the loftiest forms of artistic creativity as a musician, poet, writer, and musical entrepreneur. In a parallel to his life, Mingus had a volatile temperament that could lead from one explosive extreme to another. I knew Mingus very well and can testify to the fact that he was at times a Jekyll and Hyde, a devil and an angel: one day as sweet and harmless as a little baby, the next day losing all control in terrifying, temperamental outbursts and physical assaults. Many musicians — Max Roach and Jimmy Knepper are the most famous among them — felt the wrath of his anger and capacity for physical violence. He would vacillate between feelings of high exuberance on the one hand and total depression on the other. He felt deep down that he was a hunted man, oppressed by his environment, and his feelings of vulnerability and hurt were often converted into uncontrollable rage and tyrannical behavior to others — at times even those closest to him.

I say all this not as a bit of amateur psychologizing, let alone as an attempt at character assassination, but rather because Mingus's music in its vast emotional range reflects all these varied sides of his personality — in all its extremes, from the most gentle and lyrical to the most violent and enraged. As he once said of himself, "I am a mongrel musician who plays beautiful, who plays ugly, who plays lovely, who plays masculine, who plays feminine — who plays all sounds, loud, soft — who plays music."

Mingus was born in Nogales, Arizona, in 1922, but grew up in the Watts area of Los Angeles. He showed a great interest in music at an early age, particularly in the cello, but after realizing that his aspiration to play in the Los Angeles Philharmonic could not be satisfied under the existing social conditions and racial climate, he took up the larger relative of the cello, the double bass, studying both classical music and jazz bass, the one with a member of the Los Angeles Philharmonic, the other with Red Callender, one of the bass stalwarts of the Los Angeles jazz scene. Mingus also studied with Lloyd Reese, a much-sought-after teacher, arranger, composer, and trumpet player (in the Les Hite orchestra). But Mingus seems additionally to have studied the more advanced classical contemporary music of the time, of Béla Bartók, Arnold Schönberg, and Igor Stravinsky, at a time (in the late 1930s), be it noted, when the two first-named composers' works were still virtually unknown and unperformed in the United States. Some of Mingus's earliest compositions reflect this interest in and considerable knowledge of contemporary classical music, for which he, however, as a black musician could find very little professional outlet.

In and out of music at various times, Mingus worked with many bands as a bass player sideman — such as Barney Bigard, Louis Armstrong, Lionel Hampton — as well as leading his own *ad hoc* groups. For Hampton, he wrote and recorded in 1947 one of his early experiments in nontraditional forms, *Mingus Fingers*, a kind of virtuoso "Concerto for bass and jazz orchestra," a complex, partly atonal work, which greatly puzzled Hampton and his musicians, resulting in a far from adequate or satisfactory recorded performance [Mingus: *Mingus Fingers*].

Mingus soon attracted a great deal of attention as a new breed of bass virtuoso, especially when he was heard and recorded with the Red Norvo Trio. In 1950 Mingus settled in New York, working with such greats as Art Tatum, Charlie Parker, Dizzy Gillespie, and Stan Getz.

He soon formed what he called "Jazz Workshop sessions," surrounding himself with many of the bright young talents of the early 1950s. Here he began to experiment — almost in the Ellingtonian sense — with new and extended forms in jazz, advanced harmonic explorations, radically new and original ways of structuring improvisations (including bringing back collective ensemble improvisations); blurring the lines (i.e., by way of integration) between composition and improvisation; experimenting with extended pedal point and/or modal (i.e., nondiatonic) improvisations, sporadically abjuring writing out his compositions and instead dictating them line by line, almost note by note, to his musicians, and leading his groups not by conducting but from the bass by shouting, singing, haranguing.

With works such as *Pithecanthropus Erectus*, *Faubus Fables*, *Meditations on Integration*, and *Mr. Jelly Roll Soul*, Mingus developed both a dramatic side to his music and a political edge, often resulting in biting musical satire and social/political commentary, as in the series of *Faubus* (the infamous governor of Arkansas of the late 1950s and early 1960s) pieces.

In 1960 Mingus teamed up with Eric Dolphy, and those two, along with drummer Dannie Richmond, became virtually inseparable, also touring a great deal in Europe. After Dolphy's death in 1964, Mingus withdrew for some years from public life, suffering from depression and severe financial problems.

A Guggenheim Fellowship and the publication of his autobiography in 1971 revived Mingus's creative spirits. He traveled again with his "Workshop" — a new crop of musicians now, including John Handy, the late George Adams, and his longtime associate Jimmy Knepper — but in 1977 he fell seriously ill and, partially paralyzed, was confined to a wheelchair for the rest of his life. Mingus died in January 1979.

I haven't mentioned Mingus's *magnum opus*, *Epitaph*, a nineteen-movement nearly two and a half hour work for a 31-piece jazz orchestra, which remained mostly unperformed during his lifetime, but which I had the privilege of posthumously bringing to life, to acoustical reality, in 1989.

Because I was involved with *Epitaph* not only as the conductor of the premiere and the next thirty or so performances in the United States and Europe, but also as editor of the score from Mingus's manuscript, I would like to tell some of the history of the piece and to comment on certain aspects and movements of the work.

Unperformed in Mingus's lifetime, as I said, the score to *Epitaph* was found, quite by accident, some six years after his death, after resting peacefully for years in a box in a closet in his widow's apartment. The music was discovered by Andrew Homzy, the excellent Canadian jazz musicologist, who had been hired by Mrs. Mingus — Susan — to catalogue all of Charles's existing musical manuscripts.

Mingus seems rarely to have talked about *Epitaph* — and then only in cryptic, embittered terms. He once said to Susan: "I've been writing this big, goddamn symphony, but it'll never be played"; on another occasion, "that's music for my tombstone" — hence *Epitaph*.

The work is clearly inspired by and, in a way, a retroactive tribute to Duke Ellington, not at all in style or language — that is entirely Mingus's own — but in the concept of extended form and a multimovement work of "symphonic" proportions. An interesting sidelight to this aspect of Mingus's work is the fact that he discovered Ellington rather late, not until the mid-1940s. Oddly enough, he had studied Bartók, Schönberg, Stravinsky, and Maurice Ravel, but not much Ellington. He had written atonal, free-form pieces such as "Chill of Death" (he also gave it its German title, "Todeskälte") in 1939 and "Half-Mast Inhibition" in 1940, quite a few years before his immersion in Ellington's music and large-scale works. Mingus, who was not averse to making exaggerated claims — he often claimed that he had played in as advanced a style as Ornette Coleman years *before* Coleman, that is, in the early 1940s — may have embellished the truth somewhat in regard to the early creation of "Chill of Death" and "Half-Mast Inhibition."

What is more likely is that he first began to conceive of a piece like "Chill of Death" in 1939 and completed it over a period of time during the next decade. What argues for this scenario is that "Chill of Death" in its first version was more in a classical contemporary vein and also lacking in any form of jazz improvisation; what argues against this scenario is that none of Mingus's other known early works ("This Subdues My Passion," "Weird Nightmare," "Shuffle Bass Boogie") have any of the characteristics and originality of conception heard in "Chill of Death." The work was shelved and not heard again until forty years later in the premiere of *Epitaph*.

I don't think anyone really knows over what span of time this gigantic eighteen-movement work was written, nor when all the individual movements were composed. Indeed we may never know the full details of *Epitaph*'s creation. Some sections — "Better Get It in Your Soul," "Freedom," "Peggy's Blue Skylight" — were composed in the late 1950s and early 1960s and are, in fact, known to us in other versions for smaller instrumentations (his Jazz Workshop quintets, sextets, septets) and then rescored and expanded for *Epitaph*. Others seem to have been composed specifically for *Epitaph* — pieces like "O.P.," "Monk, Bunk & Vice Versa (Osmotin')" — and later played in small group versions. Still other *Epitaph* movements, such as "Main Score," "The Children's Hour of Dream," and certain originally untitled pieces, were surely conceived directly for the 31-piece ensemble.

But taking all we do know (or seem to know) into account, and taking the magnitude of the work, its ambitious grand plan, its vision and scope into consideration, my best guess is that Mingus worked on *Epitaph* intermittently over a period of many years — say, between the early or mid-1940s and 1962.

The manuscript score of *Epitaph* was discovered, as I mentioned, by Andrew Homzy in 1985, written mostly in Mingus's own hand, with many pages smudged, frayed, worn, and torn and as a result in some places virtually illegible. Upon closer inspection, the score, despite its 3,446 continuous measures — a stack of pages a foot high — seemed not to be entirely complete. For example, it seemed not to have any ultimate ending, and some short sections existed only in verbal description. Moreover, whatever instrumental parts may have existed (especially those for the abortive 1962 Town Hall concert and United Artists recording session) had all but disappeared. With no usable set of parts extant and only a far from presentable score to work with, it was immediately clear to Mrs. Mingus and me that before a performance of *Epitaph* could ever take place, the score would require extensive editing, occasional reconstructing, and even, in some movements, some construction and completing.

This is certainly not the appropriate place to list in detail all the editorial and reconstructive decisions that had to be made to make *Epitaph* performable. But a brief summary of the types or categories of editings is probably in order: (1) Apart from deciphering the often illegible manuscript, the correction of obvious note errors or inadvertent note misspellings (many of these by other copyists); (2) renotation of Mingus's many idiosyncratic rhythmic notations; (3) the correction of many faulty octave positions (particularly in timpani, trombone, and bass parts); (4) determining the use of percussion instruments, left mostly unspecified by Mingus; (5) resolving the profusion of shortcut "col" indications, many of which were technically impossible or unclear; (6) adding or reconciling discrepancies of dynamics and phrasings; (7) clarifying the numerous doubling requirements in the nine-piece reed section; (8) determining the ultimate sequence of movements, which, despite Mingus's consecutive numbering of all the measures — up to 3,446 — and because of many contradictory verbal instructions, remained in many respects unclear and confusing in the score; and finally (9) creating an ending for the entire work, alluded to only rather cryptically (verbally) in the manuscript.

Obviously, as was his wont in performing his music, Mingus would have resolved all of these questions in rehearsals, fleshing out missing parts or sections, refining balances, dynamics, phrasings, and many other performing details, directing and inspiring his musicians in performance with his bass playing and shouted instructions. Mingus was masterful at eliciting from his musicians the precise sound and character and mood he heard (and required) in his pieces, beyond the limited capacity of musical notation.

I regarded it as an honor and privilege to have edited and prepared *Epitaph* for performance, a truly awesome task, which I approached not only with profound reverence and respect for Mingus's creative talent, but also with an intimate knowledge of his music and performance practices, based on a close and extensive twenty-five-year professional association with him.

The first movement of *Epitaph*, its primary position unequivocally indicated by Mingus and confirmed by his titling, "Main Score," sets the tone for the entire work. The remarkable gutsy sound, driving energy, and powerful punctuations we hear at the beginning of the movement represent a substantial quotation of an earlier major work, Mingus's 1956 *Pithecanthropus Erectus*, here reorchestrated for the much larger 31-piece ensemble. Adding a particular excitement to the music is the prominent timpani part, imparting ominous subterranean rumblings to the music (incidentally, much of it originally written an octave too low by Mingus). The dark mixture of low brass and low reeds — a favorite Mingus sound — reinforces the sombre yet urgent, propulsive character of the music. Indeed, *Epitaph* is full of low-register sounds of incredible density and overtone-rich complexity, amassing instruments such as tuba, two bass trombones, contrabass-clarinet, baritone sax, bowed bass, timpani into powerful tonal conglomerates. Let us hear the opening section of *Epitaph* [excerpt from "Main Score"].

The second movement, "Percussion Discussion," was conceived originally in 1955 as a virtuoso drums-and-bass duet for Mingus himself and Max Roach. For *Epitaph*, "Percussion Discussion" was expanded and elaborated into a substantial work for a 10-piece ensemble of brass, saxes, and rhythm. It is one of the more unusual pieces in *Epitaph*, more in the realm of "Third Stream" music, in that much of the piece, although jazz related, is in a modern classical and atonal vein, involving very few typical jazz structures but instead many tempo and meter changes.

A lugubrious-sounding opening marked "very slow, ad lib. with expression" for tuba and bowed string bass, soon joined by piano and baritone saxophone, sets the essentially stern mood of this piece. Much of its discourse pits the rhythm section against terse sustained harmonies in the "horns." Eventually improvised bass/drum duets and alternating solos emerge. Then suddenly the music bursts joyously into full swing, dispelling the previous sombre mood ["Percussion Discussion"].

We skip now to the fourth movement, called "Started," based on Vernon Duke's great classic "I Can't Get Started," a song that Mingus dearly loved and played — improvised upon — hundreds of times in his life. Here in *Epitaph*, he conceives it as a gigantic series of variations, virtually a monumental classical *passacaglia*, conceived on a truly grand scale. I don't know of anything quite as ambitious in jazz, certainly not prior to 1962, and it is hard to think of anything since then of similar scope. Designed in eight long 32-bar choruses, plus an expansively complex, bursting-at-the-musical-seams coda, at a moderately slow ballad tempo the piece lasts upward of a staggering sixteen minutes. But in our world-premiere recorded performance we cut two and a half choruses (nearly five minutes). It may draw a smile from the listener when Mingus late in "Started," in the space of only six bars, quotes Anton Dvořák's *Humoresque*, Aram Khatchaturian's *Gayne* ballet "Saber Dance," David Rose's *Holiday for Strings*, and the ever-popular bugle favorite "Reveille." A little later he quotes—though almost hidden in the densely opaque sonorities — Ellington's *Reminiscing in Tempo*. As the movement progresses, and the gradually thickening textures preclude any individual "solos" from projecting above the orchestra, Mingus adds more and more layers of thick harmonies; all sense of Vernon Duke's tune and its "changes" are gone, buried in a veritable avalanche of atonal counterpoint. An almost agonizing chaotic outcry is suddenly, unexpectedly relieved by a brief cadenza of massive atonal held chords: the music has moved suddenly from polyphonic chaos to homophonic solidarity. The previous chaotic music returns briefly, only to lead this time to a quietly sad ending in five muted trumpets and low brass instruments, coming to rest on a tonally ambiguous final chord. Obviously we don't have time here to play even the full eleven minutes of "Started," but I would like you to hear the amazing sixth chorus and coda [excerpts from "Started"].

Skipping to the eighth movement, "Self Portrait/Chill of Death," we find what is in some ways Mingus's most original creation in *Epitaph*. Its basic premise is that during its multivaried course, some of it on the outer borderline of jazz, every one — literally every one — of the thirty-one musicians will have had several chances to "solo," to improvise, and thus significantly contribute to the final outcome of the piece. But even more unusual is the idea that most of these solos are very brief: four measures, six measures, three and a half measures, and so on, although a few are much longer. The uniqueness of this conception lies in the fact that this vast scattering of different-length and differently placed solos across the eleven minutes of this piece produces a complex, ever-changing kaleidoscope of instrumental textures and colors. Solos come and go at a rapid rate, more often than not overlapping with each other, and in highly varied combinations, everything from a single solo line to (at several points) as many as nine soloists improvising simultaneously. It is as if Mingus not only wanted to have improvisation lend a looseness, a sense of spontaneity, to the piece's continuity, but wanted even the point and order in which these improvisations occurred to be random and improvisatory — the improvisatory element built into the very architecture and structural fabric of the work.

As complex as this overall design of solos is structurally, the underlying harmonic scheme is all the more simple, consisting mostly of prolonged pedal points in stationary harmonies. The contrast between these long harmonic expanses and the constantly busy, variable network of epigrammatic solos is a stroke of genius and makes this piece one of the most visionary and daring in conception in all of jazz [excerpts from "Self Portrait/Chill of Death"].

I'd like to make a big jump now to movement 14, "The Children's Hour of Dreams." This piece is certainly in some respects again one of the more unusual movements in *Epitaph*. It contains absolutely no improvisation, makes no attempt to swing, is indeed more contemporary classical than jazz (but acquires a certain jazz feeling by being performed by jazz players with their natural jazz inflections), and, finally, is built formally on the structural principle, first explored by such composers as Stravinsky and Edgard Varèse, of composing a number of relatively short segments of music — themes, ideas, phrases — and then repeating and manipulating the sequence of these units (eight such separate, distinctive units in "Children's Hour") in constantly changing patterns. Indeed, the work seems to hark back again to Mingus's early studies of classical twentieth-century music by Bartók, Stravinsky, Ravel, and Debussy. At times one hears subtle allusions to the *Sacre du Printemps*. Although in principle I hate to play only a short segment of a piece, since this piece is rather sectionalized and, in a wonderfully cumulative way, repetitive in construction, perhaps a minute or two will suffice [excerpts from "The Children's Hour"].

Now we come to one of the strangest, most puzzling situations in Mingus's *Epitaph*: an originally untitled piece — Susan Mingus and I have now called it "The Underdog Rising," a near-quote from Mingus's autobiography — a piece that almost did not get included in this (or any) *Epitaph* performance. Indeed, as editor I am proud of the fact that I was able to rescue this piece from oblivion, because the condition of this movement in Mingus's manuscript score was so chaotic that not only could no instrumental parts be extracted from it but it seemed that even an intelligible score could not be assembled.

I don't know how it came to pass, but Mingus's score for this piece, as it was left after his death, for some reason contained numerous Scotch-taped partial overlays, which, unfortunately, made no musical sense whatsoever and in no instance fitted with the rest of the given score page. For example, a trumpet section overlay that was pasted onto pages 1–5 could not logically belong on those pages. Similarly, a reed section overlay of *five* bars was pasted onto another score page that, in all other instruments, had only *four* bars. In these and many other misplaced overlays harmonies did not line up vertically, musical ideas did not fit either horizontally or vertically, overlaid passages stopped abruptly and nonsensically, measure numbers in the overlays did not match those on the rest of the page, and so on. It was the strangest and most frustrating musical puzzle I had ever seen.

The thought occurred to me rather soon that I ought to dislodge all the paste-overs to see what was underneath them, hoping to find, presumably, some initial version that Mingus had attempted to revise with the overlays. To my utter surprise the staff lines beneath the overlays were all blank (!) and, therefore, yielded no useful information, not even a clue.

Wishing to trust and respect Mingus's score, I was truly puzzled as to what to make of this incomprehensible hodgepodge. But I was determined to solve the riddle, because I had by now seen that many of the disparate pieces of the puzzle contained remarkable musical ideas and that some of these related back to other movements in *Epitaph*, especially "Main Score." After studying and analyzing the movement for almost three full days, trying to make sense of it and trying to find logical relationships between and among different segments of the score, it dawned on me that Mingus (or somebody) for reasons unknown — whether in a drunken stupor or out of sheer incompetence — must have pasted the various revisions (overlays) onto the wrong pages. I further realized, since there were a dozen of these misplacements, that I would never solve the mystery of this movement unless I actually cut up the score pages into all of the separate fragments — some forty or so snippets of paper — and, as in a picture puzzle, tried to match up the various pieces into a whole that made sense vertically and horizontally, harmonically and melodically.

It took me another two days to accomplish that. Finally not only was I able to line up the separate pieces properly, but I found a logical place for *every* piece, even the minutest scrap — an important clue, I believe, confirming the correctness of my editorial puzzle solving. Modesty compels me to admit that some other solution to the puzzle is theoretically possible and that Mingus may have had something else in mind, differing from my solution. But given all the imponderables of the situation — not even knowing anything about the origin of or reason for the overlays, and until some other better information is forthcoming — my edition will have to stand.

I am happy that I was able to rescue this piece, for it turns out to be one of Mingus's most remarkable creations. Tuba, bass, and contrabass clarinet, set in a very slow tempo and accompanied by bitonal piano and guitar chords, percussion, and low timpani rumblings, create a murky *misterioso* opening atmosphere. Muted trombones in unison add to the gloom and pessimism, but soon bluesish saxophones and woodwinds introduce a mild sense of optimism. Once again, dark timpani rolls keep the music temporarily anchored in the depths. Now a talking "plunger" trombone solo (played by Britt Woodman) — which will dominate the rest of the piece — tries to enliven the mood, but sliding plunger-muted trumpets and sombre saxophone harmonies keep the "intruder" down, at least initially. As the trombone "preaching" builds, heavy chords in the other trombones and low saxes form a potent counterargument. Very gradually the trombone's chattering lifts the overall mood. Almost like a ray of midwinter sunshine, brighter high-register sonorities in open trumpets and reeds now penetrate the gloom. The rhythmic surge and deep swing of the music finally become overwhelming. A series of highly chromatic trumpet chords turn into close-voiced clusters, signaling the end of the movement (which in fact had no ending in Mingus's score). A brief free trombone cadenza (by Woodman) seemed an appropriate way to bring this remarkable movement to a fitting close ["Underdog Rising"].

I feel that I must now, in closing, present to the reader another side of Mingus's talents: his work as a bass player and improvisor. There can be no better way to demonstrate his gifts in these areas than to play for you parts of a 1960 recording, "Stormy Weather" (the famous ballad by Harold Arlen), in which Mingus is brilliantly partnered with Eric Dolphy, the great alto saxophonist — and "conqueror" of several other wind instruments, especially the bass clarinet.

Your ears will certainly discern the greatness of this rendition. I would therefore like the music to speak to you directly. But I can't resist the temptation to mention two aspects of this one-take recorded performance. In view of the fact that in his lifetime, and even often now, thirty years after his death, Dolphy is underrated or maligned and/or ignored by many jazz critics and musicians, I want to say something on his behalf, not that he really in the long run needs my defense. This trashing and ignorance of Eric Dolphy's work is quite incomprehensible to me. But I guess when famous musicians such as Miles Davis blasted Dolphy, claiming that he had no ears, played artificial nonsense, and couldn't play on changes, many people, impressed by Miles, blindly followed suit with similar criticisms. Dolphy's performance on "Stormy Weather" — with its inspired devotion to Harold Arlen's harmonic changes, Dolphy's incredible melodic invention, never letting the original tune melody too far out of mind, and extraordinary technical and creative virtuosity, with his beautiful tone at times imparting the cry and anguish of the blues — should put all such aberrant criticisms to rest.

My second suggestion is to listen to how Mingus, in his bass playing, fulfills not one, not two, but three musical functions simultaneously. He is, first, in his bass lines the keeper of the fundamental harmonies of the song; second, he is the main rhythmic keeper (the drums are often barely audible), and in his pulse and swing manages to achieve a tremendous amount of expressive and dynamic variety, from pp whispers to suddenly plangent outbursts; third, he is — on his bass — a melodist, playing beautiful melodic countermelodies to Dolphy's alto. Indeed, I dare say, some of the counterpoint between the two players is so perfect — and remember that this was totally improvised — that it could not, cannot, be bettered by even the greatest contrapuntist taking, say, three hours or three days to achieve a similar high result.

I rest my case, and let the music now speak for itself.

Music Played

"Dippermouth Blues"	King Oliver's Creole Jazz Band	1923
"Big Butter and Egg Man"	Louis Armstrong	1926
"Potato Head Blues"	Louis Armstrong	1926
"Muggles"	Louis Armstrong/Earl Hines	1928
"Mahogany Hall Stomp"	Louis Armstrong	1933
"Toby"	Bennie Moten	1932
"Lady Be Good"	Lester Young/Count Basie	1936
"Shaw 'Nuff"	Dizzy Gillespie/Charlie Parker	1945
"I Can't Get Started"	Lennie Tristano	1946
"Apple Honey"	Woody Herman	1945
"Misterioso"	Thelonious Monk	1948
Variants on a Theme of Thelonious Monk	Gunther Schuller	1960
"Mood Indigo"	Duke Ellington	1930
"Azure"	Duke Ellington	1937
"Daybreak Express"	Duke Ellington	1933
Reminiscing in Tempo	Duke Ellington	1935
"Cotton Tail"	Duke Ellington	1940
"The Clothed Woman"	Duke Ellington	1947
"Where's the Music"	Duke Ellington	1958
Mingus Fingers	Charles Mingus	1947
Epitaph	Charles Mingus	1940(?)–1962

Peacemaking from the Grassroots in a World of Ethnic Conflict

MAIREAD CORRIGAN MAGUIRE

THE TANNER LECTURES ON HUMAN VALUES

Delivered at

University of California, Riverside
March 4, 1996

MAIREAD CORRIGAN MAGUIRE has dedicated her life to promoting a peaceful resolution of the conflict in Northern Ireland, and is cofounder of the Community of the Peace People. She was drawn into her leadership position as the result of the tragic death, in August 1976, of two of her nephews and a niece, who were struck and killed on a Belfast street corner by an IRA gunman's getaway car. The driver of the car had been shot dead by a British Army patrol. Working with Betty Williams and Ciaran McKeown, she organized some of the largest peace demonstrations in the history of Northern Ireland, including rallies in Belfast, Derry/Londonderry, Dublin, and London. Working with other leading human rights activists, she also played an important role in the formation of the Committee on the Administration of Justice, a non-sectarian organization that has become a leading advocate for change in the Northern Ireland legal system. A powerful speaker, she has traveled widely throughout the United States and Europe to advance the work of the Peace People. She was a guest speaker at the Third International Conference on Human Rights in Helsinki, and at the invitation of Walter Mondale gave the keynote address at the Peace Prize Forum at Augustana College in 1992. She received the Norwegian People's Prize, and has been awarded honorary doctorates from Yale University, the College of New Rochelle, and St. Michael's College in Vermont. She was named a joint recipient of the Nobel Peace Prize in 1976.

I can think of no more urgent subject for us to be discussing today than ethnic conflict. It is not merely a topic that stimulates a passing interest. It is perhaps the greatest challenge facing the human family. What we must consider today is this question: how can we begin to solve nonviolently some of the deep ethnic conflicts in our world today and thus give hope and inspiration to each other?

When the Soviet Union collapsed there was a sense around the world that one repression had stopped and perhaps there was an opportunity for the human family to really begin to make peace, to divert those vast resources allocated to militarism and redirect them to areas of the world where the true enemies of the human family might be tackled — the enemies of collapsing environments, poverty, and inhumanity. At that moment there was great hope in the world that we were a family and perhaps we could make it together.

Tragically, within a very short time, we began to hear of countries such as Chechnya, essentially unknown before, countries in the Soviet Bloc that had been held together by military might, countries suddenly beginning to make their voices heard. Yugoslavia, once united under Tito's regime, soon followed the Soviet Union's dissolution. Suddenly republics appeared having survived seventy years of repression — Slovenia, Bosnia, Herzegovina — strange countries with unfamiliar languages, practising little-understood religions. We soon discovered that these countries had survived decades of repression with historic hatreds intact, and the people were armed, and that internal conflict was actually easy due to the availability of armaments to be used against each other or against outsiders.

At this point in time we began to realise that nuclear and conventional weapons and our armies were absolutely no use in these situations. One cannot drop a nuclear bomb on an ethnic conflict. The weapons we have developed, as a means of solving our problems, are no longer of any use to us.

This became ever more evident to me when, in 1995, I travelled to Burundi in Africa. I was part of a small delegation of women from Ireland who were invited into the country in order to see, from inside the country, the situation at a true and intimate level. There was enormous pressure to send in the United Nations from the international community, which was deeply concerned that Burundi would follow the path taken by Rwanda, leading certainly to genocide.

This pressure was exacerbated by the international world press, which would lead its television broadcasts with images of refugees fleeing from Burundi. Upon our arrival we discovered terrible problems in Burundi: people were fleeing and the army had killed people in their villages. We asked the people, "How can the outside world help? What can we do?" They very clearly responded, "Don't send us any guns. Don't send us any military forces. The place is awash with guns and while, in these refugee camps, our children need food and we haven't enough money ourselves to buy food, a child with a few cents can buy a weapon. For too long the West has given us weaponry. Send us no more." This was a plea from the heart. The Burundi people said their ethnic/political problem cannot be solved by any kind of violence.

When I visit a place like the United States of America, I stress how very important it is to recognise that we are interconnected in these ethnic conflicts: what happens in a place like Burundi literally affects all of us around the world. We play a key role in Burundi; let us not forget that eighty-five percent of the weapons being sold to Third World countries come from the USA and the European community.

Eighty-five percent of the weapons going to poor Third World countries come from the wealthy "First World" nations. We must delude ourselves no longer; we are arming the Third World. In return, a high percentage of their budgets and international aid is coming back to the West. While some of these countries cannot feed their people, they can and do buy our guns and send our money back to us. By any reckoning, this is so unjust and causes so much suffering. The world's people have got to unite their voices to stop this genocide of the poor today.

Some years ago together with a delegation of Nobel Laureates, I visited refugee camps on the Thai/Burma border. In the refugee camp, we listened to stories of Karen women who had been taken out of their villages by force and made to act as human porters by the Burmese soldiers. Many of these women told us of how they had themselves been raped by Burmese soldiers and witnessed killings and massive abuse of human rights of the ethnic minorities and Burmese dissidents by the Burmese military. This is again a situation of political/ethnic conflict where Western interests are interwoven.

In the mid-1970s, the Burmese military was on the brink of financial collapse but was kissed alive by Western oil companies (French and American) investing in Burma. The military use much of the oil revenue to buy military equipment to control and kill many Burmese and ethnic nationals. We are fast moving into a world where big businesses, etc., are controlling national and international economies and are in danger of becoming more politically powerful than national and international governments and political institutions.

In Northern Ireland our situation is one of deep ethnic/political problems. If we do not begin to understand the forces behind this ethnicity and to try to control them, we will find ourselves in a very dangerous situation. Too often the media and others within the island of Ireland look at Northern Ireland and create excellent propaganda by implying that ours is a conflict between the British government and the Irish Republican Army. This is not true! Historically, when the Troubles started in the North of Ireland in 1969, people died on the streets of Belfast before the British army was brought in. And in 1969, when the British army was brought in, the Irish Republican Army was barely in existence and unarmed. Nearly two years passed before the Irish Republican Army became a real guerrilla armed force in the North of Ireland. So we should lay to rest all the imagined intrigues about the British government and the British army and the Irish Republican Army.

Allow me to give you a glimpse at what actually happened between the people in Northern Ireland before these influences and forces began to fight with each other.

I will paint a broad picture because there isn't enough time to explore in detail the history. Northern Ireland is a community of only one and a half million people. Of this population, one million are Protestants who call themselves Unionists, who are British, who want to maintain links with the British government, who would die before they would agree to joining a united Ireland, who would die before they would agree to drop their links with Britain because that is their heritage and roots.

Northern Ireland also has a minority community representing one-third of its population. This minority group is Catholic and nationalist, who are aggrieved by the fact that seventy-five years ago Ireland was partitioned and they were separated from their hinterland, who are very conscious that they have been treated for a long time as second-class citizens, who are very proud to be Irish.

A very deep fear developed between people of two distinct ethnic groups who have lived apart for seventy-five years. Ethnicity and identity are characteristics that can be extremely dangerous when disturbed. It is fine to be very proud of one's identity when living in a quiet community, but once a conflict situation arises, when two communities begin to threaten each other because population figures are shifting towards an equal balance, then identity and ethnicity can become quite murderous. We must never underestimate the human being's capacity for absolute murder! Each one of us is murderous given the right circumstances and that is why we quickly need to learn and understand nonviolence.

Visitors to Northern Ireland find our situation quite confusing. They meet people who are white, Christian, very friendly, very civil — peace-loving people. People who visit our country cannot understand how, in 1969, these seemingly peace-loving people actually burned each other out of their homes. But due to the fact that we have been divided, that the level of fear is so high, and that the siege mentality resides in Northern Ireland, we are, in fact, absolutely capable of killing each other. Therefore, anyone working within the field of identity and ethnicity must see the importance of moving individuals above these tribal instincts.

It is fine to celebrate our diversity and our roots, but somehow we must rise above those ideas that divide us so that we may begin to work together and understand the most important identity that we have: we are the human family. Surely what we have in common is more important than what divides us. Surely as a human family we can find ways to build bridges and work together. Celebrate our diversity, yes, but always recognise that we are men and women who are interconnected in our world today, that each of us is more important than the flags and the religions, and somehow we must rise above these things that have kept us so divided.

In order to overcome the fear of differences and learn to celebrate diversity we need to study and understand nonviolence. My journey in Northern Ireland, searching and asking the questions of what it means to live in West Belfast in this particular historic period, has meant that I have had to question everything, absolutely everything. I grew up in an area where some people accepted as fact that young men joined the IRA, arguing that there was such a thing as a just war. This thinking included justifications such as: Haven't churches always blessed war? or When you live in a situation of state injustice, it is right to arm yourself and work for justice. I grew up seeing state injustice, and I grew up believing that I could not sit back — that no one should sit back — doing nothing because doing nothing is in itself wrong. But could I ever take up arms?

To deal with these issues, I went on my own spiritual journey and came to recognise that life is sacred; each human life is sacred; we are involved in a mystery that is life; and we are given life as a gift and we have no right to take that gift from another human being. I also came to my absolute belief that, as a Christian, the greatest symbol of nonviolence was Jesus hanging on a cross saying, Love your enemy and do not kill — a very simple message that Christians lived out for the first 300 years of Christianity, but tragically have moved away from since the third century.

I believe that the major religions of the world stem from roots of love, tolerance, respect, and nonviolence. Therefore I passionately believe that the only way to accomplish real change is through the power of love operating in the world.

How do we solve our problems without killing each other? At home in Northern Ireland we try to accomplish this through teaching nonviolence at every level of our society — courses on conflict resolution, prejudice reduction, human rights. This is a new direction for us. Within the human family, we teach our children reading, writing, and arithmetic from the time they are very young so that when they grow up they will be literate. Yet why, when they are very young, don't we teach them conflict resolution, peacemaking, prejudice reduction? Why don't we teach them about the world's different faiths, religions, and creeds? In teaching respect for life and respect for diversity we will create a tolerant and more compassionate world.

I firmly believe that we must teach nonviolence at every level of our society — in the home, which is surely where it starts, in the community, at universities and colleges, and in the country. We must begin building a nonviolent world.

In Northern Ireland we desperately need to build community. The only solution in a deep ethnic conflict, the only way to reduce fear, is to increase tangible human contact by bringing people together. Certainly we have the Internet and television, which are marvellous technologies, but they must not be a supplement and they cannot be a replacement for human contact. That would be a lazy and dangerous road to take. The human being needs to be loved and to love, to feel a sense of dignity, acceptance, and respect.

Human beings know when they are being treated with contempt by another whether or not words are spoken. The human being is expert at body language, expert too at picking up the vibes. More than economics, social status, or jobs, never underestimate the worth or importance of human dignity shared between individuals, communities, and nations. Respect for human dignity and human diversity are much needed to be taught in today's world — we were never taught this; we never learned to share this.

Respect for human dignity can be realised only when people communicate directly with one another. For this to occur, there can be no dramatic overnight solutions. Let us look at Belfast, a city where fourteen walls sadly help keep our people segregated. Our schools are segregated too. This of course leads to fear and mistrust. We have to do all we can to build trust; one of our programmes is that we transport, by bus, Loyalist and Republican wives and children to visit their relatives in the prisons. This bus takes people from one community to another community and allows individuals who often feared each other to sit, ride, and communicate.

There are tragic cases of violence and oppression when there is no respect for dignity, no understanding or communication. East Timor, one of the most tragic countries in our world today, is a tiny country that was invaded twenty years ago by Indonesia. One-third of its population has been cruelly murdered and Indonesia continues its colonisation practices while the world does little to help. Bishop Belo, a dedicated spokesperson for the East Timorese people, visited us in Belfast in late 1995. I took him to West Belfast and showed him the walls between Catholic and Protestant communities. Bishop Belo kept saying, But these are a Christian people. These people are Christians. Why are there walls between Christian people?

When people are not communicating with one another, or listening to each other to alleviate their fears, then fear increases. In Northern Ireland we seem to have lost the ability to hear the other person. When the ceasefire was called eighteen months ago, I went to the Falls Road, where the Catholic community was saying, The ceasefire is wonderful. We can move forward for a real change. There was a real sense of euphoria. Then I went to the Protestant Shankill, where a young minister confided to me, It's a sad day for the Protestant people here. A deal has been done between the British and the IRA. He was so fearful that somehow he and his community were being sold out.

This inability to listen has made us culturally deaf and blind in one ear and one eye so that we can no longer sense what the other person is feeling. Our very language divides. Our Protestant or Catholic traditions use language so differently. The word "justice," for example, has a completely different meaning for Protestants and Catholics in Northern Ireland. Therefore, when we attempt to tackle issues such as prisoner release, or police reform, we approach them from completely different perspectives and different priorities. This makes the work much more difficult. We have got to learn to listen and stay together as we move forward.

The only hope for nonviolence is building community. Once people feel that they can and do make a difference, and are important in their communities, they will feel a sense of power. They can then be powerful in the right sense of the use of that word, not abusers of power. So how do we give people in their communities that sense of power? We must, from the bottom up, build community nonviolently to really begin to break down at the top what we have as ethnic politics.

Northern Ireland is home to one and a half million people — about 600 tiny villages, each with populations of about 2,000 people. It will be only when these villages begin to mobilise, to solve problems, to elect local citizens to represent them, to develop resources and finances for jobs, etc., that nonviolence will grow out of their sense of empowerment. Having finances, resources, and power at this grassroots level allows communities to feel they can make a difference. Only then can they begin to solve problems nonviolently. These citizens feel free to go over to the different community, reach out, and share the road that connects one to the other.

In Northern Ireland we have never voted on a social economic spectrum; we've voted on "the flag" — for nationalism or for unionism. If we return to a devolved government based on ethnic division, we may have a stalemate for the next ten or fifteen years, until someone comes along to remind us of our differences. Then, once again, our fragile country will blow apart. Changing politics from the bottom up is therefore not only idealistic but essential for a peaceful future.

I believe we can effect this change because we are a highly disciplined, good community. Before the trouble started we had about 200 prisoners! We believe that once the guns are taken out of Irish politics, once everyone is brought into the dialogue, we will go forward. Yes, identities are changing as a Northern Irish identity evolves, the result of two communities coming together for resolution, and political change. In seventy-five years of partition, things have changed.

Still the Unionists fear they will be pulled into a unitary Ireland, but there will be no unitary Ireland in the foreseeable future. The Nationalists fear they will be pulled back into an unjust government as before, but there can be no going back to injustice. The hope lies in the growing recognition that we are of two main traditions and growing minority groups — and that there must be a pluralist political movement — not majoritarianism. There is now a recognition that majoritarianism in divided societies is not democracy and doesn't work.

We are moving forward in Northern Ireland; we have a great deal of hope. We hope to solve, nonviolently, our ethnic political problem, giving a sense of safe future to our people. There will be hiccups, of course; changing attitudes will be a life's commitment and all sides must be prepared to change and to give a little. It will not be easy, but we believe we have no alternative.

What can the ordinary person do? What can one individual do? First and foremost, we each must find time to examine our own spiritual values, because a personal revolution must precede any other change. Once we understand our own religious convictions, we assess if we truly believe in what we profess. Do we really believe in love and reconciliation and forgiveness, or are we bogged down and cemented in old attitudes, old ways, and old thinking? The need for self-reflection is obvious as we witness new spiritual movements arising in our world today, especially among the young. As they move away from traditional religions, we realise that there are many paths to God. We have to allow people to find their own way, provide the space for something new to grow.

As individuals, in our own lives we should examine our own spirituality through our prayer, also listen for the voices of today's prophets. Regard the doomsday voices and scenes of devastation on television with balance. For even in the midst of devastation, there is hope for the world. On the streets of Burundi I saw great hope. Young Americans were in the refugee camps with their mobile phones and aid trucks, working in partnership with the Burundi people and helping them where and when asked to do so. In the heart of the forests of Burma I saw young Americans helping pro-democracy students work the Internet and learning from them. It is a two-way process now and we all have to learn from each other. You don't see these heartwarming stories on television.

This is as true and important to know and see as the disturbing accounts, and it is happening all around our world today. We are interconnected; we are helping; there is real growth taking place and real compassion in and for humanity that does not often appear on television. The media, especially television, have to be made accountable and responsible. Pictures that television news crews sent around the world from Burundi showed a country burning, a civilisation falling apart. The world watched with utter helplessness. However, what news crews chose not to broadcast was the Burundi people working to solve their problems with great courage, with great dignity.

With great dignity they will continue to deal with their problems — in their way, in their time. Western nations exude an arrogance to people who are barefoot; we feel they have nothing to offer but rather need, desire what we have to give. We have no right to impose Western models on these new political movements; yes, we can help, but only on their terms, not ours.

Wonderful changes are taking place in our world today, but with great care we must learn to recognise prophetic voices, those politicians prepared to serve their people by providing political leadership in service, not only to their people, but to the world. The United States of America should not close its back or its doors to the rest of the world; you have too much to offer. Find political leadership that will be prophetic, men and women who will give hope, and help lead the human family toward a new horizon. As Martin Luther King tried to build the "beloved community," encourage those leaders who have as their goal and vision to build the "beloved community" with all the nations of the world.

The United States needs to be reminded not to value materialism too highly in a very poor world. Growth cannot be everlasting because the cake is too small. The Western world has kept the vast majority of the cake for so long, leaving nothing for our brothers and sisters in the Third World countries. This must change and we must be prepared to change, make sacrifices, go without, and share what we have. We have to do without that second helping, because the world can no longer afford the excesses of several cars, several houses, of people living a high lifestyle. Unless we are prepared to live simply so others may simply live then things will not change.

I believe that there is movement towards reassessing, reaffirming, and "refinding" spiritual values that provide us with the strength to demand social justice, for a community without social justice is a community that will never have peace. Violence is only the symptom. What we have to understand is what drives people to take a gun, people who for so long have held anger and frustration in, who bear more than their share of injustice, inhumanity, and unfairness.

Eventually they explode and their community explodes as a result. I pray to God that America can defuse the bomb before the explosion, for once the evil genie of violence gets out of the bottle, it is very nearly impossible to get it back in again. Be aware of the signs for they are here.

You know what to do — make real changes and work tirelessly as we do in the streets of Belfast. We knock on doors; we sell our little paper and build peace in Belfast one home, one family at a time. We will know that you are doing the same here in the United States, as people are doing it in Burundi, as people are doing it in Burma. Together the human family can build a civilised world.

Kant on Reason and Religion

ONORA O'NEILL

THE TANNER LECTURES ON HUMAN VALUES

Delivered at

Harvard University
April 1–3, 1996

ONORA O'NEILL is principal of Newnham College, Cambridge University. She was educated at Somerville College, Oxford University, and received her Ph.D. from Harvard University, where she was awarded the Carrier prize for her dissertation *Universilizability*. She has taught at Barnard College and the University of Essex, serves on the council of the Royal Institute of Philosophy, the Nuffield Council on Bioethics, and the Oxford Commission of Inquiry, and is a past president of the Aristotelian Society. She is also a fellow of the British Academy and a foreign honorary member of the American Academy of Arts and Sciences. She has written widely on ethics and political philosophy, and her most recent books include *Faces of Hunger: An Essay on Poverty, Development, and Justice* (1986), *Constructions of Reason: Exploration of Kant's Practical Philosophy* (1989), and *Towards Justice and Virtue* (1996).

LECTURE I. REASONED HOPE

Kant's philosophy of religion has perplexed even his warmest admirers. Nobody has pointed this out more amusingly than Heinrich Heine, who saw in Kant the Robespierre of the intellect. The orderly philosopher of Königsberg, whose daily constitutional was attended and sheltered by his servant Lampe, armed with a modest umbrella, was really a terrorist who destroyed the *ancien régime* of European religion and philosophy. The *Critique of Pure Reason* was the sword that killed deism in Germany. Yet Kant, Heine suggests, derailed this sublime and terrifying philosophy, that pointed toward the death of God, when a domestic difficulty arose. He relented and patched a God together because his servant, old Lampe, was disconsolate. Heine lampoons Kant:

> Immanuel Kant traced his merciless philosophy up to this point, he stormed heaven, . . . there was no more allmercyfulness, no more fatherly goodness, no otherworldly rewards for this worldly restraint, the immortality of the soul was at its last gasp . . . and old Lampe stood there with his umbrella under his arm, a miserable onlooker with anxious sweat and tears running down his face. And so Immanuel Kant had mercy and

---

As a graduate student at Harvard in the 1960s I read Kant's philosophy of religion and was both fascinated and baffled. My interest was rekindled when I gave a number of seminars on the subject as Read-Tuckwell lecturer at the University of Bristol in 1986. I am grateful to the Read-Tuckwell committee and to the University of Bristol for the stimulus and opportunity to explore the topic with knowledgeable and helpful colleagues. At the time I remained puzzled by Kant's conception of reason, and consequently about his intent in giving the title *Religion within the Limits of Reason Alone* to a work that seems so remote from other writing on reason and religion. In the years since then I have worked extensively on Kant's conception of reason. When invited to deliver the Tanner Lectures at Harvard University I hoped that I would at last be in a position to speak about the ways in which Kant's writing on religion connects reason, hope, and interpretation. I am deeply grateful to the Tanner Foundation for the opportunity to present this work and to Harvard University for making the occasion both intellectually engaging and enjoyable.

showed that he wasn't just a great philosopher, but also a good person. He thought it over and said, half kindly and half in irony: "Old Lampe must have a God, or the poor fellow can't be happy — but man ought to be happy on earth — practical reason says so (at least according to me); so let practical reason also disclose the existence of God." By this argument Kant distinguished theoretical from practical reason and, as with a magic wand, brought back to life the corpse of deism which theoretical reason had killed.[1]

If Heine and other critics are right, Kant's retreat is ignominious. In the first Critique he asserts the death of God: "No one indeed will be able to boast that he *knows* that there is a God and a future life" (*CPR* A828–29/B856–57);[2] in the second Critique he argues for God and immortality. Can practical reason really produce a magic wand to revive the corpse of deism — let alone of a more comfortable religion for old Lampe? Or does it provide no more than an old man's umbrella as defence against the terrifying weapons of theoretical reason? Heine is not the only critic who concludes that Kant's "practical" arguments fail, that there is no

---

[1] Heinrich Heine, *Zur Geschichte der Religion und Philosophie*, in his *Gesammelte Werke*, 6 vols. (Berlin and Weimar: Aufbau Verlag, 1951), vol. 5, 110.

[2] Kant references are given parenthetically using abbreviated titles and the following translations; except where indicated the page numbers are those of the translation.

Critique of Pure Reason, tr. Norman Kemp Smith (London: Macmillan, 1933). (*CPR*; pagination of first and second editions)

Critique of Practical Reason, tr. L. W. Beck (Indianapolis: Bobbs-Merrill, 1977). *CPrR*; Academy pagination)

Critique of Judgement, tr. James Creed Meredith (Oxford: Clarendon Press, 1978). (*CJ*)

Religion within the Limits of Reason Alone, tr. Theodore M. Greene (New York: Harper and Row, 1960). (*R*)

Groundwork of the Metaphysic of Morals, tr. H. J. Paton as *The Moral Law* (London: Hutchinson, 1953). (*G*; Academy pagination)

The Conflict of the Faculties, tr. Mary Gregor (New York: Abaris Books, 1979). (*CF*; Academy pagination)

Theory and Practice, What Is Enlightenment? and *What Is Orientation in Thinking?* — all tr. H. B. Nisbet in Hans Reiss, ed., *Kant: Political Writings*, 2nd ed. (Cambridge: Cambridge University Press, 1991). (*TP*, *WE*, *WOT*)

real consolidation to be had, and that we cannot escape the colossal wreck of rationalist metaphysics and theology and the threat to religious faith.

1. *The Great Gulf*

If these critics are right, the defects of Kant's account of religion are symptoms of wider problems in his philosophy. The arguments for God and immortality that Kant advances in the *Critique of Practical Reason* are supposed to bridge a "great gulf" (*CJ* 14, 36) between Kant's accounts of the natural world and of human freedom. If no bridge can be built, Kant is committed to a spectacular but wholly implausible metaphysical position that claims that human beings live in two unconnected worlds. They are part of a natural, phenomenal world that is temporally structured, causally ordered, and knowable by theoretical reason. Yet they are also free agents who are part not of the natural, phenomenal world but of a noumenal or intelligible world that is inaccessible to theoretical reason and neither temporally structured nor causally ordered.

I shall take it that Kant and Heine are both right in thinking that the critical philosophy leads us toward the brink of a great gulf, which seemingly separates self from world, freedom from nature, and acting from knowing. It is therefore entirely reasonable to ask what sort of bridge Kant tries to build across the great gulf, and whether it reinstates the God for whom Lampe pined, or is as flimsy as Heine suspected, or whether there are other ways of looking at the matter.

In these lectures I shall offer reasons for thinking that the critical philosophy indeed destroys and neither revives nor aims to revive either deism or more familiar forms of theism. Nevertheless, I shall argue, Kant offers good reasons for thinking that the bridge across the great gulf can be bridged by an account of religion, and also for thinking that this account of religion can lie "within the limits of reason alone." The key to this alternative understanding of "religion within the limit of reason alone" lies, I shall argue, in proper attention to Kant's distinctive account of reason.

This evening I shall begin by sketching the great gulf that is to be bridged and by outlining Kant's conception of reason. I shall then turn to his view that the bridge that is to cross the great gulf is a bridge of hope, and finally shall try to say something about what it would take for hopes to be reasonable. Tomorrow I shall build on this account of reasoned hope to understand why in his last writings on religion Kant constantly cites (and miscites) the texts of Christian Scripture,[3] while still claiming to offer an account of "religion within the limits of reason alone."

2. *The Two Standpoints*

A common view of the predicament in which Kant believes we find ourselves, and of his solution to it, is that it is a predicament of his own making, which he could have avoided. There is no gulf between self and world, between nature and freedom, between knowledge and action, and so there is no need to work out how the gulf might be bridged. Put more prosaically, the proper task of philosophy is to provide an adequate account of human freedom and action that is not only compatible with but integrated into an adequate account of our knowledge of a causally ordered world. By avoiding Kant's problem we would also avoid any need for his desperate remedy.

I cannot within the framework of two lectures trace the arguments that led Kant to the contrary view, but shall outline the position that he reaches, and some of the reasons he offers for thinking that it is not internally incoherent. The point can be put in a compressed form by noting that Kant thought that he was making not an ontological but an epistemological claim. The predicament in which we find ourselves is not that of having to lead

---

[3] For discussion of Kant's use of Scripture see Henri d'Aviau de Ternay, *Traces Bibliques dans la Loi Morale chez Kant* (Paris: Beauchesne, 1986), and "Kant und die Bibel: Spuren an den Grenzen," in Friedo Ricken und François Marty, *Kant über Religion* (Stuttgart: Kohlhammer, 1992).

our lives in two distinct ontological orders, but that of having to adopt two mutually irreducible standpoints in leading our lives. The theoretical standpoint is naturalistic: from it we see the world and human life as subject to natural law and causal inquiry. The practical standpoint is that of human freedom: from it we see ourselves as agents who intervene in limited ways in that natural order. Only the theoretical standpoint can accommodate science; only the practical standpoint can accommodate morality.

We are unavoidably, deeply, and thoroughly committed both to the naturalistic standpoint and to the standpoint of freedom. We can dispense with neither standpoint, since neither makes sense without the other. If we do not see ourselves as free we can give no account of activity, hence none of the activities of judging and understanding by which we establish the claims of knowledge; if we do not see ourselves as parts of a causally ordered world we can give no account of the effective implementation of human projects, including moral action, in the world. Our lives would be impossible without commitment to freedom *and* to causality in the robust sense in which Kant understands these terms: neither can stand alone. Yet we do not understand, let alone know, what makes them compatible. The strangeness of human life is that we find a hiatus at the core of our self-understanding, which cannot be comprehended within any single perspective. We have to adopt both standpoints: neither is dispensable and neither is subordinate or reducible to the other — yet their conjunction is a challenge and an affront to the very project of reasoning, which aims at coherence. This hiatus is the "great gulf" that threatens Kant's philosophy.[4]

A traditional reading of Kant — Heine's is one among many — is that Kant resolves this problem by reinstating some form of transcendent realism, within which the coordination of nature and

---

[4] For epistemological readings of Kant's account of the two standpoints see Henry Allison, *Kant's Theory of Freedom* (Cambridge: Cambridge University Press, 1990), and Onora O'Neill, "Reason and Autonomy in Grundlegung III," in *Constructions of Reason: Explorations of Kant's Practical Philosophy* (Cambridge: Cambridge University Press, 1989), 51–65.

freedom is to be secured by metaphysical means — as it were offstage. I believe that the strategies Kant mainly deploys to solve the problem are more modest. The first and the most fundamental aspect of his more modest approach is a surprisingly minimalist view of the powers of human reason.

3. *Human Reason*

From the very beginning of *The Critique of Pure Reason* Kant insists on the limits of human knowledge: our knowledge cannot reach beyond human experience and our experience is confined to the natural world. The deficiency is not easily remediable, since it arises from the limits and failings of human reason, which "is burdened by questions which, as prescribed by the very nature of reason itself, it is not able to ignore, but which as transcending all its powers, it is also not able to answer." (*CPR*, Avii).

Even everyday methods of reasoning can lead into incoherent conceptions of the soul (the paralogisms), of cosmology (the antinomies), and of God (the critique of rational theology). Try as we will, we find ourselves torn between insatiable desires to know metaphysical truths and the frustrated realization that attempts to do so repeatedly lead us into dialectical illusion. The problem of providing a proper account of the character and tasks of human reason is postponed for many hundreds of pages, until the discussion of philosophical method in the *Doctrine of Method*, which begins with a candid acknowledgment that the whole edifice of the critical philosophy remains insecure because we still lack any account of the methods to be used if these cognitive shipwrecks are to be avoided.

All that Kant proposes as remedy for this uncomfortable situation is that we *accept* that our grandest cognitive ambitions must be set aside and that we *adopt* a form of cognitive *discipline* to protect ourselves from error:

> The greatest and perhaps the sole use of all philosophy of pure reason is therefore only negative; since it serves not as an

organon for the extension but as a discipline for the limitation of pure reason, and, instead of discovering truth, has only the modest merit of guarding against error. (*CPR* A795/B823; cf. A709/B737)

He admits that this is an uncomfortable conclusion to reach after long philosophical efforts:

> that reason, whose proper duty it is to prescribe a discipline for all other endeavours, should itself stand in need of such a discipline may indeed seem strange. (*CPR* A710/B738)

At first consideration the proposal may seem worse than strange. If reason is or is to be subordinated to a *discipline*, then it seems that Kant must have given up the ambitions of philosophy, or perhaps have settled for some antirational appeal to common sense or shared understandings or the like, which usurps the claims and title of reason. However, the *Transcendental Doctrine of Method* offers quite another picture, in which reason itself is construed as a certain sort of negative self-discipline.

Kant's account of the discipline of reason can be summarized in three claims. First, in calling reason a discipline, he is claiming that it is a *negative* constraint on the ways in which we think and act: there are no substantive axioms of reason, whose content can fully steer processes of reasoning; there are merely constraints.[5] Reason is indeed merely formal.

Second, the discipline of reason is *nonderivative*. Reason does not derive from any more fundamental standards. On the contrary, it appeals to no other premises, so can be turned on *any* claim or belief or proposal for action. Neither church nor state,

---

[5] Kant uses the term *discipline* for a form of *negative instruction*, "by which the constant tendency to disobey certain rules is restrained" (*CPR* A709–10/B737–38). See more generally chapter I of the *Transcendental Doctrine of Method*, called *The Discipline of Pure Reason* (*CPR* A707/B735ff.), especially the first few pages and the considerations that lie behind rejecting the geometric method that are rehearsed in section I of the chapter titled *The Discipline of Pure Reason in Its Dogmatic Employment*.

nor other powers, can claim exemption from the scrutiny of reason for their pronouncements and assumptions. The authority of reason would be nullified by any supposition that it is subordinate to the claims of one or another happenstantial power:

> Reason must in all its undertakings subject itself to criticism; should it limit that freedom of criticism by any prohibitions, it must harm itself, drawing upon itself damaging suspicions. Nothing is so important through its usefulness, nothing so sacred, that it may be exempted from this searching examination, which knows no respect for persons. (*CPR* A738/B766)

If reason has *any* authority, it must be *its own* rather than *derivative*. Although reason does not have derivative authority, authority it must have. Authority is needed to distinguish between ways of organizing thought and action that are to count as reasoned and those that are to be dismissed as unreasoned. Kant traces this nonderivative authority to the requirement that reasons be public, in the sense that they can be given or exchanged, shared or challenged. Nothing then can count as reasoned unless it is followable by others, that is, unless it is *lawlike*. Ways of organizing thought and action that are not lawlike will be unfollowable by at least some others, who will view them as arbitrary or incomprehensible.

The minimal, modal requirement that reasons be followable by others, without being derivative from other standards, is Kant's entire account of the authority of reason. Yet mere nonderivative lawlikeness has considerable implications for the organization of thought and action: in the domain of theory it amounts to the demand that reasons be intelligible to others; in the domain of action it amounts to the requirement that reasons for action be ones that others too could follow.[6]

---

[6] This formulation covers both the partially reasoned case of *heteronomous* action, where principles are lawlike, but derivative from or conditional on desires, and the fully reasoned case of *autonomous* action, whose principles are lawlike and not derivative from or conditional on any particular desires. Reasons for action whether partial or complete must be followable by those for whom they are to be reasons for action.

The three aspects of Kant's conception of reason are summarized in the thought that reason requires a "wholly nonderivative and specifically negative law-giving" ("da scheint eine ganz eigene und zwar negative Gesetzgebung erforderlich zu sein," *CPR* A711/B739, my translation). The same trio of requirements — that reason be negative, underivative, and lawlike — are linked in numerous Kantian formulations, and most notably in the best-known version of the Categorical Imperative, which demands action only on maxims that can at the same time be willed as universal laws. Here the supreme principle of practical reason is presented as a *negative* (formal) requirement that is *underivative* because it appeals to no other spurious "authorities" (that would be heteronomy) and demands adherence to *lawlike* maxims (i.e., to maxims that could be adopted by all).[7]

How far does this meagre conception of reason help us to understand Kant's claim to offer an account of religion within the limits of reason alone? Evidently it cannot offer reasons for thinking that the impasses to which speculative reasoning leads are likely to be overcome. This meagre conception of reason is unlikely to yield proofs of human freedom or immortality or of God's existence. However, Kant notes that our reasons for being interested in the soul and in God are primarily practical (*CPR* A800–804/B828–32) and raises the question whether "reason may not be able to supply us from the standpoint of its practical interest what it altogether refuses to supply in respect of its speculative interest" (*CPR* A805/B833; cf. A796/B824).

4. *Kant's Fundamental Questions*

Kant's surprising move far into his discussion of method, almost at the end of the *Critique of Pure Reason* (*CPR* A805/B833),

---

[7] For further textual evidence for this interpretation of Kant's conception of reason see Onora O'Neill, "Reason and Politics in the Kantian Enterprise" and "The Public Use of Reason," in *Constructions of Reason*, 3–27, 28–50, and "Vindicating Reason," in *The Cambridge Companion to Kant*, ed. Paul Guyer (Cambridge: Cambridge University Press, 1992), 280–308.

is to assert that human reason is fundamentally interested not in *two* questions — one about knowledge, one about action — but in *three* questions:[8]

1. What can I know?
2. What ought I do?
3. What may I hope?

The grouping of questions was hardly new. For example, a summary of Christian commitment would comprise answers to each question: I can know God; I ought to love God and my neighbour as myself; I may hope for the life to come. Each answer picks out the underlying principle of one of the traditional theological virtues, faith, hope, and charity: faith centres on knowledge of God; hope centres on the life to come; charity centres on love for God and neighbour.[9]

Kant does far more than take over and resequence these three traditional questions. His answers to "What can I know?" and

---

[8] Elsewhere Kant adds a fourth question: what is man? (e.g., *Logic*, tr. Robert Hartman and Wolfgang Schwarz [Indianapolis: Bobbs-Merrill, 1974], 29). However, this fourth question is viewed as comprising the other three, which would need to be answered within any adequate answer to the fourth. Since the fourth question is to be answered by anthropology (in Kant's understanding of the term), this arrangement of the fundamental question confirms the view — evident from the outset of the *Critique of Pure Reason* — that Kant's philosophy begins from an anthropocentric rather than a theocentric starting point.

[9] It is notable that Kant displaces hope from the middle place that it holds in the theological triad. That intermediate position has been thought to suggest that hope is less fundamental than faith and less perfect than charity (cf. Aquinas, *Summa Theologiae*, IaIIae.62.4); or even that it is only an aspect of imperfect, doubting faith, to be superseded in the future fuller faith of those who "possess" God, as mundane hopes are superseded when a hoped-for goal is achieved. However, some recent theologians — influenced in part by Kant — lay more weight on hope. For example, Karl Rahner writes that "hope does not express a modality of faith and love" and that "hope is . . . the basic modality of the very attitude to the eternal" (Karl Rahner, *A Rahner Reader*, ed. G. A. McCool [London: Darton, Longman and Todd, 1975], 231). Jürgen Moltmann too in some ways places hope ahead of faith and charity: "Christian proclamation is not a tradition of wisdom and truth in doctrinal principles. Nor is it a tradition of ways and means of living according to the law. It is the announcing, revealing, publishing of an eschatological event" (Jürgen Moltmann, *Theology of Hope: On the Ground and the Implications of a Christian Eschatology*, tr. James W. Leitch [London: SCM, 1967], 299.

"What ought I do?" are developed without any reference to God and without use of religious discourse; it is these answers that supposedly open up the great gulf that Heine, and many others, think will swallow up Kant's whole philosophy. Kant thought that he could avert this disaster by showing how a reasoned answer to the third question — "What may I hope?" — could bridge the great gulf.

5. Faith and Hope

It is easy to miss the central place that hope has in Kant's philosophy, and in particular in his philosophy of religion, because his discussion of religion often focuses on faith rather than on hope. In the preface of the second edition of the *Critique of Pure Reason* he famously asserted that "I have therefore found it necessary to deny knowledge to make room for faith" (*CPR* Bxxx; cf. A745/B773). In the *Doctrine of Method* and in the *Critique of Practical Reason* he identifies three postulates of God, freedom, and immorality, of which two are readily construed as articles of faith.

These passages taken in isolation might suggest that Kant expects to show that traditional theological claims, although they are not supported by the rational proofs to which deists aspired, can yet be reached by some nonrational "leap of faith." Yet neither in the account of faith offered in the discussions of the Postulates of Pure Practical Reason in the *Critique of Practical Reason* nor in *Religion within the Limits of Reason Alone* does Kant take this line. He doesn't assert that if we are prepared to overlook the claims of reason, then we can embrace religious truths without needing reasons. Rather he proposes that although articles of faith cannot be known or proven, the grounds of faith lie within the limits of reason. He is, it seems, neither deist nor fideist.[10] What then is his account of faith?

[10] For a contrary view see Alan Wood, "Kant's Deism," in *Kant's Philosophy of Religion Reconsidered*, ed. Philip J. Rossi and Michael Wreen (Bloomington and

6. Meinen, Wissen, Glauben

Late in the *Critique of Pure Reason* (*CPR* A820-B848ff.; cf. *CJ* 140ff.) and shortly after he poses the three questions that interest human reason, Kant distinguishes three forms of cognitive attitude. Mere *opining* (*meinen*) is holding something true, being consciously aware that one has no sufficient grounds, and that there are no objective grounds. Even opinion requires some grounds — or it would be no more than imagination — but the grounds of opinion are not even subjectively sufficient. *Knowing* (*wissen*) is holding something to be true for reasons that are both subjectively and objectively sufficient. Between opinion and knowledge Kant places *Glaube*, whose obvious translation would be *belief* or *faith*, and which he characterises as holding something for reasons that are objectively insufficient but subjectively sufficient, indeed subjectively unavoidable.

Glaube is a form of cognitive propositional attitude that is neither mere opinion nor knowledge. What can it be to have faith in this sense? Kant draws on an image (*CPR* A825/853), familiar both in Blaise Pascal and in Søren Kierkegaard, that strength of faith or belief can be understood in terms of a wager. *Glaube* is apparently to be understood as commitment, or trust. We know how strong our trust or commitment is when we realise how much we would stake on it. A measure of commitment is not, however, the same thing as a reason for making the commitment, and unless Kant can show reasons (even if not the objective reasons that can ground knowledge) for religious commitment he will not have shown that it is other than credulity. If religion is to be considered

---

Indianapolis: Indiana University Press, 1991), 1–21, and also in his earlier work, *Kant's Rational Theology* (Ithaca, N.Y.: Cornell University Press, 1973). Wood sees Kant as a deist despite his insistence that we can make no religious knowledge claims, and even speaks of Kant's *Religion* as a rationalist interpretation of Christian doctrine. This expansive use of the terms *deist* and *rationalist* obscures the fact that Kant nowhere endorses the knowledge claims of natural religion, and so takes a position very distant from deism as usually understood. The same disregard for Kant's insistence that we do not know religious truths can be seen throughout the articles by Joseph Runzo and Nicholas Wolterstorff in the same volume.

within the limits of reason alone, it must not merely be possible to make religious commitments: there must be reasons to do so. The reasons that Kant offers interpret religious trust or commitment fundamentally as a mode of hope: religious faith cannot be a matter of knowledge, and must be a matter of taking a hopeful view of human destiny.

Kant stakes a great deal on the claim that religious commitment is not any sort of knowledge. He claims that if the rationalist dream were fulfilled and we knew the truths of deism, religious belief would be coerced and morality impossible. In the second Critique he asserts that it is because faith is not provable and human beings have to struggle with doubt and commitment that morality is possible:

> [If] God and eternity in their awful majesty would stand unceasingly before our eyes. . . . Transgression of the law would indeed be shunned, and the commanded would be performed. But . . . because the spur to action would in this case always be present and external . . . most actions conforming to the law would be done from fear, few would be done from hope, none from duty. The moral worth of actions . . . would not exist at all. The conduct of man would be changed into mere mechanism. . . . (*CPrR* 147)

It would be a religious and moral disaster if *per impossibile* God were the demonstrable God of the rationalist tradition: religion (as Pascal also understood) *requires* a hidden God. *Deus absconditus* coerces neither belief nor action. Far from it being a misfortune that "no one indeed will be able to boast that he knows that there is a God and a future life" (*CPR* A828–29/ B856–57), this cognitive limitation is indispensable for uncoerced morality; moreover, it leaves the space in which the question "What may I hope?" can be asked. In this respect, as in so many others, Kant is wholly at odds with his rationalist predecessors, who grounded optimism about human destiny in the conviction that no less-than-optimal destiny would have been created for us by the demonstrable creator of the best of all possible worlds. Enlightenment optimism, unlike hope, is grounded in knowledge.

If Kant had offered *only* an argument from ignorance and the limits of human knowledge, his claim to show that we have reason to adopt any form of faith or hope, let alone specific faiths or hopes, would be quite unsatisfactory. However, the argument from the limits of human knowledge is only part of the picture. The other part of the picture consists of arguments for the indispensability and the irreducibility of the two standpoints. We cannot fail to act on the assumption of our own freedom, if only because the very activities of cognition require us to assume our own freedom; conversely, in acting we cannot fail to assume that we know a causally ordered world in which our action is to intervene. Hence we have to make sense not simply of the thought that our knowledge is limited, but of the further thought that we must accept some set of assumptions under which the answers we give to the first two questions that interest human reason are rendered mutually consistent. In short we must assume that there is some sort or degree of coordination of nature and freedom that ensures that our future is one in which we can act, and in which the aim of moral action is not absurd: it must be possible to insert the moral intention into the world (cf. *CPR* A807–8/B836–37; *CJ* 143, 146 [470, 472]).

Of course, this is not to say that we *know* how or how far the natural and the moral orders are coordinated, let alone that their full integration is possible, or will come to pass. It is only to say that for practical purposes we must take it that some degree of their coordination is possible. In doing so we commit ourselves to the view that the future in which we act is not inevitably frustrating — in short we must entertain at least a minimal hope that the future on which we take our action to bear is a future on which it can bear. The core of any answer to the third question "What may I hope?" is the thought that whatever I may hope must incorporate a hope that human destiny leaves some room for action and specifically for the moral intention to be realised by acting in the world. Rather than grounding hope in faith, Kant in fact construes the basics of faith as a form of hope.[11]

Several large questions arise at this point. I shall take up three of them. First, does the reality that hope can fail show that, contrary to Kant's view, we do not need to live in the light of (any sort of) hope? Second, does he show that *only* religious hopes as traditionally conceived will provide the right light? Third, does he show that religious hopes as traditionally understood, or any other specific hopes, can be reasoned hopes?

7. *Hope and Despair*

We may begin with the most general difficulty: is Kant right to insist that human reason must ask a third question that points to the future, and whose answers point to hopes for that future? Isn't hope a splendid but optional matter? What makes the question of the future an unavoidable interest of human reason, and not merely a topic of emotional or personal concern to each of us? The very idea that commitment to action and morality requires hope can seem implausible. Do not many reasonable people with strong moral commitments look to the future more with fear or foreboding, or even with indifference and despair, than in hope? Do not others hope unreasonably, building their lives around illusory or even self-deceiving aspirations or wishes? In short, isn't hope unnecessary?

The most plausible of Kant's moves is surely the claim that we must be committed to *some* view of the future if we are committed to action of any sort. If we were entirely noncommittal about the future, we could make no sense of any commitment to action. We see this clearly when we remember what it would be to think that there is no possible future: *complete* despair overwhelms all commitment and stifles action. In acting we look to the future; if we

---

[11] Cf. *Critique of Judgement*, 146: "Faith, in the plain acceptance of the term, is a confidence of attaining a purpose the furtherance of which is a duty. . . ."

can bring about any change, it can only be change in the world, in the future. Those who think action that changes the future impossible can aim for nothing: commitment to action that is thought impossible is not really commitment; we cannot aim to achieve what we know to be unachievable. Conversely, if we act at all we reveal at least a minimal commitment to, a minimal hope for, some future in which some action may take place and may have some results. That we have some intimation of a future that is open to action in some respects is constitutive not only of the moral life, but of the life of action, and so on Kant's view also of cognition.[12]

Kant does not, of course, claim that despair is impossible. His claim is conditional: commitment to action and morality, that is, commitment to acting morally within a causally ordered world, demands that we hope that our commitments are to some extent realisable in that world. He aims to show not simply that lack of hope is psychologically hard, but that it is incoherent unless action and morality too are given up.

8. *Modalities of Hope*

The second large question is whether a requirement for hope must be or must include religious hopes as traditionally conceived. On this Kant apparently gives several differing answers. The different views are in part a reflection of the different modalities of hope.

Kant formulates the third question in which human reason is unavoidably interested permissively. He asks not "What *must* I hope?" but rather "What *may* I hope?" Yet in many passages in

---

[12] What happens in dark conditions when action is barely possible is instructive. Consider Nadja Mandelstam's *Hope against Hope: a Memoir*, tr. Max Hayward (London: Collins Harvill, 1971), or Bruno Bettelheim, *The Informed Heart: The Human Condition in Modern Mass Society* (London: Thames and Hudson, 1960), with its poignant discussion of those who gave up hope in the death camps, became walking dead, and were dubbed "Musselmänner" by others. It may be sober truth rather than whistling in the dark when we tell one another that while there is life there is hope.

various works he concentrates on what must rather than on what may be hoped. Of course, any adequate account of what we *may* hope will have to incorporate some account of anything that we *must* hope. There might, however, be many distinct answers to the question "What may I hope?" that had in common only those aspects of hope that are required. It may, for example, be the case that various quite distinct hopes for human destiny incorporate a convincing account of what we must hope.

Notoriously Kant puts forward a very strong account of what we must hope in the *Critique of Practical Reason*. He there argues not only that we must hope that the moral intention can be inserted into the world to some extent, but that we must hope that the moral and natural orders can be *fully* coordinated in an optimal way in which happiness and virtue, our natural and our moral ends, are eventually perfectly coordinated in each of us.

These demanding hopes are presented as requiring certain Postulates of Practical Reason. On Kant's account a postulate is

> a theoretical proposition which is not as such [i.e., theoretically] demonstrable but which is an inseparable corollary of an *a priori* unconditionally valid practical law. (*CPrR* 122)

In the second Critique Kant argues for the demanding claim that we must aim not only to introduce the moral intention into the world but to work toward the *summum bonum* or *complete* coordination of natural and moral good, of happiness and virtue, in each free agent, so must hope for a correspondingly strong and complete degree of coordination between the natural and the moral order, and so must postulate or hope for our own immortality and for the existence of God:

> This infinite progress is possible, however, only under the presupposition of an infinitely enduring existence and personality of the same rational being; this is called the immortality of the soul. Thus the highest good is practically possible only on the supposition of the immortality of the soul.... (*CPrR* 122)

Accordingly each of us

> may hope for a further uninterrupted continuance of this progress, however long his existence may last, even beyond this life. (*CPrR* 123)

Hence, Kant holds, we must also postulate

> the existence ... of a cause of the whole of nature, itself distinct from nature, which contains the ground of the exact coincidence of happiness with morality ... the highest good is possible in the world only on the supposition of a supreme cause of nature which has a causality corresponding to the moral disposition. (*CPrR* 125)

If we aimed only for a lesser degree of happiness or of virtue, or for a lesser degree of their coordination, we might need to adopt only lesser postulates or hopes. However, the maximal aim would make little sense unless one also hoped for or assumed an eternity to achieve it and a deity to make it possible. The strong and specific claims about what we must hope that Kant defends in the *Critique of Practical Reason* are plausible if, but only if, we find good reasons for the assumption that we *must* take it that a *complete* coordination of happiness and virtue in each of us is on the cards.

Yet might we not make sense of our dual commitment to knowledge of a causally ordered world and to action, including moral action, within that world on the basis of lesser assumptions? Why should action not posit or hope for the possibility of moral progress, but make no assumptions about the possibility of achieving natural and moral perfection? Might it be enough to postulate that we can insert the moral intention into the world as and how we can, rather than with total efficacy? If so might we not construe the task of moral progress as a this-worldly, shared and historical, perhaps incompletable task, rather than as one that will provide each of us an occupation for an eternal afterlife?

In some of his political and historical writings Kant takes a this-worldly view of reasoned hope, in which neither God nor immortality is taken to be an indispensable corollary of our commitment to his views of our dual commitment to the natural and the moral orders. In place of the religious interpretation of the Postulates of Pure Practical Reason of *Critique of Practical Reason*, he articulates the hopes we must have as hopes for an earthly future, for the possibility of progress in which nature and morality are coordinated not in another life but on this earth. If moral action is seen as a historical goal, reasoned hope may fasten not on God and immortality, but on history and progress.[13]

There are many passages in which Kant articulates a this-worldly counterpart to the Postulates of Pure Practical Reason. Here one instance may serve for many; in *Theory and Practice* he wrote:

> I may thus be permitted to assume that, since the human race is constantly progressing in cultural matters (in keeping with its natural purpose), it is also engaged in progressive improvement in relation to the moral end of its existence. . . . I do not need to prove this assumption. . . . I base my argument upon my inborn duty of influencing posterity in such a way that it will make constant progress. . . . History may well give rise to endless doubts about my hopes . . . however uncertain I may be and may remain as to whether we can hope for anything better for mankind, this uncertainty cannot detract from the maxim I have adopted, or from the necessity of assuming for practical purposes that human progress is possible. (*TP* 88)

Many moves in this passage mirror those by which Kant argued in the second Critique to God and immortality: we are committed to moral aims whose feasibility we cannot prove theoretically; to make sense of this we need to postulate, assume, or hope for a

---

[13] Cf. Yirmiahu Yovel's discussion of the Postulates of Pure Practical Reason and the Regulative Ideal of History in his *Kant and the Philosophy of History* (Princeton, N.J.: Princeton University Press, 1980), 72.

human future that allows room for human progress (not in this case necessarily for progress to perfection); these hopes for the future of humankind cannot be renounced if we are committed to morality. Here and elsewhere Kant pictures human destiny in this-worldly terms.

Only if any answer to the question "What may I hope?" must include hope for God and immortality will Kant's answer to his third question vindicate theistic religious claims; even if reasoned hope were to vindicate some rather abstract religious claims, it might not vindicate all the familiar Christian tenets that would restore Lampe's happiness. Heine's comments on Kant's strategy for consoling Lampe can be read as doubts whether the supposed constraints that reason places on what we *may* hope are sufficient to show that we *must* have any sort of religious hope. Even if the abstract claims of deism and the tenets of traditional Christian faith provide two specific answers to the question "What may I hope?" Kant's arguments may not show that either forms part of *every* answer to the narrower question "What must I hope?"

Could Kant have supplied an argument for the unique status of hopes for God and immortality, so showing that we not merely may but must hold such hopes? Does he establish his claim that it is "morally necessary to assume the existence of God," so proving that any answer to the question "What *may* I hope?" must incorporate a theistic claim? If he does not, Kant will have shown only that we must make *some* assumption about the grounds of the possibility of coordination between the natural and moral orders. He would not have offered reasons to think that we must hope for God and immortality, let alone for the specifics of Christian faith. He would have left it open that our hopes need not have a specifically religious form, and even that they might be more coherent if they do *not* take a religious form.

What are we to make of this apparent shift in Kant's views? Was he constantly revising his account of human hopes and destiny, searching for the most convincing answer? Or does he take it that there are no reasons to think that our hopes must take a unique form? Does he think that we may hope either for God and immortality or for historical progress? Or is there evidence that either religious hope or historical hope is his final view of human destiny and that he rejects other views? Or does he merely vacillate between alternative answers to this third question?

9. *Hope and Reason*

The broad sense in which hopes for a future in which action and morality are possible may be reasoned is that they render Kant's theoretical and practical philosophies consistent. The theoretical and practical uses of reason lead us to positions that seem to be far apart — separated indeed by a great gulf. Hopes for a future in which action in the world is possible provide at least a slender bridge across that great gulf. The bridge is slender in that nothing demonstrates that or how the natural world and the moral order come to be coordinated. Kant does not provide any basis for boasting that we *know* that there is a God and a future life, or even that we *know* that history will allow for progress. His account of what we must hope is, after all, only an account of the required core of hope that we must adopt to achieve consistency.

It may be only this required core of hope that we are given grounds to think of as *reasoned hope* (a successor to *docta spes*). This core of hope is cognitively simple and indeterminate. It is merely formal, or *negative*, unlike more determinate hopes for God and immortality or for specific modes of historical progress. It is *nonderivative* in the sense that it does not invoke or presuppose the authority of any particular metaphysical system or religious revelation, or of any church, or state, or other power. Moreover it is *lawlike* in the sense that these minimal hopes are hopes that everyone can have, indeed hopes that everyone who is committed to knowledge and action has reason to share.

However, much of Kant's writing on hope goes beyond this picture and invokes more specific religious or historical hopes. One way in which his various accounts of more specific hopes might be understood is as answers to his broader question "What may I hope?" In the second of these lectures I shall consider some of the accounts of permitted hope that can be found in *Religion within the Limits of Reason Alone* and ask whether Kant offers us reason to think that these more resonant hopes too lie within the limits of reason.

LECTURE II. INTERPRETATION WITHIN THE LIMITS OF REASON

Kant pursued his inquiry into the links between reason and religion into his final years. His last major complete work is his extraordinary, and in many ways disconcerting, *Religion within the Limits of Reason Alone*. At first encounter there seems to be a great distance between this convoluted work, with its numerous discussions of Scripture and of Christian dogma, of ancient authors and of anthropology, of comparative religion and of church governance, its speculations on etymology and on ethical associations, and the abstract arguments that lie behind the Postulates of Practical Reason of the *Critique of Practical Reason*.

The publication of *Religion within the Limits of Reason Alone* got Kant into wearisome troubles with the anxious Prussian censors. At first consideration this is a surprising response to a work that seems more respectful of established faith than his numerous earlier writings on religion, which had brought him no trouble.[1] Christian concerns and Christian Scriptures are in evidence throughout the book. It consists of four long linked essays, the first published in 1792 and the others in 1793. Each takes up

---

[1] The explanation is usually said to lie in the more conservative regime in Berlin, where Frederick William II had appointed as minister of justice J. C. Wöllner, who introduced a more restrictive Censorship Edict in 1788, which permitted religious freedom provided that dissidents kept unorthodox opinions to themselves. Yet it is surely relevant that Kant confronted the censors with an entirely new and unsettling tone and approach in his late writing about religion. In the event publication was permitted, but Kant was required to publish nothing further on religion.

an ancient and resonant thematization of good and evil. The first discusses the *common root* of good and evil in human freedom; the second the *conflict* between good and evil; the third the *victory* of good over evil; and the last the life lived in *service* of the good. This sequence follows a traditional Christian articulation of human origins and destiny: *original sin, temptation, conversion,* and *ministry* are moments of the encounter of the pilgrim soul with good and evil. This Christian tenor is sustained by numerous discussions of Christian Scripture.

Yet Kant's underlying line of thought appears to question rather than to endorse much of Christian faith and tradition. His task, he asserts, is that of the *philosophical theologian*, who approaches religion *within the limits of reason*. This task, he insists, is quite different from that of the *biblical theologian*, who defends ecclesiastical faith by appealing to church authority to guide his reading of Scripture, and whose defence of faith does not appeal to reason.[2] The discussions of Christian Scripture in *Religion within the Limits of Reason Alone*, however, are to be reasoned. Indeed, in the preface to the second edition Kant asserts that "reason can be found not only to be compatible with Scripture but also at one with it" (*R* 11). How can religion within the limits of reason conceivably be "at one with" the Scripture of a particular religious tradition?

Much here will depend on one's understanding of Kant's conception of reason. This evening I shall try to show how the minimalist account of reason that Kant presents in the *Doctrine of Method* of the *Critique of Pure Reason* can be used to unravel his interpretations to Christian Scripture, and to make sense of his

[2] The distinctions between philosophical and biblical theology are a major theme also of Kant's *Conflict of the Faculties*, published a year later. There (as also in *What Is Enlightenment?*; also in *Kant: Political Writings*) he cites obedience to the state as the ultimate reason why biblical theologians may not appeal to reason: "the biblical theologian . . . draws his teaching not from reason but from the *Bible*; . . . As soon as one of these faculties presumes to mix with its teachings something it treats as derived from reason, it offends against the authority of the government that issues orders through it" (*CF* 23).

claim to approach religion within the limits of reason alone by way of interpretation of the sacred texts of one tradition.

1. *Relation to the Second Critique*

Unsurprisingly there are many continuities between Kant's earlier and his later writing on religion. Like the second Critique, *Religion within the Limits of Reason Alone* argues to religious claims from moral claims. The book begins with the claim that "morality leads ineluctably to religion" (*R* preface 1, 5) and ends with the thought that "the right course is not to go from grace to virtue but rather to progress from virtue to pardoning grace" (*R* 190). Morality once again appears as the parent rather than as the child of religion; charity once again does not build on but precedes faith. Once again we are presented with a reversal of tradition that old Lampe might not have found consoling.

Moreover, like the *Critique of Practical Reason, Religion within the Limits of Reason Alone* takes up the question "What may I hope?" Here too Kant insists that hope forms the bridge that renders our dual commitment to knowledge and to moral action coherent. Our moral ambitions, indeed our moral intentions and our very plans of action, cannot be fully grounded in knowledge: we lack not only the relevant knowledge that the world is open to the possibility of moral or other intervention, but even the self-knowledge that would assure us that we are committed to moral action:

> Man cannot attain naturally to assurance concerning such a [moral] revolution ... for the deeps of the heart (the subjective first grounds of his maxim) are inscrutable to him. Yet he must be able to *hope* through his *own* efforts to reach the road which leads hither ... because he ought to become a good man. (*R* 46)

Yet at many points *Religion within the Limits of Reason Alone* is less definite than the *Critique of Practical Reason* about the form that hope, even hopes for the highest good, must take. Often the text does not make it clear whether the hope that makes sense of our aspirations to morality is this-worldly or other-worldly; sometimes it is not obvious whether the hope is religious or historical. Near the end of the work Kant claims that

> reason . . . says that whoever, with a disposition genuinely devoted to duty, does as much as lies in his power to satisfy his obligation . . . may hope that what is not in his power will be supplied by the supreme Wisdom *in some way or other*. (*R* 159; cf. 130)

The same very abstract structure of hope is the appropriate corollary to intentions to seek the highest good:

> The idea of the highest good, inseparably bound up with the purely moral disposition, cannot be realized in man himself . . . yet he discovers within himself the duty to work for this end. Hence he finds himself impelled to believe in the cooperation or management of a moral Ruler of the world, by means of which this goal can be reached. And now there opens up before him the abyss of a mystery regarding what God may do . . . , whether indeed *anything* in general, and if so, *what* in particular should be ascribed to God. (*R* 130)

Whether we not merely *may* hope but have good reasons, indeed *ought*, to hope that supreme Wisdom will act in this life or the next, in history or in the hereafter, or in both, whether indeed anything in particular should be ascribed to God, is often left quite obscure.

2. *Scripture as Symbol of Morality*

There are also many ways in which the discussion of religion in *Religion within the Limits of Reason Alone* differs from and is far more specific than that in the *Critique of Practical Reason*. The most obvious puzzle is to understand how anything we would call *philosophical theology* can appeal to Scripture — or for that matter can be advanced by commenting on Roman and tribal religion, on superstition and clericalism. What part can discussion of the Fall of Man or the Virgin Birth or the Second Coming have in an account of religion within the limits of reason? Surely a work on the religion of reason should invoke particular tales and traditions only as examples of lack of reason.

In the preface to the first edition Kant remarks (rather unhelpfully) that it would be a good idea to have a

> special course of lectures on the purely *philosophical* theory of religion (which avails itself of everything including the Bible), with such a book as this, perhaps, as the text (or any other if a better can be found). (*R* 10)[3]

He is quite right that the text avails itself, if not quite of everything, still of too much; but this seemingly will make it harder rather than easier for us to read it as an account of religion within the limits of reason.

The reasons that Kant offers for thinking that his discussion of Scripture is appropriate to his task lie scattered in comments on narrative and interpretation at various stages of the book. The initial discussion of interpretation is interspersed with comments on the Adamic myths in book one. Here Kant suggests that Scripture may be understood as a group of narratives that offer a temporal *model* or *symbol* of a rational (hence atemporal) structure. For example, his reading of the story of Adam's sin and of the expulsion from Eden sees it as symbolizing the subordination of moral principles to natural inclinations.

> Holy Scripture (the Christian portion) sets forth this intelligible moral relationship in the form of a narrative, in which two principles in man, as opposed to one another as heaven is

---

[3] The censors reacted rather promptly to this thought, if in the wrong way. In 1795, a year after the second preface, they issued an order to the academic senate at Königsberg expressly forbidding *any* professor to lecture on *Religion within the Limits of Reason Alone*. Cf. "Translator's Introduction" to *The Conflict of the Faculties*.

to hell, are represented as persons outside him; who not only pit their strength against each other but also seek (the one as man's accuser and the other as his advocate) to establish their claims *legally* as before a supreme judge. (R 73)[4]

The drama of temptation and salvation may be read as symbolizing a conflict between the moral principle and the principle of subordinating morality to desire. Although, Kant writes, the "natural inclinations, *considered in themselves*, are *good*" (R 51; cf. 31),[5] the subordination of morality to inclination would be freely chosen evil. This is appropriately symbolized in the story of the Fall, where an originally innocent being comes to moral awareness, is reminded by a good spirit of the demands of morality, is tempted by a spirit who personifies the principle of evil, freely chooses to subordinate morality to desire, and yet leaves open the possibility of a return to the good (R 37).

Since the details of the Adamic myths can be read as symbols of the interrelationship between freedom, knowledge, and morality in our lives, we can understand the story as told of ourselves, but symbolically. Kant quotes a line from Horace, who admonishes us not to scoff even at ludicrous tales about the gods, reminding us that *mutato nomine de te fabula narratur* (R 37).[6] A story does not have to be literally true, or even (as Kant suggests by quoting a pagan author) taken from the Bible, in order to be read in the interests of morality. The myth of the Fall can be *rehabilitated* rather than *repudiated* if it is read as a narrative that symbolically

---

[4] The restriction of this claim to the Christian portion of Scripture is immediately disregarded; later in the book it is clear that a restriction to the Bible is also to be set aside.

[5] This point is notoriously missed in reading Kant's ethics. Yet it is an unavoidable corollary both of his view that happiness, which is the satisfaction of natural inclinations, is a component of the *summum bonum* and of his theory of action, which demands that maxims be freely adopted.

[6] "Under another name the tale is told of you." Horace, *Satires*, in *Q. Horati Flacci Opera*, ed. E. C. Wickham, revised H. W. Garrod, Oxford Classical Texts (Oxford: Oxford University Press, 1984), Book I, i, line 69, 135.

represents our understanding of evil as freely chosen and yet rejectable:

> For man, therefore, who despite a corrupted heart possesses a good will, there remains a hope of a return to the good from which he has strayed. (R 39)

Nobody will be surprised that the Adamic myths *can* be read in this way, or more generally that Scripture *can* be given an interpretation that makes it an appropriate symbol of Kant's views of the relation between knowledge and morality, and so of hope; but it is surprising that Kant makes this move. Why should *Religion within the Limits of Reason Alone* discuss Scripture at all? In making sympathetic use of the myths and symbols of biblical traditions Kant is very distant from the spirit of reasoned religion as generally understood. Deism, for example, aspired to a quite limited salvage job on the most abstract propositions of Christian faith — and was content to jettison the rest, and to deride bits of it as superstition. Kant can be as scathing as any deist in his denunciation of popular superstition, which he castigates as religious illusion (R 156ff.), and of clericalism, which he denounces as fetishism "which borders very closely on paganism" (R 168): yet he does not denounce or renounce Scripture. Rather he regards it as important to show that Scripture can or may be read in a certain way.

3. *In the Interests of Morality*

The second element of Kant's account of the role of interpretation of Scripture within religion within the limit of reason is summarized by the thought that sacred texts not merely *can* be read as symbols of morality, but that they *ought to* be read in this way:

> this narrative must at all times be taught and expounded in the interests of morality. (R 123)

It would be easy to think that what Kant means is simply that we ought to seek a morally edifying meaning in the stories of Scripture, that it is a matter, as we say, of bringing out the moral of the story. This is a common enough view of how Scripture can or even of how it ought to be interpreted "in the interests of morality," which has provided the basis for countless sermons and homilies. However, it will not serve Kant's purposes, since the idea of "bringing out the moral" presupposes that a text of Scripture has an intrinsic, if sometimes obscure, moral meaning (which other secular or pagan texts may lack) and that this meaning is to be brought out.

Kant, however, does not attribute either special standing or moral wisdom to Christian Scripture. The Bible is no more than a book that has "fallen into men's hands" (R 98); traditional faith may be no more than something that "chance . . . has tossed into our hands" (R 100). There is no reason to suppose that such contingent cultural documents and traditions are morally admirable or even sound. Nevertheless Kant insists not only that we can, but that we ought to read them "in the interests of morality." Doing so is not a matter of looking for their true meaning. The relevant

> interpretation may, in the light of the text . . . appear forced — it may often really be forced; and yet if the text can possibly support it, it must be preferred to a literal interpretation which either contains nothing at all [helpful] to morality or else actually works counter to moral incentive. (R 101)

This conception of proper interpretation can get going on the sacred texts of any tradition. Christian texts are neither unique nor indispensable. This can be illustrated by the fact that the philosophers of classical antiquity managed to interpret the crudest of polytheistic stories in ways that approximate a moral doctrine intelligible to all (R 101–2), and by equivalent moves in Judaism, Islam, and Hinduism (R 102).

The issue behind these interpretive moves is highlighted by posing the question:

> whether morality should be expounded according to the Bible or whether the Bible should not rather be expounded according to morality. (R 101n)

Kant's firm answer is that morality rather than Scripture comes first:

> since . . . the moral improvement of men constitutes the real end of all religion of reason, it will comprise the highest principle of all Scriptural exegesis. (*R* 102)[7]

4. Reasoned Interpretation and Authority

These moves show why Kant speaks of his work as defending *moral religion*; they do not make it entirely clear why he should speak of himself as defending *religion within the limits of reason*. It is, of course, true that Kant sees morality as based on practical reason, but it does not follow that all interpretation of Scripture "in the interest of morality" must itself lie within the limits of reason. Even if morality is based on reason, the readings of texts that support or express moral principles might, as Kant notes, be forced rather than reasoned.

However, interpretations that are forced by the standards of literal or fundamentalist interpretation may conform to Kant's minimalist account of reason. Kant depicts reason as a way of disciplining thinking and acting, which is *negative*, in that it lacks all specific content, *nonderivative*, in that it does not invoke authorities other than reason, and *lawlike*, in that it uses principles that all can adopt. If there are reasoned ways of interpreting, they will have to meet these three standards, and in doing so will also meet the criteria that are combined in the Categorical Imperative, so will constitute guidelines for moral as well as for reasoned interpretation.

The first two standards are readily apparent in Kant's account of the sorts of interpretation that would be appropriate for the philosophical theologian. The philosophical theologian lacks any

---

[7] In *The Conflict of the Faculties* Kant also identifies reason as "the highest interpreter of Scripture" (*CF* 41).

substantive standards of interpretation and may not invoke any authority other than that of reason to guide interpretation. Scriptural exegesis "within the limits of reason" may not appeal to revelation, state or ecclesiastical authority, or historical scholarship, let alone authorial intentions (cf. *R* 39n; cf. 101ff.), on which traditions of biblical theology may build.[8] Equally, scriptural exegesis within the limits of reason does not appeal to the no less suspect "authority" of individual religious experience, conscience, or feeling — a mode of interpretation that Kant thinks leads to enthusiasm or fanaticism (*R* 104–5; cf. *WOT* 246ff.).

However, none of this explains why religion within the limits of reason should refer to Scripture, except for polemical purposes, let alone why it should seek interpretations that rehabilitate rather than repudiate. Does not the activity of interpreting particular texts suggest some covert, if very indeterminate, assumption that they have some authority? If so, should not their interpretation be firmly excluded from religion within the limits of reason?

5. *Reasoned Interpretation and Popular Religion*

Kant's central comments on interpretation deal mainly with issues of authority and do not show why religion within the limits of reason should engage with Scripture. At most they show that *if* (for some still obscure reason) reasoned religion did interpret Scripture, it would do so without assuming substantive starting points and in particular without taking any other authority for granted. However, the third aspect of Kant's account of reason — that it is lawlike — can, I believe, explain why Kant thinks that an engagement with accepted traditions and texts is an indispensable part of reasoned religion.

[8] Kant acknowledges that as things are the *philosophical theologians*, who interpret Scripture by reference to the principles of morality and hence of reason, are far outnumbered by *scriptural scholars* or *biblical theologians*, who are usually expositors of one or another historically specific ecclesiastical faith, and who rely on the authoritative tenets of a particular church or tradition to guide their *doctrinal* interpretation (*R* 103–5; *CF* 23–24; 36ff., 61ff.).

Kant puts his reason for thinking that the philosophical theologian needs to engage with Scripture as follows:

> the authority of Scripture ... as ... *at present* the only instrument *in the most enlightened portion of the world* for the union of all men into one church, constitutes the ecclesiastical faith, which, as the popular faith, cannot be neglected, because no doctrine based on reason alone seems to the people qualified to serve as an unchangeable norm. (*R* 103; my italics)

These reasons for interpreting Christian Scripture refer to a time and a place: they are reasons for eighteenth-century Europe. Somehow, at some juncture, the philosophical theologian has to reason in ways that engage with actual religious conceptions as they are held and cherished by the people. Otherwise an "appeal to pure reason as the expositor" could have nothing to say to the many millions who held to the time-honoured religion that sustained old Lampe and countless others, or to adherents of the other religions.

Kant accepts that such reasoning must take account of its audience:

> It is also possible that the union of men into one religion cannot feasibly be brought about or made abiding without a holy book and an ecclesiastical faith based on it. (*R* 123)

Reasoned religion must be lawlike, not just in the sense that it can be followed by any rational being, but also in taking account of the fact that rational beings, as things are, are adherents of particular religious traditions. So reasoned religion too must engage with the sacred texts and traditions of popular religion; it must start on familiar ground and show how the familiar sayings of Scripture can be interpreted without appeal to groundless authorities: otherwise it will be accessible only to a few philosophical theologians.

It follows that the philosophical theologian *must* interpret whichever sacred texts are actually widely understood and respected. Without this move, religious teaching cannot fully meet the requirements of reason. Surprising as it may seem, religion within the limits of reason not merely *may* but *must* interpret accepted texts, and their ordinary reception. Only this focus and strategy of interpretation can secure a conception of religion that is guided by principles that are negative (formal), underivative, and also lawlike, so support religion within the limits of reason.

Lawlikeness is, however, a slender constraint. Kant is not appealing to any conception of *lawfulness*, which would invoke some further, separate authority to guide the interpretation of Scripture. That is the unreasoned strategy of biblical theologians, whose problem is that the separate authority to which they appeal stands in need of but does not receive justification. So it is to be expected that the interpretations that the philosophical theologian reaches, although they lie within the limits of reason, may not be unique or even highly determinate reasoned interpretations. Reason will not fully fix the reading of Scripture, any more than it fully fixes the content of permissible hope.

6. *Reasoned Interpretation and Polymorphous Hope*

This account of Kant's conception of reasoned interpretation is corroborated by the fact that he repeatedly states simply that we *may* or that we *can* read a passage of Scripture in a certain way, rather than that we *must* do so. For example, in speaking of the incarnation he writes:

> ... just because we are not the authors of this idea [of moral perfection], and because it has established itself in man without our comprehending how human nature could have been capable of receiving it, it is more appropriate to say [*kann* man hier besser sagen] that this archetype has *come down* to us from heaven and has assumed our humanity. ... Such union with us *may* therefore be regarded [*kann* ... angesehen werden] as a state of *humiliation* of the Son of God. (R 54–55; my italicization of modal terms)

In speaking of the temptation of Christ he writes:

> So it is not surprising [literally: it *may not* be taken amiss: "es *darf* also *nicht* befremden"] that an Apostle represents this *invisible* enemy, who is known only through his operations upon us and who destroys basic principles, as being outside us and, indeed, as an evil *spirit*. (*R* 52; my italicization of modal terms)

And in speaking of the end of the world he writes:

> The appearance of the Antichrist, the millennium, and the news of the proximity of the end of the world — all these *can* take on, before reason, their right [gute] symbolic meaning. (*R* 126; my italicization of modal terms)

The reason Kant takes this tentative approach should now be clear. He himself puts it this way:

> Nor can we charge such interpretations with dishonesty, provided we are not disposed to assert that the meaning which we ascribe to the symbols of the popular faith, even to the holy books, is exactly as intended by them, but rather allow this question to be left undecided and merely admit the *possibility* that their authors may be so understood. (*R* 102)

When Kant speaks of his approach to religion as lying *within the limits of reason* he does not mean that he identifies a unique set to reasoned beliefs or hopes, but only that he identifies a range of beliefs or hopes whose structure places them within the limits of reason. The sense in which reason is "not only ... compatible with Scripture but also at one with it" (*R* 11) is therefore weaker than it may initially have seemed: reasoned faith and hope are polymorphous.

7. *Hope without Doctrine*

If Kant's minimalist account of reason and of reasoned interpretation allows for a plurality of interpretations of the Scriptures on which popular faith rests, it is not surprising that he thinks that his account of faith and of hope will be undogmatic and undoctrinal, even when it engages with the texts and tenets of received religion. Reasoned religion is, after all, to answer the third question that interests human reason, the question of human destiny, which asks not "What must I hope?" but more openly "What may I hope?" In asking this question Kant leaves open not only various ways in which identifiably religious hopes for human destiny may be articulated, but also the possibility that hopes for human destiny may be articulated in social, political, and historical, this-worldly terms rather than in other-worldly terms.

The pure religious faith for which philosophical theology is to provide reasons lies *within the limits* of reason, but it is not the only articulation of hope that lies within those limits. Every articulation of hope and belief that lies within the limit of reason must incorporate the *canon* of reasoned faith, that is to say, an answer to the question "What *must* we hope?" Each ecclesiastical faith also proposes one *organon* of religious faith, that is to say, a specific answer to the question "What may I hope?" Another ecclesiastical faith might use quite another vocabulary to support a different account of what we may hope.[9]

In *Religion within the Limits of Reason Alone*, as one might expect, the accent is on religious articulations of the hopes we may have. And yet even here, in a work that constantly comments on Christian Scripture and that refers repeatedly to Christian and more broadly to religious articulations of hope, the traditional, other-worldly formulations of Christian hope are constantly put in question.

The first and evidently the most basic way in which Christian hope is put into question is by the shift of religious concern from the first to the third question of human reason, from a question

[9] See Friedo Ricken, "Kanon und Organon im Streit der Fakultäten," in *Kant über Religion*, ed. François Marty and Friedo Ricken (Stuttgart: Kohlhammer Verlag, 1992), 181–94.

about knowledge to a question about hope. Although Kant views the language of Scripture as an appropriate articulation of the hopes we may have, nothing that he claims restores a realist interpretation of God or immortality. Hope is not backed by knowledge. Human destiny remains a matter not of knowledge but of hope.

The second way in which Christian hope, as traditionally understood, is put into question in *Religion within the Limits of Reason Alone* is by the fact that the essential core of Kant's answer to the question "What may I hope?" establishes so little about what I must hope. All that Kant argues is that we must postulate, assume, hope for the possibility that our moral commitments are not futile: we must hope for the possibility of inserting the moral intention into the world. This bare structure of hope — the canon of hope — can be expressed in a range of vocabularies whose permissible articulations of hope will be accessible to different people, who may hope for varying conceptions of grace or of progress that might bridge and gap between moral intention and empirical outcomes.[10] Religious articulations of hope are not to be rejected, but other forms of hope are also permissible. We may hope for grace, for progress, or for both, and for each in many forms.

8. *Ecclesiastical Faith and the Ethical Commonwealth*

Behind these varied hopes lies a common commitment to action, which does not vary. Both in his accounts of religious hope and in his accounts of historical hope, Kant depicts the action to which we are committed as social as well as individual, and as this-worldly.[11] In *Religion within the Limits of Reason Alone* he puts

---

[10] Consider Kant's central claims about service to God at the beginning of book 4 of the *Religion*. He starts from the thought that "religion is the recognition of all duties as divine commands," which on the surface appears to require that God exists. But in the note to the text he immediately rebuts this reading by claiming that "no assertorial knowledge is required (even of God's existence)" and that "the *minimum* of knowledge (it is possible that there may be a God) must suffice" (R 142).

[11] Kant does not think that we have any special duties to God (R 142n). However, viewing our duties as divine commands takes us beyond individual duty.

it in the following terms at the beginning of his account of the victory of good over evil:

> As far as we can see, therefore, the sovereignty of the good principle is attainable, so far as men can work towards it, only through the establishment and spread of a society in accordance with, and for the sake of, the laws of virtue, a society whose task and duty it is to rationally impress these laws in all their scope upon the entire human race. For only thus can we hope for a victory of the good over the evil principle. (*R* 86 and cf. the following pages)

The fully achieved version of such a society would be what Kant terms an *ethical commonwealth* ("ethisches gemeines Wesen"). An ethical commonwealth is a "union of men under merely moral [as opposed to juridical] laws"; it can exist in the midst of a political commonwealth; it may even include all the members of a political commonwealth (*R* 86). However, in human hands this ethical ideal "dwindles markedly" (R 91), although it can be approximated, more or less well, by the visible church (*R* 91ff.).

Both in *Religion within the Limits of Reason Alone* and in *Conflict of the Faculties* Kant depicts the visible church as a *vehicle*, which will finally be superseded as a purer, more fully reasoned faith supplants mere ecclesiastical faith:

> In the end all religion will gradually be freed from all empirical determining grounds and from all statutes which rest on history and which through the agency of ecclesiastical faith provisionally unite all men for the requirements of the good; and thus at last the pure religion of reason will rule over all, "so that God may be all in all." . . . The leading-string of holy traditions with its appendages of statutes and observances,

---

One important passage is the following: "Now here we have a duty which is *sui generis*, not of men toward men, but of the human race towards itself. For the species of rational beings is objectively, in the idea of reason, destined for a social goal, namely, the promotion of the highest as a social good. . . . the highest moral good cannot be achieved merely by the exertions of a single individual towards his own moral perfection but requires rather the union of such individuals into a whole towards such a goal — into a system of well-disposed men" (*R* 89).

which in its time did good service, becomes bit by bit dispensable, yea, finally when man enters upon his adolescence it becomes a fetter. (*R* 112)[12]

If all of the outward and visible elements of church life and liturgy could be shed, we would be left with the abstract demands of purely moral religion. What we are left with is not however a mere hope, for whose realization we must wait, whether patiently or impatiently. We are also left with the moral commitment that underlies hope. This commitment sets a task that we may not sit back and leave either to Providence or to others:

> ... man [must] proceed as though everything depended on him; only on this condition dare he hope that higher wisdom will grant the completion of his well-intentioned endeavours. (*R* 92; cf. 149ff.)
>
> The only thing that matters in religion is deeds [Alles kommt in der Religion aufs Tun an]. (*CF* 41)

The context of action may but need not be framed by the life of a church. Kant's account of reasoned religion allows at least a *transitional* role to ecclesiastical faith and to the visible church, but it is not clear whether it allows more. Can the empirical realities and institutional structures of a church (or of another social but secular "vehicle") be wholly superseded? If so, what is to bind the members of the ethical commonwealth together? If there are shared duties "of the human race," will their enactment not require shared public practices and institutions? If so, will not our hopes, including our shared hopes, have to be connected to shared

---

[12] Compare this account to the secular, political, and historical account of the maturing of reason that Kant offers in *What Is Enlightenment?* where he describes the gradual emergence of human beings from immaturity to rationality, from a private, other-directed use of their incomplete capacities to reason to a public, autonomous use of their more developed capacities to reason. For a fuller discussion see Onora O'Neill, "Reason and Politics in the Kantian Enterprise," in *Constructions of Reason: Explorations of Kant's Practical Philosophy* (Cambridge: Cambridge University Press, 1989), 3–27.

activities and institutional structures, whether religious or this-worldly? Even if we hope for God and immortality it does not follow that a time will come at which joint action in this life can dispense with all specific institutions and practices: the religious may always need to take the structures of a visible church seriously on this earth.[13]

. . . by reason of a peculiar weakness in human nature, pure faith can never be relied on as much as it deserves, that is a church cannot be established on it alone. (R 94)

Equally, if the future for which we may hope is conceived of in this-worldly terms, it seems clear that we could not dispense with all social structures in building toward an ethical commonwealth. The history of would-be purely intentional communities is discouraging, despite the fact that they have in fact built on many shared social structures. It seems that the only point at which joint action without shared structures might be possible is in the afterlife — of which we know nothing.

So a third way in which at least some forms of Christian hope are put into question is by the fact that, in the end, in this world, religious and social and political hopes must be closely connected. All types of hope are expressed in action, indeed in collective action, that aims toward an ethical commonwealth; all are a matter of taking it that the moral intention can be expressed in the world. However, different genres of hope answer the question "What

---

[13] Kant himself seems to hesitate on the dispensability of institutional structures in this life. In some passages both in *Religion within the Limits of Reason Alone* and in *The Conflict of the Faculties* he relegates all institutional forms to the status of a *vehicle* by which a transition from ecclesiastical faith to pure religious faith, shorn of observances and liturgy, of tradition and history, can be achieved (cf. R 106). At other times he suggests that the vehicle is indispensable, at least in this life (cf. R 126n). See Hans Michael Baumgartner, "Das 'Ethische gemeine Wesen' und die Kirche in Kant's 'Religionsschrift,' " in *Kant über Religion*, ed. François Marty and Friedo Ricken, 156–67, and Allen Wood, "Rational Theology, Moral Faith, and Religion," in *The Cambridge Companion to Kant*, ed. Paul Guyer (Cambridge: Cambridge University Press, 1992), 394–416, for thoughtful discussion of this problem.

may I hope?" using different vocabularies and images, which can be woven into differing this-worldly practices and institutions. The religion of reason, on Kant's account, shows us that many religious and historical articulations of hope are permissible, that some articulations are congruent and compatible with others, but does not show that one type of hope is required to the exclusion of all others.

The censors of Prussia are long dead, but they were, I think, right to be worried. Although the surface of *Religion within the Limits of Reason Alone* presents a view of reasoned religion that seemingly takes Christian faith and Scriptures seriously, Kant's philosophical theology does not endorse religion in any straightforward way. Slightly below the surface of the work is a view of reason and of reasoned interpretation that assigns no unique status to religious hopes, to Christian hope, to Christian Scriptures, to the Christian church, or to all that old Lampe held sacred. The only moves Kant makes toward the specificities of the faith that Lampe knew and loved are that he gives general reasons for taking existing popular religion seriously in reading texts and existing ecclesiastical faith seriously in moving toward an ethical commonwealth. The outcome allows that traditional faith and hopes *may* be retained, but Kant's own hope is that both popular and ecclesiastical faith will be interim measures, and serve as vehicles to a purer faith and more abstract hopes that need no institutions and lack all specificity. The guardians of established religion could hardly be expected to endorse — even if they did not need to censor — a vision of religion that demotes the particular inflection of faith and hope that was in their care to the status of one among many permissible variants.

THE TANNER LECTURERS

1976–77

OXFORD Bernard Williams, Cambridge University
MICHIGAN Joel Feinberg, University of Arizona
"*Voluntary Euthanasia and the Inalienable Right to Life*"
STANFORD Joel Feinberg, University of Arizona
"*Voluntary Euthanasia and the Inalienable Right to Life*"

1977–78

OXFORD John Rawls, Harvard University
MICHIGAN Sir Karl Popper, University of London
"*Three Worlds*"
STANFORD Thomas Nagel, Princeton University

1978–79

OXFORD Thomas Nagel, Princeton University
"*The Limits of Objectivity*"
CAMBRIDGE C. C. O'Brien, London
MICHIGAN Edward O. Wilson, Harvard University
"*Comparative Social Theory*"
STANFORD Amartya Sen, Oxford University
"*Equality of What?*"
UTAH Lord Ashby, Cambridge University
"*The Search for an Environmental Ethic*"
UTAH STATE R. M. Hare, Oxford University
"*Moral Conflicts*"

1979–80

OXFORD Jonathan Bennett, University of British Columbia
"*Morality and Consequences*"
CAMBRIDGE Raymond Aron, Collège de France
"*Arms Control and Peace Research*"
HARVARD George Stigler, University of Chicago
"*Economics or Ethics?*"

MICHIGAN	Robert Coles, Harvard University *"Children as Moral Observers"*
STANFORD	Michel Foucault, Collège de France *"Omnes et Singulatim: Towards a Criticism of 'Political Reason' "*
UTAH	Wallace Stegner, Los Altos Hills, California *"The Twilight of Self-Reliance: Frontier Values and Contemporary America"*

1980–81

OXFORD	Saul Bellow, University of Chicago *"A Writer from Chicago"*
CAMBRIDGE	John Passmore, Australian National University *"The Representative Arts as a Source of Truth"*
HARVARD	Brian M. Barry, University of Chicago *"Do Countries Have Moral Obligations? The Case of World Poverty"*
MICHIGAN	John Rawls, Harvard University *"The Basic Liberties and Their Priority"*
STANFORD	Charles Fried, Harvard University *"Is Liberty Possible?"*
UTAH	Joan Robinson, Cambridge University *"The Arms Race"*
HEBREW UNIV.	Solomon H. Snyder, Johns Hopkins University *"Drugs and the Brain and Society"*

1981–82

OXFORD	Freeman Dyson, Princeton University *"Bombs and Poetry"*
CAMBRIDGE	Kingman Brewster, President Emeritus, Yale University *"The Voluntary Society"*
HARVARD	Murray Gell-Mann, California Institute of Technology *"The Head and the Heart in Policy Studies"*
MICHIGAN	Thomas C. Schelling, Harvard University *"Ethics, Law, and the Exercise of Self-Command"*
STANFORD	Alan A. Stone, Harvard University *"Psychiatry and Morality"*

UTAH	R. C. Lewontin, Harvard University *"Biological Determinism"*
AUSTRALIAN NATL. UNIV.	Leszek Kolakowski, Oxford University *"The Death of Utopia Reconsidered"*

1982-83

OXFORD	Kenneth J. Arrow, Stanford University *"The Welfare-Relevant Boundaries of the Individual"*
CAMBRIDGE	H. C. Robbins Landon, University College, Cardiff *"Haydn and Eighteenth-Century Patronage in Austria and Hungary"*
HARVARD	Bernard Williams, Cambridge University *"Morality and Social Justice"*
STANFORD	David Gauthier, University of Pittsburgh *"The Incompleat Egoist"*
UTAH	Carlos Fuentes, Princeton University *"A Writer from Mexico"*
JAWAHARLAL NEHRU UNIV.	Ilya Prigogine, Université Libre de Bruxelles *"Only an Illusion"*

1983-84

OXFORD	Donald D. Brown, Johns Hopkins University *"The Impact of Modern Genetics"*
CAMBRIDGE	Stephen J. Gould, Harvard University *"Evolutionary Hopes and Realities"*
MICHIGAN	Herbert A. Simon, Carnegie-Mellon University *"Scientific Literacy as a Goal in a High-Technology Society"*
STANFORD	Leonard B. Meyer, University of Pennsylvania *"Music and Ideology in the Nineteenth Century"*
UTAH	Helmut Schmidt, former Chancellor, West Germany *"The Future of the Atlantic Alliance"*
HELSINKI	Georg Henrik von Wright, Helsinki *"Of Human Freedom"*

1984–85

OXFORD	Barrington Moore, Jr., Harvard University *"Authority and Inequality under Capitalism and Socialism"*
CAMBRIDGE	Amartya Sen, Oxford University *"The Standard of Living"*
HARVARD	Quentin Skinner, Cambridge University *"The Paradoxes of Political Liberty"*
	Kenneth J. Arrow, Stanford University *"The Unknown Other"*
MICHIGAN	Nadine Gordimer, South Africa *"The Essential Gesture: Writers and Responsibility"*
STANFORD	Michael Slote, University of Maryland *"Moderation, Rationality, and Virtue"*

1985–86

OXFORD	Thomas M. Scanlon, Jr., Harvard University *"The Significance of Choice"*
CAMBRIDGE	Aldo Van Eyck, The Netherlands *"Architecture and Human Values"*
HARVARD	Michael Walzer, Institute for Advanced Study *"Interpretation and Social Criticism"*
MICHIGAN	Clifford Geertz, Institute for Advanced Study *"The Uses of Diversity"*
STANFORD	Stanley Cavell, Harvard University *"The Uncanniness of the Ordinary"*
UTAH	Arnold S. Relman, Editor, *New England Journal of Medicine* *"Medicine as a Profession and a Business"*

1986–87

OXFORD	Jon Elster, Oslo University and the University of Chicago *"Taming Chance: Randomization in Individual and Social Decisions"*

The Tanner Lecturers 313

CAMBRIDGE Roger Bulger, University of Texas Health Sciences Center, Houston
"*On Hippocrates, Thomas Jefferson, and Max Weber: The Bureaucratic, Technologic Imperatives and the Future of the Healing Tradition in a Voluntary Society*"

HARVARD Jürgen Habermas, University of Frankfurt
"*Law and Morality*"

MICHIGAN Daniel C. Dennett, Tufts University
"*The Moral First Aid Manual*"

STANFORD Gisela Striker, Columbia University
"*Greek Ethics and Moral Theory*"

UTAH Laurence H. Tribe, Harvard University
"*On Reading the Constitution*"

1987–88

OXFORD F. Van Zyl Slabbert, University of the Witwatersrand, South Africa
"*The Dynamics of Reform and Revolt in Current South Africa*"

CAMBRIDGE Louis Blom-Cooper, Q.C., London
"*The Penalty of Imprisonment*"

HARVARD Robert A. Dahl, Yale University
"*The Pseudodemocratization of the American Presidency*"

MICHIGAN Albert O. Hirschman, Institute for Advanced Study
"*Two Hundred Years of Reactionary Rhetoric: The Case of the Perverse Effect*"

STANFORD Ronald Dworkin, New York University and University College, Oxford
"*Foundations of Liberal Equality*"

UTAH Joseph Brodsky, Russian poet, Mount Holyoke College
"*A Place as Good as Any*"

CALIFORNIA Wm. Theodore de Bary, Columbia University
"*The Trouble with Confucianism*"

BUENOS AIRES Barry Stroud, University of California, Berkeley
"*The Study of Human Nature and the Subjectivity of Value*"

MADRID Javier Muguerza, Universidad Nacional de Educación a Distancia, Madrid
"The Alternative of Dissent"

WARSAW Anthony Quinton, British Library, London
"The Varieties of Value"

1988–89

OXFORD Michael Walzer, Institute for Advanced Study
"Nation and Universe"

CAMBRIDGE Albert Hourani, Emeritus Fellow, St. Antony's College, and Magdalen College, Oxford
"Islam in European Thought"

MICHIGAN Toni Morrison, State University of New York at Albany
"Unspeakable Things Unspoken: The Afro-American Presence in American Literature"

STANFORD Stephen Jay Gould, Harvard University
"Unpredictability in the History of Life"
"The Quest for Human Nature: Fortuitous Side, Consequences, and Contingent History"

UTAH Judith Shklar, Harvard University
"American Citizenship: The Quest for Inclusion"

CALIFORNIA S. N. Eisenstadt, The Hebrew University of Jerusalem
"Cultural Tradition, Historical Experience, and Social Change: The Limits of Convergence"

YALE J. G. A. Pocock, Johns Hopkins University
"Edward Gibbon in History: Aspects of the Text in The History of the Decline and Fall of the Roman Empire"

CHINESE
UNIVERSITY OF
HONG KONG Fei Xiaotong, Peking University
"Plurality and Unity in the Configuration of the Chinese People"

1989–90

OXFORD Bernard Lewis, Princeton University
"Europe and Islam"

The Tanner Lecturers

CAMBRIDGE	Umberto Eco, University of Bologna "*Interpretation and Overinterpretation: World, History, Texts*"
HARVARD	Ernest Gellner, Kings College, Cambridge "*The Civil and the Sacred*"
MICHIGAN	Carol Gilligan, Harvard University "*Joining the Resistance: Psychology, Politics, Girls, and Women*"
UTAH	Octavio Paz, Mexico City "*Poetry and Modernity*"
YALE	Edward N. Luttwak, Center for Strategic and International Studies "*Strategy: A New Era?*"
PRINCETON	Irving Howe, writer and critic "*The Self and the State*"

1990–91

OXFORD	David Montgomery, Yale University "*Citizenship and Justice in the Lives and Thoughts of Nineteenth-Century American Workers*"
CAMBRIDGE	Gro Harlem Brundtland, Prime Minister of Norway "*Environmental Challenges of the 1990s: Our Responsibility toward Future Generations*"
HARVARD	William Gass, Washington University "*Eye and Idea*"
MICHIGAN	Richard Rorty, University of Virginia "*Feminism and Pragmatism*"
STANFORD	G. A. Cohen, All Souls College, Oxford "*Incentives, Inequality, and Community*" János Kornai, University of Budapest and Harvard University "*Market Socialism Revisited*"
UTAH	Marcel Ophuls, international film maker "*Resistance and Collaboration in Peacetime*"

YALE — Robertson Davies, novelist
"Reading and Writing"

PRINCETON — Annette C. Baier, Pittsburgh University
"Trust"

LENINGRAD — János Kornai, University of Budapest and Harvard University
"Transition from Marxism to a Free Economy"

1991–92

OXFORD — R. Z. Sagdeev, University of Maryland
"Science and Revolutions"

CALIFORNIA

LOS ANGELES — Václav Havel, former President, Republic of Czechoslovakia
(Untitled lecture)

BERKELEY — Helmut Kohl, Chancellor of Germany
(Untitled lecture)

CAMBRIDGE — David Baltimore, former President of Rockefeller University
"On Doing Science in the Modern World"

MICHIGAN — Christopher Hill, seventeenth-century historian, Oxford
"The Bible in Seventeenth-Century English Politics"

STANFORD — Charles Taylor, Professor of Philosophy and Political Science, McGill University
"Modernity and the Rise of the Public Sphere"

UTAH — Jared Diamond, University of California, Los Angeles
"The Broadest Pattern of Human History"

PRINCETON — Robert Nozick, Professor of Philosophy, Harvard University
"Decisions of Principle, Principles of Decision"

1992–93

MICHIGAN — Amos Oz, Israel
"The Israeli-Palestinian Conflict: Tragedy, Comedy, and Cognitive Block — A Storyteller's Point of View"

CAMBRIDGE — Christine M. Korsgaard, Harvard University
"The Sources of Normativity"

UTAH	Evelyn Fox Keller, Massachusetts Institute of Technology "*Rethinking the Meaning of Genetic Determinism*"
YALE	Fritz Stern, Columbia University "*Mendacity Enforced: Europe, 1914-1989*" "*Freedom and Its Discontents: Postunification Germany*"
PRINCETON	Stanley Hoffmann, Harvard University "*The Nation, Nationalism, and After: The Case of France*"
STANFORD	Colin Renfrew, Cambridge University "*The Archaeology of Identity*"

1993-94

MICHIGAN	William Julius Wilson, University of Chicago "*The New Urban Poverty and the Problem of Race*"
OXFORD	Lord Slynn of Hadley, London "*Law and Culture — A European Setting*"
HARVARD	Lawrence Stone, Princeton University "*Family Values in a Historical Perspective*"
CAMBRIDGE	Peter Brown, Princeton University "*Aspects of the Christianisation of the Roman World*"
UTAH	A. E. Dick Howard, University of Virginia "*Toward the Open Society in Central and Eastern Europe*" Jeffrey Sachs, Harvard University "*Shock Therapy in Poland: Perspectives of Five Years*" Adam Zagajewski, Paris "*A Bus Full of Prophets: Adventures of the Eastern-European Intelligentsia*"
PRINCETON	Alasdair MacIntyre, Duke University "*Truthfulness, Lies, and Moral Philosophers: What Can We Learn from Mill and Kant?*"
CALIFORNIA	Oscar Arias, Costa Rica "*Poverty: The New International Enemy*"
STANFORD	Thomas Hill, University of North Carolina at Chapel Hill "*Basic Respect and Cultural Diversity*" "*Must Respect Be Earned?*"
US SAN DIEGO	K. Anthony Appiah, Harvard University "*Race, Culture, Identity: Misunderstood Connections*"

1994-95

YALE — Richard Posner, United States Court of Appeals
"*Euthanasia and Health Care: Two Essays on the Policy Dilemmas of Aging and Old Age*"

MICHIGAN — Daniel Kahneman, University of California, Berkeley
"*Cognitive Psychology of Consequences and Moral Intuition*"

HARVARD — Cass R. Sunstein, University of Chicago
"*Political Conflict and Legal Agreement*"

CAMBRIDGE — Roger Penrose, Oxford Mathematics Institute
"*Space-time and Cosmology*"

PRINCETON — Antonin Scalia, United States Supreme Court
"*Common-Law Courts in a Civil-Law System: The Role of the United States Federal Courts in Interpreting the Constitution and Laws*"

UC SANTA CRUZ — Nancy Wexler, Columbia University
"*Genetic Prediction and Precaution Confront Human Social Values*"

OXFORD — Janet Suzman, South Africa
"*Who Needs Parables?*"

STANFORD — Amy Gutmann, Princeton University
"*Responding to Racial Injustice*"

UTAH — Edward Said, Columbia University
"*On Lost Causes*"

1995-96

PRINCETON — Harold Bloom, Yale University
I. "*Shakespeare and the Value of Personality*," and II. "*Shakespeare and the Value of Love*"

OXFORD — Simon Schama, Columbia University
"*Rembrandt and Rubens: Humanism, History, and the Peculiarity of Painting*"

CAMBRIDGE — Gunther Schuller, Newton Center, Massachusetts
I. "*Jazz: A Historical Perspective*," II. "*Duke Ellington*," and III. "*Charles Mingus*"

RIVERSIDE	Mairead Corrigan Maguire, Belfast, Northern Ireland *"Peacemaking from the Grassroots in a World of Ethnic Conflict"*
HARVARD	Onora O'Neill, Newham College, Cambridge *"Kant on Reason and Religion"*
STANFORD	Nancy Fraser, New School for Social Research *"Social Justice in the Age of Identity Politics: Redistribution, Recognition, and Participation"*
UTAH	Cornell West, Harvard University *"A Genealogy of the Public Intellectual"*
YALE	Peter Brown, Princeton University I. *"The End of the Ancient Other World: Death and Afterlife between Late Antiquity and the Early Middle Ages,"* and II. *"The Decline of the Empire of God: From Amnesty to Purgatory"*